KNOCK 'EM DEAD 1999

BY
Martin Yate

Adams Media Corporation
Holbrook, Massachusetts

To your successful job hunt

Published by
Adams Media Corporation
260 Center Street, Holbrook, Massachusetts 02343

ISBN: 1-58062-070-1

Manufactured in the United States of America.

J   I   H   G   F   E   D   C   B   A

Library of Congress Cataloging-in-Publication Data
Yate, Martin John.
Knock 'em dead 1999 / by Martin Yate.
p.   cm.
Rev. ed. of: Knock 'em dead.
Includes bibliographical references and index.
ISBN 1–58062–070–1
1. Employment interviewing. I. Title. II. Title: Knock 'em dead.
HF5549.5.I6Y37   1998
650.14—dc21   98–39569
CIP

Author photo: Nick Basillion

This book is available at quantity discounts for bulk purchases.
For more information, call 1-800-872-5627 (In Massachusetts 781-767-8100).

Visit our home page at http://www.careercity.com

Contents

III. Great Answers to Tough Interview Questions   121

This section tells you not only what to answer but also how to answer. It provides the real preparation for getting the job you want and deserve.

IV. Finishing Touches   211

Statistics show that the last person to interview usually gets the job. Here are some steps you can take that will keep your impression strong.

V.   In Depth   263

Appendices   289

Acknowledgments

My thanks to the following people, who, in different ways, have helped this book become what it is today—the only internationally published job hunting guide of its kind.

I'd like to recognize a couple of people in the media who have given me support and encouragement over an extended period of time. These include Tony Lee and the staff of NBEW at Dow Jones, Bill Thompson of AP, the Famous Dolans of WOR and CNBC, Fred and the gang at Morning Exchange (for putting me through my paces at the beginning of every tour, every year), and the entire editorial staff at *Working Woman*.

Of course, grateful thanks are also in order to my old friend Gary down in the Lone Star State, to Lisa Fisher, and to Anker Heergaard.

From the employment services world: Dunhill Personnel System presidents—Brad Brin of Milwaukee, Warren Mahan of Maine, Leo Salzman of Columbus, Dave Bontempo of Southampton, Paul and Pat Erickson of Shawnee Mission, Jim Fowler (and Ray Johnson) of Huntsville, Stan Hart of Troy, Mike Badgett of Cherry Hills Village, and John Webb and everyone in beautiful San Antonio.

Thanks also to Don Kipper of Ernst & Whinney, Dan O'Brien of Grumman, Amy Marglis and Kathy Seich of Merrill Lynch, Roger Villanueva of I.M.S., Victor Lindquist of Northwestern University, Ed Fitzpatrick of the University of Michigan, and Mary Giannini of Columbia University.

Gratitude is due to Eric Blume for his editorial assistance in the first three editions, to my second editor, Brandon Toropov; and of course to my current editorial genius, Ed Walters. In 1998 I especially like to thank Will McNeill and Perry Yate for their research efforts. Thanks go also to that man of vision, my publisher Bob Adams, and the people who got this hot little book into your hands—the tireless sales representatives of Adams Publishing.

Why *Knock 'em Dead?*

In 1985, when this book was first published, we began by answering the question "Why another book about interviewing?" Because the others stop at that critical point when the tough questions start flying. Sadly, that critique of the many other books out there is still valid. And with over three million *Knock 'em Dead* books in print worldwide, there seems ample evidence that readers agree with my 1985 assessment.

Still, *Knock 'em Dead* has not stood still. In the years since that first edition, this book has grown in size and scope every year; it has doubled in length and now covers the entire job search process. I am confident that it does so with a broader scope, and with more depth and originality, than any other book in the field.

The ever-expanding page count reflects my responses to the constantly changing realities of the world of work. Although we have revised the work throughout, this flexible approach is perhaps best exemplified by one of the new sections to be found in this year's edition, "When You See Clouds on the Horizon." This new appendix takes into account the sobering reality that you can no longer rely on long years of service to a single company to keep a career in high gear.

I wrote *Knock 'em Dead* because too much of the job search advice I could find on the shelves of my bookstore was infantile at best and detrimental to one's professional health at worst. The vast majority of job hunting books lack the practical advice of what to do in the heat of battle. *Knock 'em Dead* will take you through the whole process—from putting the paperwork together to negotiating salary to your best advantage. Of course, the core of the book still helps you resolve the job seeker's most dreaded question: "How on earth do I answer *that* one?"

Here, you'll get hundreds of the tough, sneaky, mean, and low-down questions that interviewers love to throw at you. With each question, I will show you what the interviewer wants to find out about you, and explain how you should reply. After each explanation, you'll get a sample answer and suggestions on how to customize it to your individual circumstances. The examples themselves come from real life, things people like you have done on the job that got them noticed. I'll show you how they packaged those experiences, how they used their practical experience to turn a job interview into a job offer.

Perhaps you are trying to land your first job or are returning to the workplace. Maybe you are a seasoned executive taking another step up the ladder of success. Whoever you are, this book will help you, because it shows you how to master any interview and succeed with any interviewer. You will learn that every interviewer tries to evaluate each candidate by the same three criteria: Is the candidate *able* to do the job? Is he or she *willing* to put in the effort to make the job a success? And last but not least, is he or she *manageable*? You will learn how to demonstrate your superiority in each of these areas, under all interview conditions.

The job interview is a measured and ritualistic mating dance in which the best partners whirl away with the glittering prizes. The steps of this dance are the give-and-take, question-and-response exchanges that make meaningful business conversation. Learn the steps and you, too, can dance the dance.

Your partner in the dance, obviously, is the interviewer, who will lead with tough questions that carry subtleties hidden from the untrained ear. You will learn how to recognize those questions-within-questions. And with this knowledge, you will be cool, calm, and collected, while other candidates are falling apart with attacks of interview nerves.

How do you discover hidden meanings in questions? I recently heard a story about a young woman who was doing very well on an interview for a high-pressure job in a television studio. The interviewer wanted to know how she would react in the sudden, stressful situations common in TV, and got his answer when he said, "You know, I don't really think you're suitable for the job. Wouldn't you be better off in another company?" With wounded pride, the job hunter stormed out in a huff. She never knew how close she was, how easy it would have been to land the job. The interviewer smiled: He had caught her with a tough question. Did the interviewer mean what he said? What was really behind the question? How could she have handled it and landed the job? The great answers to tough questions like that and many others are waiting for you in the following pages.

The job interview has many similarities to good social conversation. Job offers always go to the interviewee who can turn a one-sided examination of skills into a dynamic exchange between two professionals. In *Knock 'em Dead*, you will learn the techniques for exciting and holding your interviewer's attention, and at the same time, for promoting yourself as the best candidate for the job.

This book will carry you successfully through the worst interviews and job hunting scenarios you will ever face. It is written in five interconnected parts. "The Well-Stocked Briefcase" gets you ready for the fray. You will quickly learn to build a resume with broad appeal and to use a unique customizing technique guaranteed to make your application stand out as something special. You will also learn how to tap into thousands of job openings at all levels that never reach the newspapers.

Once you are ready for action, "Getting to Square One" examines all the approaches to getting job interviews and teaches you simple and effective ways to set up multiple interviews. This section ends with techniques to steer you successfully through those increasingly common telephone screening interviews.

"Great Answers to Tough Interview Questions" gives you just that, and teaches you some valuable business lessons that will contribute to your future success. All successful companies look for the same things in their employees, and everything they're looking for you either have or can develop. Sound impossible? I will show you the twenty key personality traits that can convey your potential for success to any interviewer.

"Finishing Touches" assures that "out-of-sight, out-of-mind" will not apply to you after you leave the interviewer's office. You will even discover how to get a job offer after you have been turned down for the position, and how to negotiate the best salary and package for yourself when a job offer is made. Most important, the sum of those techniques will give you tremendous self-confidence when you go to an interview: No more jitters, no more sweaty palms.

The final section, "In Depth," includes new ideas for long-term career survival and some important advice on keeping your financial boat afloat during tough times.

If you want to know how business works and what savvy businesspeople look for in an employee, if you want to discover how to land the interview and conquer the interviewer, then this book is for you. *Knock 'em Dead* delivers everything you need to win the job of your dreams. Now get to it, step ahead in your career, and knock 'em dead.

— *Martin John Yate*
New York

Part I | The Well-Stocked Briefcase

This section will show you how to discover, define, and package your skills and strong points, and to do the necessary legwork that will prepare you to sell them.

Have you heard the one about the poor man who wanted to become a famous bear-slayer? Once upon a time, in a town plagued by bears, lived a man. The man had always wanted to travel but had neither the right job nor the money. If he could kill a bear, then he could travel to other places plagued with bears and make his living as a bear-slayer. Every day he sat on the porch and waited for a bear to come by. After many weeks of waiting, he thought he might go looking for bears. He didn't know much about them, except that they were out there.

Full of hope, he rose before dawn, loaded his single-shot musket, and headed for the forest. On reaching the edge of the forest, he raised the musket and fired into the dense undergrowth.

Do you think he hit a bear or, for that matter, anything else? Why was he bear hunting with a single-shot musket, and why did he shoot before seeing a bear? What was his problem? Our hero couldn't tell dreams from reality. He went hunting unprepared and earned what he deserved. The moral of the tale is this: When you look for a job, keep a grip on reality, go loaded for bear, and don't go off half-cocked.

Out there in the forest of your profession hide many companies and countless opportunities. These are major corporations, small family affairs, and some in between. They all have something in common, and that's problems. To solve those problems, companies need people. Think about your present job function: What problems would occur if you weren't there? You were hired to take care of those problems.

Being a problem solver is good, but companies prefer to hire and promote someone who also understands what business is all about. There are three lessons you should remember on this score.

Lesson One: Companies are in business to make money. People have loyalty to companies; companies have loyalty only to the bottom line. They make money by being economical and saving money. They make money by being efficient and saving time. And if they save time, they save money, and have more time to make more money.

Lesson Two: Companies and you are exactly alike. You both want to make as much money as possible in as short a time as possible. That allows you to do the things you really want with the rest of your time.

Lesson Three: There are buyer's markets (advantage: prospective employer) and there are seller's markets (advantage: prospective employee). Job offers put you in a seller's market, and give you the whip hand.

Lesson One tells you the three things every company is interested in. *Lesson Two* says to recognize that you really have the same goals as the company. *Lesson Three* says that anyone with any sense wants to be in a seller's market.

If you look for jobs one at a time, you put yourself in a buyer's market. If you implement my advice in *Knock 'em Dead,* you will have multiple job offers. And job offers, however good or bad they are, will put you in a seller's market, regardless of the economic climate.

Operating in a seller's market requires knowing who, where, and what your buyers are in the market for, then being ready with the properly packaged product.

In this section you will find out how to identify *every* company that could be in need of your services. You will learn how to discover the names of the president, those on the board, and those in management; the company sales volume; complete lines of company services or products; and the size of the outfit. You will evaluate and package your professional skills in a method guaranteed to have appeal to every employer. And you will discover highly desirable professional skills you never knew you had.

It will take a couple of days' work to get you loaded for bear. You are going to need to update your resume (or create a new one), generate some cover letters, research potential employers, and create a comprehensive marketing plan.

While I cover each of these areas in sequence, I recommend that, in the execution, you mix and match the activities. In other words, when the direct research begins to addle the gray matter, switch to resume enhancement, and so on. An hour of one activity followed by an hour of another will keep your mind fresh and your program balanced.

Your first action should be a trip to the library (taking sufficient paper and pens). On the way, purchase some push-pins, a large-scale area map, and some stick-on labels—and rustle up a three-foot piece of string. Take some sandwiches; there is no feeling in the world like eating lunch on the library steps.

1 | All Things to All People

A resume's goal is to show that you are a problem solver. Here are the five exercises to help you identify the important aspects of your work history, the three types of resumes you can use, and the seven rules for creating a broad, powerful curriculum vitae.

At the library, walk in purposefully and ask for the reference section. When you find it, wander around for a few minutes before staking a claim. You will discover that libraries are a good place to watch the human race, so get the best seat in the house. Make sure you have a clear view of the librarian's desk. When you need a rest, that's where all the comic relief takes place.

Interviewers today are continually asking for detailed examples of your past performance. They safely assume you will do at least as well (or as poorly) on the new job as you did on the old one, and so the examples you give will seal your fate. Therefore you need to examine your past performance in a manner that will empower you to handle these questions in a professional and competent manner.

This chapter will show you how to identify examples of problems solved, projects completed, and contributions made that will impress any interviewer. As you complete the exercises in this chapter and concurrently proceed with your research, your added self-knowledge and confidence could well open your eyes to as-yet-unimagined professional opportunities. You will also get the correctly packaged information for a workmanlike resume. Two birds with one stone.

Resumes, of course, are important, and there are two facts you must know about them. First, you are going to need one. Second, no one will want to read it. The average interviewer has never been trained to interview effectively, probably finds the interview as uncomfortable as you do, and will do everything possible to avoid discomfort. Resumes, therefore, are used more to screen people out than screen them in. So your resume must be all things to all people.

Another hurdle to clear is avoiding too much of your professional jargon in the resume. It is a cold hard fact that the first person to see your resume is often in the personnel department. This office screens for many different jobs and cannot be expected to have an in-depth knowledge of every specialty within the company— or its special language.

For those reasons, your resume must be short, be easy to read and understand, and use words that are familiar to the reader and that have universal appeal. Most important, it should portray you as a problem solver.

While this chapter covers ways to build an effective resume, its main goal is to help you perform better at the interview. You will achieve that as you evaluate your professional skills according to the exercises. In fact, you are likely to discover skills and achievements you didn't even know you had. A few you will use in your resume (merely a preview of coming attractions); the others you will use to knock 'em dead at the interview.

A good starting point is your current or last job title. Write it down. Then, jot down all the other different titles you have heard that describe that job. When you are finished, follow it with a three- or four-sentence description of your job functions. Don't think too hard about it, just do it. The titles and descriptions are not carved in stone—this written description is just the beginning of the resume-building exercises. You'll be surprised at what you've written; it will read better than you had thought.

All attributes that you discover and develop in the following exercises are valuable to an employer. You possess many desirable traits, and these exercises help to reveal and to package them.

☐ **Exercise One**: Reread the written job description, then write down your most important duty/function. Follow that with a list of the skills or special training necessary to perform that duty. Next, list the achievements of which you are most proud in that area. It could look something like this:

Duty: Train and motivate sales staff of six.
Skills: Formal training skills. Knowledge of market and ability to make untrained sales staff productive. Ability to keep successful salespeople motivated and tied to the company.
Achievements: Reduced turnover 7 percent; increased sales 14 percent.

The potential employer is most interested in the achievements—those things that make you stand out from the crowd. Try to appeal to a company's interests by conservatively estimating what your achievements meant to your employer. If your achievements saved time, estimate how much. If you saved money, how much? If your achievements made money for the company, how much? Beware of exaggeration—if you were part of a team, identify your achievements as such. It will make your claims more believable and will demonstrate your ability to work with others.

Achievements, of course, differ according to your profession. Most of life's jobs fall into one of these broad categories:

- Sales and service
- Management and administration
- Technical and production

While it is usual to cite the differences between those major job functions, at this point it is far more valuable to you to recognize the commonalities. In sales, dollar volume is important. In management or administration, the parallel is time saved, which is money saved; saving money is just the same as making money for your company. In the technical and production areas, increasing production (doing more in less time) accrues exactly the same benefits to the company. Job titles may differ, yet all employees have the same opportunity to benefit their employers, and in turn, themselves.

Today, companies are doing more with less; they are leaner, have higher expectations of their employees, and plan to keep it that way. The people who get hired and get ahead today are those with a basic understanding of business goals. And successful job candidates are those who have the best interests of the company and its profitability constantly in mind.

☐ **Exercise Two**: This simple exercise helps you get a clear picture of your achievements. If you were to meet with your supervisor to discuss a raise, what achievements would you want to discuss? List all you can think of, quickly. Then come back and flesh out the details.

☐ **Exercise Three**: This exercise is particularly valuable if you feel you can't see the forest for the trees.

Problem: Think of a job-related problem you had to face in the last couple of years. Come on, everyone can remember one.
Solution: Describe your solution to the problem, step by step. List everything you did.
Results: Finally, consider the results of your solution in terms that would have value to an employer: money earned or saved; time saved.

☐ **Exercise Four:** Now, a valuable exercise that turns the absence of a negative into a positive. This one helps you look at your job in a different light and accents important but often overlooked areas that help make you special. Begin discovering for yourself some of the key personal traits that all companies look for.

First, consider actions that if not done properly would affect the goal of your job. If that is difficult, remember an incompetent co-worker. What did he or she do wrong? What did he or she do differently from competent employees?

Now, turn the absence of those negatives into positive attributes. For example, think of the employee who never managed to get to work on time. You could honestly say that someone who did come to work on time every day was punctual and reliable, believed in systems and procedures, was efficiency-minded, and cost- and profit-conscious.

If you have witnessed the reprimands and ultimate termination of that tardy employee, you will see the value of the positive traits in the eyes of an employer. The absence of negative traits makes you a desirable employee, but no one will know unless you say. On completion of the exercise, you will be able to make points about your background in a positive fashion. You will set yourself apart from others, if only because others do not understand the benefit of projecting all their positive attributes.

☐ **Exercise Five:** Potential employers and interviewers are always interested in people who:

- Are efficiency-minded
- Have an eye for economy
- Follow procedures
- Are profit-oriented

Proceed through your work history and identify the aspects of your background that exemplify those traits. These newly discovered personal pluses will not only be woven into your resume but will be reflected in the posture of your answers when you get to the interview, and in your performance when you land the right job.

Now you need to take some of that knowledge and package it in a resume. There are three standard types of resumes:

Chronological: The most frequently used format. Use it when your work history is stable and your professional growth is consistent. The chronological format is exactly what it sounds like: It follows your work history backward from the current job, listing companies and dates and responsibilities. Avoid it if you have experienced performance problems, have not grown professionally (but want to), or have made frequent job changes. All those problems will show up in a glaring fashion if you use a chronological resume.

Functional: Use this type if you have been unemployed for long periods of time or have jumped jobs too frequently, or if your career has been stagnant and you want to jump-start it. A functional resume is created without employment dates or company names, and concentrates on skills and responsibilities. It can be useful if you have changed careers, or when current responsibilities don't relate specifically to the job you want. It is written with the most relevant experience to the job you're seeking placed first, and de-emphasizes jobs, employment dates, and job titles by placing them inconspicuously at the end. It allows you to promote specific job skills without emphasizing where or when you developed those skills.

Combination: Use this format if you have a steady work history with demonstrated growth, and if you have nothing you wish to de-emphasize. A combination resume is a combination of chronological and functional resumes. It starts with a brief personal summary, then lists job-specific skills relevant to the objective, and segues into a chronological format that lists the how, where, and when these skills were acquired.

Notice that each style is designed to emphasize strengths and minimize certain undesirable traits. In today's world, all of us need a powerful resume. It is not only a door opener, it is also there long after we are gone and will almost certainly be reviewed just before the choice of the successful candidate is made by the interviewer.

Examples of each style follow; for more detailed information on assembling a winning resume, you may wish to purchase this book's companion volume, *Resumes That Knock 'em Dead*.

If you already have a resume and just want to make sure it measures up, check it against these seven basic rules of resume writing.

☐ **Rule One:** Use the most general of job titles. You are, after all, a hunter of interviews, not of specific titles. Cast your net wide. Use a title that is specific enough to put you in the field, yet vague enough to elicit further questions. One way you can make a job title specifically vague is to add the term *specialist* (e.g., Computer Specialist, Administration Specialist, Production Specialist).

☐ **Rule Two:** If you must state a specific job objective, couch it in terms of contributions you can make in that position. Do not state what you expect of the employer.

☐ **Rule Three:** Do not state your current salary. If you are earning too little or too much, you could rule yourself out before getting your foot in the door. For the same reason, do not mention your desired salary.

☐ **Rule Four:** Remember that people get great joy from getting pleasant surprises. Show a little gold now, but let the interviewer discover the mother lode at the interview.

☐ **Rule Five:** Try to keep your resume to one page; take whatever steps necessary to keep the resume no more than two pages long. No one reads long resumes—they are boring, and every company is frightened that if it lets in a windbag, it will never get him or her out again.

☐ **Rule Six:** Your resume must be typed. As a rule of thumb, three pages of double-spaced, handwritten notes make one typewritten page.

☐ **Rule Seven:** Finally, emphasize your achievements and problem-solving skills. Keep the resume general.

A Resume Only a Computer Could Love

In 1993, *78 percent* of companies surveyed had an automated resume-tracking system in place. If you're applying to a large company, or if you suspect that a potential employer is using computers instead of human beings to scan resumes, then you should prepare a computer-friendly resume as well as a more traditional version.

To prepare a resume especially for a computerized recruiter:

- Always send an original resume, never a photocopy.
- Put your name on the *first line* of your resume, and put nothing else before it.
- Use a laser jet printer or a typewriter rather than a dot matrix printer.
- Use common typefaces, such as Times, Palatino, Optima, and Courier. Avoid serif (letters with curlicues on them) or script typefaces that the computer might not recognize.

- Keep the point sizes between 10 and 14.
- If you want to use boldface, save it for headings. Never use it to type your name, address, or telephone number.
- Use few horizontal lines, and no vertical lines, if you can help it.

And:

- Never use double columns or other complicated layouts.
- Never use any paper except white or beige, sized 8½" x 11".
- Never incorporate graphics, shading, ellipses, brackets, parentheses, italics, script, underlining, or compressed type.
- Never staple, fold, or fax your resume.

Keying into Buzzwords

Begin and end your computer-friendly resume with a short section of eighty words or less, called keywords, or talents. Talents encompass technical jargon and other nouns that can be used to label the job or yourself.

To compile a list of talents, check the classifieds for positions similar to the one you're looking for, and cull any recurring nouns. Make sure to put the most important words first, in case the computer is limited in the amount of buzzwords it can remember.

No Plain, No Gain

Remember, when you're preparing a resume to be scanned and understood by a computer, you are not necessarily writing one that would appeal to a human. Your goal is not to catch the recruiter's eye with fancy fonts, a jazzy layout, and exciting language, but simply to make it through the scanner intact with enough information—in the appropriate order—that when the computer is looking for somebody with your qualifications, your resume will pop up.

What follows is a selection of standard, non-computer-specific resumes for you to adapt as you see fit.

CHRONOLOGICAL RESUME

Jane Swift, 9 Central Avenue, Quincy, MA 02269. (617) 555-1212

SUMMARY: Ten years of increasing responsibilities in the employment services industry. Concentration in the high-technology markets.

EXPERIENCE: Howard Systems International, Inc.   1994-Present
Management Consulting Firm
Personnel Manager

Responsible for recruiting and managing consulting staff of five. Set up office and organized the recruitment, selection, and hiring of consultants. Recruited all levels of MIS staff from financial to manufacturing markets.

Additional responsibilities:
- coordinated with outside advertising agencies
- developed P.R. with industry periodicals—placement with over twenty magazines and newsletters
- developed effective referral programs—referrals increased 32 percent

EXPERIENCE: Technical Aid Corporation   1987-1994
National Consulting Firm. MICRO/TEMPS Division

Division Manager   1993-1994
Area Manager   1990-1993
Branch Manager   1988-1990

As Division Manager, opened additional West Coast offices, staffed and trained all offices with appropriate personnel. Created and implemented all divisional operational policies responsible for P & L. Sales increased to $20 million from $0 in 1988.

- Achieved and maintained 30 percent annual growth over seven-year period.
- Maintained sales staff turnover at 14 percent.

As Area Manager, opened additional offices, hiring staff, setting up office policies and training sales and recruiting personnel.

Additional responsibilities:
- supervised offices in two states
- developed business relationships with accounts—75 percent of clients were regular customers
- client base increased 28 percent per year
- generated over $200,000 worth of free trade-journal publicity

As Branch Manager, hired to establish the new MICRO/TEMPS operation. Recruited and managed consultants. Hired internal staff. Sold service to clients.

EDUCATION: Boston University
B.S. Public Relations, 1987

FUNCTIONAL RESUME

Jane Swift
9 Central Avenue
Quincy, MA 02269
(617) 555-1212

OBJECTIVE: A position in Employment Services where my management, sales, and recruiting talents can be effectively utilized to improve operations and contribute to company profits.

SUMMARY: Over ten years of Human Resources experience. Extensive responsibility for multiple branch offices and an internal staff of forty-plus employees and 250 consultants.

SALES: Sold high-technology consulting services with consistently profitable margins throughout the United States. Grew sales from $0 to over $20 million a year.

Created training programs and trained salespeople in six metropolitan markets.

RECRUITING: Developed recruiting sourcing methods for multiple branch offices.

Recruited over 25,000 internal and external consultants in the high-technology professions.

MANAGEMENT: Managed up to forty people in sales, customer service, recruiting, and administration. Turnover maintained below 14 percent in a "turnover business."

FINANCIAL: Prepared quarterly and yearly forecasts. Presented, reviewed, and defended these forecasts to the Board of Directors. Responsible for P & L of $20 million sales operation.

PRODUCTION: Responsible for opening multiple offices and accountable for growth and profitability. One hundred percent success and maintained 30 percent growth over a seven-year period in ten offices.

WORK
EXPERIENCE:
1994 to Present HOWARD SYSTEMS INTERNATIONAL, Boston, MA
National Consulting Firm
Personnel Manager

1987-1994 TECHNICAL AID CORPORATION, Needham, MA
National Consulting & Search Firm
Division Manager

EDUCATION: B.S., 1987, Boston University

REFERENCES: Available upon request

COMBINATION RESUME

EMPLOYMENT SERVICES MANAGEMENT

Jane Swift
9 Central Avenue
Quincy, MA 02269
(617) 555-1212

OBJECTIVE:

Employment Services Management

SUMMARY: Ten years of increasing responsibilities in the employment services marketplace. Concentration in the high-technology markets.

SALES: Sold high-technology consulting services with consistently profitable margins throughout the United States. Grew sales from $0 to over $20 million a year.

PRODUCTION: Responsible for opening multiple offices and accountable for growth and profitability. One hundred percent success and maintained 30 percent growth over a seven-year period in ten offices.

MANAGEMENT: Managed up to forty people in sales, customer service, recruiting, and administration. Turnover maintained below 14 percent in a "turnover business." Hired branch managers, sales, and recruiting staff throughout United States.

FINANCIAL: Prepared quarterly and yearly forecasts. Presented, reviewed, and defended these forecasts to the Board of Directors. Responsible for P & L of $20 million sales operation.

MARKETING: Performed numerous market studies for multiple branch openings. Resolved feasibility of combining two different sales offices. Study resulted in savings of over $5,000 per month in operating expenses.

COMBINATION RESUME (page 2)

EXPERIENCE: Howard Systems International, Inc.   1994-Present
Management Consulting Firm
Personnel Manager

Responsible for recruiting and managing consulting staff of five. Set up office and organized the recruitment, selection, and hiring of consultants. Recruited all levels of MIS staff from financial to manufacturing markets.

Additional responsibilities:
- developed P.R. with industry periodicals—placement with over twenty magazines and newsletters
- developed effective referral programs—referrals increased 320 percent

Technical Aid Corporation   1987-1994
National Consulting Firm. MICRO/TEMPS Division
Division Manager   1993-1994
Area Manager   1990-1993
Branch Manager   1987-1990

As Division Manager, opened additional West Coast offices, staffed and trained all offices with appropriate personnel. Created and implemented all divisional operational policies. Responsible for P & L. Sales increased to $20 million from $0 in 1988.

- Achieved and maintained 30 percent annual growth over seven-year period.
- Maintained sales staff turnover at 14 percent.

As Area Manager, opened additional offices, hiring staff, setting up office policies, training sales and recruiting personnel.

Additional responsibilities:
- supervised offices in two states
- developed business relationships with accounts—75 percent of clients were regular customers
- client base increased 28 percent per year
- generated over $200,000 worth of free trade-journal publicity

As Branch Manager, hired to establish the new MICRO/TEMPS operation. Recruited and managed consultants. Hired internal staff. Sold service to clients.

EDUCATION: B.S., 1987, Boston University

2 | The Executive Briefing

If you know the specific requirements of a particular opening, the executive briefing will quickly, and impressively, line them up with your skills and qualities.

A general resume does have drawbacks. First, it is too general to relate your qualifications to each specific job. Second, more than one person will probably be interviewing you, and that is a major stumbling block. While you will ultimately report to one person, you may well be interviewed by other team members. When that happens, the problems begin.

A manager says to a subordinate, "Spend a few minutes with this candidate and tell me what you think." Your general resume may be impressive, but the manager rarely adequately outlines the job being filled or the specific qualifications for which he or she is looking. This means that other interviewers do not have any way to qualify you fairly and specifically. While the manager will be looking for specific skills relating to projects at hand, personnel will be trying to match your skills to the job-description-manual vagaries, and the other interviewers will fumble in the dark because no one told them what to look for. Such problems can reduce your chances of landing a job offer.

A neat trick I helped develop for the executive-search industry is the Executive Briefing. It enables you to customize your resume quickly to each specific job and acts as a focusing device for the person who interviews you.

While the Executive Briefing is only one form of cover letter, I am including it here for one very important reason—namely, that you are, in your research, going to come across "dream opportunities" before your new resume is finished. The Executive Briefing allows you to update and customize that old resume with lightning speed without delaying the rest of your research.

Like many great ideas, the Executive Briefing is beautiful in its simplicity. It is a sheet of paper with the company's requirements for the job opening listed on the left side, and your skills—matching point by point the company's needs—on the right. It looks like the following:

Executive Briefing

Dear Sir/Madam:

While my attached resume will provide you with a general outline of my work history, my problem-solving abilities, and some achievements, I have taken the time to list your current specific requirements and my applicable skills in those areas. I hope this will enable you to use your time effectively today.

Your Requirements:	My Skills:
1. Management of public library service area (for circulation, reference, etc.)	1. Experience as head reference librarian at University of Smithtown
2. Supervision of fourteen full-time support employees	2. Supervised support staff of seventeen
3. Ability to work with larger supervisory team in planning, budgeting, and policy formulating	3. Responsible for budget and reformation of circulation rules during my last year
4. ALA-accredited MLS	4. ALA-accredited MLS
5. Three years' experience	5. One year with public library; two with University of Smithtown

---

This briefing assures that each resume you send out addresses the job's specific needs and that every interviewer at that company will be interviewing you for the same job.

Send an Executive Briefing with every resume; it will substantially increase your chances of obtaining an interview with the company. An Executive Briefing sent with a resume provides a comprehensive picture of a thorough professional, plus a personalized, fast, and easy-to-read synopsis that details exactly how you can help with current needs.

The use of an Executive Briefing is naturally restricted to jobs that you have discovered through your own efforts or seen advertised. It is obviously not appropriate for sending when the requirements of a specific job are unavailable. Finally, using the Executive Briefing as a cover letter to your resume will greatly increase the chance that your query will be picked out of the pile in the personnel department and hand-carried to the appropriate manager.

3 | The Inside Track

Why some people stay on a plateau longer, while others get more offers at better companies.

There used to be a stigma about changing jobs or looking for a new one. Today we live in a different climate. Everyone you speak with in your job hunt has been through your experience. Career moves and unemployment are an integral part of our working lives, but how long this phase lasts is entirely up to you.

I recently met an executive who was looking for a job for the first time in twenty years. He had been looking for seven months and wasn't the least bit concerned: "I've been told that it takes a month for every ten thousand dollars of salary, so I really have another eighteen months to go." He seemed to have this mistaken idea that after two years of unemployment, someone would magically appear with another chief executive's job for him.

His method of job hunting was networking "because that is what I've been told is the best way to find jobs." It is if it works, but all too often a single-shot approach misfires.

The employment market varies from year to year. Sometimes it's a buyer's market and sometimes a seller's. But the fact remains that regardless of the state of the economy, there are good jobs out there for the job hunter who employs a systematic and comprehensive approach.

Too many job hunters rely solely on applications to the well-known companies, the IBMs of this world. They forget that the majority of growth in American industry is with small companies with less than fifty employees. Your goal is to land the best possible job for you and your needs. The problem is, you won't have the chance to pick the best opportunity unless you check them all out.

Average employee turnover in the American workplace has remained steady for some years at about 14 percent. In other words, just about every company is looking for someone during the year. What you have to do is to make sure that you are aware of the opportunity and the company, and the company in turn is aware of you when that opportunity arises.

There is a multi-pronged approach that combines active and passive job hunting strategies that every job hunter can use to cover all the bases and tap the very best opportunities.

1. Direct research. Your future could well lie with a company you never dreamed existed.
2. Newspapers. Thousands of overlooked opportunities.
3. Employment agencies. Whomever you allow to represent you will decide whom you get to meet and how seriously your initial candidacy will be considered.
4. References. The references you supply to potential employers in the later stages of the job hunt can be utilized effectively at the beginning, too.
5. College placement offices and alumni/ae organizations. Even if you have long since graduated, these organizations can be a big help.
6. Professional associations. It is sometimes said that it is not what you know, but who you know.
7. Job fairs. Home of employers in a feeding frenzy for today and tomorrow.
8. Business and trade publications. These are a much underrated resource for telling you what is happening on your profession's main street and who is making it happen.
9. Networking. It is more than an empty phrase. There are numerous networks we can all tap into effectively.
10. Job hunters' networks. If one doesn't exist, create your own.
11. Electronic databases. The newest weapon in your arsenal.

Tapping the hidden job market need not be scary if you follow a sound plan. In the following pages, you'll examine insider tricks to get you up to speed and ensure you maintain momentum in each of these areas.

4 | The Hidden Job Market

Eleven innovative interview-generating techniques to get you up to speed and ensure you maintain momentum.

On a radio talk show earlier this year I listened to a problem from a listener. She said, "I'm in the academic field and I've been unemployed for two years, and I don't know what to do." I asked her how many organizations she had contacted, and she said 250. I asked her how many possible employers there were, and she said about 3,000. I said, "Next caller please." The world owes no one a living. You have to go out and find a job.

While I was revising this chapter, I heard from the producer of a national talk show on which I had recently appeared. She told me she used the techniques described in this part of the book to get thirty interviews in three weeks!

1. Direct Research

No job search is going to be truly comprehensive without research. As we have seen, this means visiting the local library with the best research section. It is well worth traveling a few miles to get to a major library.

There are a number of reference books you can consult; they are listed in the bibliography, so I won't waste space teaching you how to use them—the librarian will be happy to do that.

Your goal is to identify and build personalized dossiers on the companies in your chosen geographic area. Do not be judgmental about what and who they might appear to be: You are fishing for possible job openings, so cast your net wide and list them all.

Take a pad of paper, and using a separate sheet for each company, copy all the relevant company information. So that we agree on *relevant*, take a look at the example (page 21).

In the example, you see the names of the company president and chairman of the board, a description of the complete lines of company services or products, the size of the company, and the locations of its various branches. Of course, if you find other interesting information, copy it down, by all means. For instance, you might come across information on growth or shrinkage in a particular area of a company, or you might read about recent acquisitions the company has made. Write it all down.

```
                    Corporation, Inc.
Headquarters:
123 Main Street
Boston, MA 01234

Main phone: 617/555-1212
Personnel (Joseph Smith, Director): 617/555-1212

President: Richard Johnson (for 3 yrs.)
COO: William Jones (for 2 yrs.)

Director of Word Processing Services: Peter Lee

Company produces a complete line of office machines:
calculators, adding machines, typewriters (electric,
electronic, manual), telephones, computerized switching
systems, and a wide range of peripheral equipment.
Employs 1,200, all in Massachusetts.

This location is primarily an administrative facility,
but it provides all services for the firm (research,
repair, operations, word processing). Manufacturing
facilities located in Worcester (calculators, telephone
equipment, peripherals) and Wakefield (typewriters,
computers).

Sales (1992): $334.4 million
Profits: plus 5 percent over last five years

Recently acquired Disko, Inc. (Braintree, MA), a software
firm (looks like it's diversifying ???). Maybe has
something big in the works (possible merger with The Bigg
Corporation).
```

This information will help you shine at the interview in three ways. Your knowledge creates a favorable impression at your first meeting; that you made an effort is noticed. That no one else bothers is a second benefit; you have set yourself apart from the others. And third, you are showing that you respect the company, and therefore, by inference, the interviewer; this sets a favorable tone.

All your effort has an obvious short-term value: It helps you win job offers. It also has long-term value because you are building a personalized reference work of your industry/specialty/profession that will help you throughout your career whenever you wish to make a job change.

Unfortunately, no single reference work you will find at the library is complete. The very size and scope of reference works means that they are just a little out of date at publication time. Also, no single reference work lists every company. Because you don't know what company has the very best job for you, you need to research as many businesses in your area as possible, and therefore you will have to look through several reference books.

Be sure to check out any specialized guides mentioned in the bibliography, including the *Standard & Poor's Register* and your state's manufacturing directory. Senior-level executives will be especially interested in volume two of this register, which gives detailed personal histories and contact information about board members and first-rank executives.

Your local *Business-to-Business Yellow Pages* is also worth a look. Information found here will range from a company name and telephone number to a full-page advertisement providing considerable "insider" data.

If you can get only names and telephone numbers, the directory can still be a valuable resource. While most directories are updated infrequently and tend only to list major players in the field, *B-to-B Yellow Pages* are updated annually. They are used extensively by growth companies as a marketing tool.

Most of our nation's economic growth (and therefore most of the promising new job opportunities) is with the small-growth companies.

Making the Battle Map

At the end of the day, pack up and head home for some well-deserved troughing and sluicing. Remember to purchase a map of your area, push-pins, and small stick-on labels for implementing the next step of your plan.

Put the map on the wall. Attach the string to a push-pin, stick the pin on the spot where you live, and draw concentric circles at intervals of one mile.

Next, take out the company biographies prepared at the library and write "#1" on the first. Find the firm's location on the map and mark it with a push-pin. Then, mark an adhesive label "#1" and attach it to the head of the pin. As you progress, a dramatic picture of your day's work appears. Each pin-filled circle is a territory that needs to be covered, and each of those pins represents a potential job. In short order you will have defaced a perfectly good map, but you'll have a physical outline of your job hunting efforts.

It is likely you will return to the library, continuing your research work and preparing your resume. The initial research might take a few days. Your goal in this stage is to generate a couple of hundred sources, enough to get you started. Then, once your campaign is up to speed, you can visit again as prudence dictates.

Try walking to the library the next time, if practical. Not only is it cheaper (a sound reason in itself), but the exercise is important. You are engaged in a battle of wits, and the healthier you are physically, the sharper you will be mentally. You need your wits about you, because there are always well-qualified people looking for the best jobs. Yet it is not the most qualified who always get the job. It is the person who is best prepared who wins every time. Job hunters who knock 'em dead at the interview are those who do their homework. Do a little more walking. Do a little more research.

Purchasing Mailing Lists

Mailing lists can be cheap and effective. With very few exceptions there is a mailing list of exactly the types of movers and shakers you want to work for. Additionally, these lists can be broken down for you by title, geography, zip code—all sorts of ways. They are affordable, too; usually about $100 for a thousand. For a list broker, just look in your *Yellow Pages* under "Mailing List Brokers/Compilers."

As even the most up-to-date lists are out-of-date by the time they get to you, it is a good investment to call and verify that Joe Schmoe, vice president of engineering, is still there. If Joe is no longer there you can find out where he went, and you will have uncovered another opportunity for yourself.

ONLINE RESOURCES

American Business Information
http://www.abii.com
ABI is one of the largest list brokers in the nation. The company advertises that their lists cover over 10 million businesses. Mailing lists can be as simple as a name and address or as detailed as including company size, annual sales, and the names of executives.

American List Counsel
http://www.amlist.com
This company maintains over 16,000 different lists. You can search online for a list by keyword, or you can request a free catalog.

2. Newspapers

Most people, unfortunately, use either the newspaper or reference books when job hunting, but rarely both. These people run the risk of ending up in a buyer's market. Not a good place to be.

Almost everybody looking for a new job buys the newspaper and then carefully misuses it. A recent story tells of a job hunter who started by waiting for the Sunday paper to be published. He read the paper and circled six jobs. He called about the first only to find it had already been filled, and in the process, got snubbed by someone whose voice had yet to break, requesting that in the future he write and send a resume rather than call. As anything is better than facing telephone conversations like this, the job hunter didn't call the other five companies, but took a week to write a resume that no one would read, let alone understand. He sent it, then waited a week for someone to call. Waited another week. Kicked the cat. Felt bad about that, worse about himself, and had a couple of drinks. Phone rang, someone was interested in the resume but, unfortunately, not in someone who slurred his words at lunchtime. Felt worse, stayed in bed late. Phone rang. An interview! Felt good, went to the interview. They said they'd contact him in a few days. They didn't, and when he called, everybody was mysteriously unavailable. The job hunter begins to feel like a blot on God's landscape.

This is obviously an extreme example, but the story is a little too close to home for many, and it illustrates the wrong way to use the newspaper when you're looking for a job. In today's changing economy it is not unusual for an advertisement in a local paper to draw upwards of 150 responses. I know of ads that have drawn almost two thousand responses. It is these odds of 1 in 150 or 1 in 2,000 that cause some to reject the want ads as a realistic method for finding employment. There are ways to answer want ads correctly and narrow the odds to 1 in 10 or even 1 in 5. This is exactly what I am going to show you how to do now.

While reference books give you bags of hard information about a company, they tell you little about specific job openings. Newspapers, on the other hand, tell you about specific jobs that need to be filled now, but give you few hard facts about the company. The two types of information complement each other. Often you will find ads in the newspaper for companies you have already researched. What a powerful combination of information this gives you going in the door to the interview!

Use newspaper ads to identify all companies in your field that are currently hiring, not just to identify specific openings. Write down pertinent details about each particular job opening on a separate sheet of paper, as you did earlier when using the reference books. Include the company's name, address, phone number, and contacts.

ONLINE RESOURCES

The New York Times
http://www.nytimes.com
http://www.nytimes.com/classified/
This site contains regular help wanted ads from the *New York Times* and a virtual job fair sponsored by Jobtrak. You can search the help wanted ads through the alphabetical index by job title or by keyword. This site, like many others, also contains a link to CareerPath, one of the best career websites available.

Chicago Tribune
http://www.chicago.tribune.com
Access the job information on this site by clicking on Marketplaces, and then, CareerPath.com. This leads you to the *Chicago Tribune* career site, which includes help wanted ads, a resume connection, a job fair, and a link to CareerPath.

Los Angeles Times
http://www.latimes.com
Click on the Classifieds menu and select Jobsource. Not only does this site contain help wanted ads from the paper, it also features job tips, information about job fairs, employer profiles, and a link to CareerPath.

Wall Street Journal
http://www.wsj.com
http://www.careers.wsj.com
Not only does this excellent site contain a job search database (which you can search by company, industry, job function, or location), but it features information on salaries and job profiles, job-hunting advice, information on executive recruiters, and links to related articles in *Barron's* and *National Business Employment Weekly*.

San Jose Mercury News
http://sjmercury.com
In the Classifieds & Services section, click on Jobs: Talent Scout. You can search the employment database, post your resume, get information on technical job fairs, or link over to CareerPath.

National Business Employment Weekly
http://www.nbew.com
This online version of the job-search and career guidance publication contains feature articles covering search tactics, resumes, networking and interviewing. The information in these articles tends to be up-to-date and quite informative. This site also contains a link to the *Wall Street Journal*'s career page, http://www.careers.wsj.com.

In addition to finding openings that bear your particular title, look for all the companies that regularly hire in your field. Cross-check the categories. Don't rely solely on those ads advertising for your specific job title. For example, let's say you are a graphic artist looking for a job in advertising. You should flag any advertising or public relations agency with any kind of need. The fact that your job is not being advertised does not mean a company is not looking for you; if a company is in a hiring mode, a position for you might be available. In the instances when a company is active but has not been advertising specifically for your skills, write down all relevant company contact data. Then contact the company. You could be the solution to a problem that has only just arisen or even one they have despaired of ever solving.

Virtually every newspaper has an employment edition each week (in addition to Sunday), when they have their largest selection of help-wanted ads. Make sure you always get this edition of the paper.

It is always a good idea to examine back issues of the newspapers. These can provide a rich source of job opportunities that remain unfilled from previous advertising efforts. I suggest working systematically through the want ads, going back twelve to eighteen months. React to ads as if they were fresh: answer the ones with your job title and contact companies in your field even if they appear to be seeking people with different skills.

When you contact by phone or letter, your opening gambit is not to say, "Gee whiz, Ms. Jones, I'm answering your ad from last July's *Sentinel.*" No. You mention that you've "heard through the grapevine that the company might be looking" or that you "have been intrigued by their company and hope they might be looking for . . ."

Sound crazy? That's what a *Knock 'em Dead* reader said to me recently in a letter. He also said this trick landed him a $90,000-a-year job from a seven-month-old want ad. Sometimes the position will never have been filled and the employer simply despaired of getting someone through advertising. Sometimes the person hired left or didn't work out. Or perhaps they are only now starting to look for another person like the one they had advertised for earlier. They might even just be coming off a hiring freeze. Whatever the case, every old ad you follow up on won't result in an opening, but when one does, the odds can be short indeed. Smart money always goes on the short odds.

In addition to your local papers, there are regional, national, and international papers that employers favor to meet their professional needs.

National and International Newspapers:

The *Chicago Tribune*	The *San Jose Mercury News* (if you are
The *New York Times*	in the high-tech field)
The *Los Angeles Times*	The *Wall Street Journal*
The *Financial Times*	The *National Business Employment*
	Weekly (NBEW)

The *NBEW* is of special interest to the professional. Published by the *Wall Street Journal*, *NBEW* is a weekly paper that carries hundreds of higher-level professional positions. It is packed with useful articles on job hunting and entrepreneurship, and carries a calendar of support groups' activities and employment events around the country. *Of special interest is the weekly profile of salaries by industry and function. NBEW* is available on selected newsstands, or you can subscribe for $35 for eight weeks by calling 1-800-JOB-HUNT.

Regional Newspapers:

Northeast
The *New York Times*
Newsday
The *Washington Post*
The *Philadelphia Inquirer*
The *Boston Globe*
The *Hartford Courant*

Midwest
The *Chicago Tribune*
The *Detroit Free Press*
The *Kansas City Star*
Rocky Mountain News
The *Denver Post*
The *St. Louis Post Dispatch*

West
The *San Francisco Chronicle*
The *San Francisco Examiner*
The *San Jose Mercury News*
The *Sacramento Bee*
The *Los Angeles Times*
The *San Diego Union*
The *Seattle Times*

Southwest
The *Dallas News*
The *Dallas Times*
The *New Orleans Times Picayune*

Southeast
The *Atlanta Constitution*
The *Miami Herald*

The reason you must use a combination of reference books and advertisements is that companies tend to hire in cycles. When you rely exclusively on newspapers, you miss those companies just about to start or just ending their hiring cycles. Comprehensive research is the way to tap what the business press refers to as the hidden job market. It is paramount that you have as broad a base as possible—people know people who have your special job to fill.

Adding all these companies to your map, you will have a glittering panorama of prospects, the beginnings of a dossier on each one, and an efficient way of finding any company's exact location. This is useful for finding your way to an interview and in evaluating the job offers coming your way.

Box Number Want Ads

Employed professionals are understandably leery of answering ads that give only box numbers. Unemployed professionals wonder whether it is worth the effort. There are many reasons not to answer blind ads, but the two reasons for action far outweigh the negatives:

One, if you don't respond you aren't in the game, and you have to play to win.

Two, you may not be suitable for the job advertised but may be suitable for another position.

If you are employed and skeptical about "blowing your cover," or unemployed and eager to increase your chances, try this technique. Call the main post office in the area and ask for the local office that handles zip code _____. Call the substation and speak to the local post office manager, or P.O. box manager. Introduce yourself as an employed job hunter and ask for the name of the box holder so that you won't jeopardize your current job. If you make your request pleasant and personal enough you might get the information you need. If not, try asking, "Is it my employer, _____?"

Your Own Want Ads

Better use the money to fire up your barbecue.

Consistency

Consistent research is the key to gathering speed and maintaining momentum. Without consistent research your job hunt will stall for lack of people and companies to approach.

A few years ago a neighbor of mine in the airline business found himself looking for a job. At the time, MGM Air, the airline that flies the super-rich between New York and Los Angeles, was just beginning operations. The neighbor had a friend already with the company who was going to get him a job. It took a year of not looking for work before this job hunter realized that things you want to happen often don't . . . unless you make them. Not only did he never work for MGM Air, he never worked in the airline industry again.

When you look like a penguin, act like a penguin, and hide among penguins, don't be surprised if you get lost in the flock. Today's business marketplace demands a different approach. Your career does not take care of itself; you must go out and grab the opportunities.

3. Public and Private Employment Agencies

There are essentially four categories: state employment agencies, private employment agencies and executive recruiters, temporary help organizations, and career counselors.

State Employment Agencies. These are funded by the state labor department and typically carry names like State Division of Employment Security, State Job Service, or Manpower Services. The names vary but the services remain the same. They will make efforts to line you up with appropriate jobs and will mail resumes out on your behalf to interested employers who have jobs listed with them. It is not mandatory for employers to list jobs with state agencies, but more and more are taking advantage of these free services. Once the bastion of minimum-wage jobs, positions listed with these public agencies can reach $50,000–$60,000 a year for some technical positions.

If you are moving across the state or across the country, your local employment office can plug you into what is known as a national job bank, which (theoretically) can give you access to jobs all over the nation. However, insiders agree that it can take up to a month for a particular job from a local office to hit the national system. The most effective way to use the service is to visit your local office and ask for an introduction to the office in your destination area.

Private Employment Agencies. Choose your agent, or "headhunter" as they are commonly called, with the same care and attention with which you would choose a spouse or an accountant. The caliber of the individual and company you choose could well affect the caliber of the company you ultimately join. Further, if you choose prudently, he or she can become a lifetime counselor who can guide you step by step up the ladder of success.

Understand that there are distinctly different types of employment services:

- Permanent employment agencies where you pay the fee
- Permanent agencies where the employer pays the fee
- Contingency and retained search firms

As this is the for-profit sector of the marketplace, the question arises: Whose pocket is the profit coming from? Employment Agencies in the private sector must be registered as either an Employer Paid Fee (EPF) or an Applicant Paid Fee (APF) agency. To avoid misunderstanding, it is best to confirm which is which before entering into any relationships.

Only employment agencies and certain contingency search firms will actively market you to a large number of companies with whom they may or may not have an existing relationship. A true executive search firm will never market your services. It will only present your credentials on an existing assignment.

So what type of company is best for you? Well, the answer is simple: the one that will get you the right job offer. The problem is there are thousands of companies in each of these broad categories. So how do you choose between the good, the bad, and the ugly?

Fortunately this is not as difficult as it sounds. Let's explode one or two myths. A retained executive search firm is not necessarily any better or more professional than a contingency search firm, which in turn is not necessarily better or more professional than a regular employment agency. Each has its exemplary practitioners and its charlatans. Your goal is to avoid the charlatans and get representation by an exemplary outfit. Make the choice carefully, and having made the choice, stick with it and listen to the advice you are given.

Check on the date of the firm's establishment. If the company has been in town ever since you were in diapers, the chances are good that they are reputable.

A company's involvement in professional associations is always a good sign. It demonstrates commitment and, through extensive professional training programs, an enhanced level of competence. In the employment services industry, the National Association of Personnel Consultants (NAPC) is the premier professional organization, with state associations in all fifty states.

Involvement in independent or franchise networks of firms can also be a powerful plus. For example, an independent network like the National Personnel Associates group has over three hundred member firms around the continental United States and Europe. Membership in one of the leading franchise groups, such as Snelling & Snelling, Sanford Rose, Management Recruiters, Dunhill, or Romac is likewise positive. These networks also have extensive training programs that help assure a high-caliber consultant. Franchise offices can be especially helpful if you are looking to change jobs and move across the country (or further) at the same time, as they tend to have powerful symbiotic relationships with other network members; in fact this is often a primary reason for their being a member of that particular franchise or network. Many of the independent and franchise network members also belong to the NAPC.

ONLINE RESOURCES

Sanford Rose Associates
http://www.sanfordrose.com
This executive recruiting firm usually caters to professionals searching in the $50K to $200K salary range. This site provides information on career opportunities and office locations.

Management Recruiters Inc.
http://www.mrinet.com
MRI is one of the world's largest search and recruitment firms. This website contains information on office locations, career advice, job openings, and allows you to post your resume.

Snelling & Snelling Inc.
http://www.snelling.com
In addition to providing office locations, this site also offers information on open positions, available personnel for employers, and franchise opportunities.

Dunhill Staffing Systems Inc.
http://www.dunhillstaff.com
With over 120 locations around the nation, Dunhill offers temporary, permanent, and executive search capabilities. This site also lets you search a job database and gain access to interview strategies.

Romac International
http://www.romac.com
This firm fills temporary, permanent, and contract positions in Information Technology, Finance, accounting, health care, engineering, and several other technical fields. This website allows you to search for available jobs.

To take your evaluation one step further, it is prudent to ask whether your contact has CPC designation. CPC or its international equivalent, CIPC, stands for Certified Personnel Consultant (or Certified International Personnel Consultant). The CPC and CIPC designations are recognized as a standard of excellence and commitment only achieved after rigorous training and study.

CIPC designation requires that the holder already have achieved CPC designation, and it requires adherence to an international code of ethics as designated by the International Personnel Services Association (IPSA).

Although certification can be applied for after two years of experience in the personnel consulting business, the studying involved usually means that even the newest holders of CPC have five years of experience, while your average CPC probably has seven to ten years of experience and contacts with top-notch employers under his or her belt.

Qualified CPCs can also be relied upon to have superior knowledge of the legalities and ethics of the recruitment and hiring process, along with the expertise and tricks of the trade that only come from years of hands-on experience. All of this can be put to work on your behalf.

It makes good sense to have a friend in the business with an ear to the ground on your behalf as you continue your upward climb. If you want my best advice: Find an NAPC member in good standing with CPC designation and listen to what he tells you.

Finally, don't get intimidated, and remember you are not obligated to sign anything. Neither are you obligated to guarantee an agency that you will remain in any employment for any specific length of time. Don't get put in a trick bag by the occasional cowboy in an otherwise exemplary and honored profession.

Executive Recruiters. These people rarely deal at salary levels under $70,000 per year. All the advice I have given you about employment agencies applies here (although you can take it for granted that the executive recruiter will not charge you a fee). They are going to be more interested in your resume for their files than in wanting to see you right then and there, unless you match a specific job they are trying to fill for a client. They are far more interested in the employed than in the unemployed, because an employed person is less of a risk (they often guarantee their finds to the employer for up to a year) and a more desirable commodity. Executive recruiters are there to serve the client, not to find you a job. They neither want nor expect you to rely on them for employment counseling, unless they specifically request that you do—in which case you should listen closely.

Working with a Headhunter

Few people realize it, but symbiotic relationships can be developed with headhunters in all these categories to help you professionally. Their livelihood depends on who and what they know. Perhaps you can exchange mutually beneficial information. But do be circumspect. An unethical headhunter can create further competition for you when you share information about companies you are talking to.

Select two or three firms that work in your field. Do not mass mail your resume to every agent in town. This can lead to multiple submissions of your resume to a single company and a resultant argument over which agency is due a fee. When such a situation arises, companies will sometimes choose to walk away from the candidate in question.

Ascertain network and association membership and how this might help in your job search. Determine who pays the fee and whether any contracts will need to be exchanged. Define titles and the employment levels they represent, along with geographical areas. Know what you want, or ask for assistance in defining your parameters. This will include title, style of company, salary expectations, benefits, and location.

If the professional is interested in representing you, expect a detailed analysis of your background and prepare to be honest. Do not overstate your job duties, accomplishments, or education. If there are employment gaps, explain them.

Find out first what the professional expects of you in the relationship and then explain what you expect. Reach commitments you both can live with, and stick with them. If you break those commitments, expect your representative to cease representation and to withdraw your candidacy from potential employers. They are far more interested in long-term relationships than passing nuisances.

Keep the recruiter informed about any and all changes in your status, such as salary increases, promotions, layoffs, or other offers of employment.

Don't consider yourself an employment expert. You get a job for yourself every three or four years. These people do it for a living every day of every week. Ask for their objective input and seek their advice in developing interviewing strategies with their clients.

Always tell the truth.

Temporary Help Companies. There are temporary help companies that provide corporate services to professionals at most levels, from unskilled and semi-skilled labor (referred to as light industrial in the trade) to administration, finance, technical, sales and marketing professionals, doctors, lawyers, and even interim executives up to the levels of CFOs and COOs.

Temporary help services can be a useful resource if you are unemployed. You can get temporary assignments, maintain continuity of employment and skills, and perhaps enhance your marketability in the process.

If you are changing careers or returning to work after an absence, temporary assignments can help get new or rusty skills up to speed and provide you with a current work history in your field. The temporary life can help you break out of your rut as well. It is becoming increasingly common to hear of the career-motivated professional who has been categorized and pigeon-holed in the workplace, but who finds a highly reputable temporary company and subsequently completely overhauls his skills to such an extent that a new career is possible.

In both these situations there are two other benefits:

1. You will get exposure to employers in the community who, if you really shine, could ask you to join the staff full time.
2. You will develop another group of networking contacts.

Working with a Temporary Help Company

Investigate the turnover of the temporary staff. If other temporaries have stayed with the company long term, chances are that company does a good job and has good clients.

Determine whether they are members of the National Association of Temporary Services (NATS) or of NAPC. These are the two leading industry associations.

Select a handful of firms that work in your field; this will increase the odds of suitable assignments appearing quickly.

Define the titles and the employment levels they represent, along with geographical areas they cover.

Do not overstate your job duties, accomplishments, or education.

Find out first what the temporary help professional expects of you in the relationship; then explain what you expect. Reach commitments you both can live with, and stick with them.

Judge the assignments not solely on the paycheck (although that can be important) but also on the long-term benefits that will accrue to your job search and ongoing career.

Keep the temporary help counselor informed about any and all changes in your status, such as offers of employment or acquisition of new skills.

Remember that the temporary company is your employer. They will appreciate extra effort when they really need it and will reciprocate.

Resolve key issues ahead of time. Should an employer want to take you on full time, will that employer have to pay a set amount, or will you just stay on as a temporary for a specific period and then go on the employer's payroll?

Career Counselors. Career counselors charge for their services: sometimes as little as $200 for a resume and a half an hour's advice, sometimes up to $10,000. For this you get assistance in your career realignment or job search skill development. What you don't get is a guarantee of employment.

If you consider this route, speak to a number of counselors and check multiple references on all of them. As you are unlikely to be given poor references, you will want to check secondary and tertiary references. This is simple to do. Check the half dozen references you request and then ask each of the referees to refer someone else they know who used the service. Then check that reference as well.

It could also be prudent to check out potential counselors with your local Better Business Bureau to see whether any complaints have been registered against them.

Find out how long the company has been in business; ascertain a complete work history of the individual counselor who is likely to be assisting you. A number of people have been known to slip into this area of the employment services business for a quick buck with little expertise and commitment.

The person who can offer you the best advice in this area is the professional who has both corporate personnel experience *and* employment agency or retained search experience. This exposure should be mandatory for anyone willing to charge you for career and employment assistance.

All the Players

To provide you with the widest possible choice of employment services, here are some contact data for the most comprehensive lists and directories available:

National Association of Personnel Services
3133 Mount Vernon Avenue
Alexandria, VA 22305
703-684-0180
National Directory of Personnel Consultants, $30.00 (including shipping and handling). Identifies companies by occupational specialization and geographical coverage. Includes employment agencies, contingency and retained search companies, and temporary help organizations in membership. The industry's premier organization. Thousands of reputable contacts. Also available as printed labels and on disk; price on request.

Directory of Executive Recruiters
Kennedy Publications
Kennedy Place, Route 12 South
Fitzwilliam, NH 03447
603-585-6544 or 800-531-0007
Directory of Executive Recruiters, $44.95. Details 2,000 retained and contingency firms throughout the USA, Canada, and Mexico. Labels; not available on disk.

National Association of Temporary Services
119 South Saint Asaph Street
Alexandria, VA 22314-3119
703-549-6287
Directory with 7,300 entries by city and state, $160. A SASE with a polite request will get you a free listing of temporary help companies by city for the state of your choice. Disk; prices on request.

The Recruiting & Search Report
Ken Cole, President
Box 9433
Panama City Beach, FL 32417
850-235-3733
This organization sells data. It should be known as "legwork central." The company provides many of the research services offered by the top outplacement firms only for the individual consumer. Its unique and exciting products for the job hunter include:

- Over one hundred industry-specific directories of top contingency and retained research firms throughout the United States. Updated quarterly. Provides pinpoint accuracy for $15 per category, with a minimum of three categories. Just specify your industry and get the heavy hitters by return mail. This is a great deal.
- *Executive Research Directory*. $88 (the eighth edition was published in January of 1998). This is a tremendous resource for the senior-level executive. Perhaps you need contact information for the board members of, say, artificial intelligence's fifty largest firms. Well, here are the researchers who can find this information for you. At the highest levels, it is paramount that your references be sound. This directory provides resources who will check your references for you.
- Senior executive research package. Includes the *Executive Search Research Directory* and a printout of the four hundred research directors at many of the nation's leading search firms. $125.
- Dun & Bradstreet Database. NJCRC has acquired this database of 230,000 firms. This combined with their state-of-the-art word processing capabilities means that they can offer direct-mail services for specifically targeted markets. Price upon request.
- Labels. Mailing lists customized by geography, occupation, and industry. Price upon request. Disks are available.

Don't restrict yourself to any single category in this area. Executives, especially, should not turn their noses up at local employment agencies. Often that local agency has better rapport and contacts with the local business community than the big-name search firm. I have also known more than one employment agency that regularly placed job candidates earning in excess of $250,000 per year. Don't get hung up on agency versus search firm labels without researching the outfits in question; you could miss some great career opportunities.

4. Your References as a Resource

As a rule, we have faith in ourselves and are confident that our references will speak well of us. The fact is that some will speak well of us, some will speak excellently, and some, we might be surprised to hear, bear us no good will.

The wrong references at a critical juncture could spell disaster. At the very start of your job hunt you need to identify as many potential references as possible. The more options you have, the better your likelihood of coming up with excellent references. When you are currently employed, however, unless you want your employer to know you are actively engaged in making a career move, you will want to avoid using current managers and coworkers as references.

Yet at this point of the job search, excellent references, though important, are simply an added bonus. Your hidden agenda is to use these contacts as job search leads.

The process is simplicity itself, starting with an introduction: "Bob, this is _____. We worked together at Acme between 1985 and 1992. How's it going?" It is appropriate here to catch up on gossip and the like. Then broach the subject of your call.

"John, I wanted to ask your advice." (Everyone loves to be asked for an expert opinion.) "We had some cutbacks at Fly-By-Night Finance, as you probably heard," or "The last five years at Bank of Crooks and Criminals International have been great, and the _____ project we are just winding down has been a fascinating job. Nevertheless, I have decided that this would be a perfect time for a career move to capitalize on my experience."

Then, "John, I realize how important references can be and I was wondering if you would have any reservations about my using you as a reference?" It's better to find out now rather than down the line when it could blow a job offer.

The response will usually be positive, so then you move to the next step. "Thanks, John, I hoped you would feel able to. Let me update you about what I have been doing recently and tell you about the type of opportunity I'm looking for." Then proceed in less than two minutes to give a capsule of what has passed since you worked together and what you are looking for. With coworkers or past managers, be sure to restate why you left your last job, since the reference is likely to be asked.

You can then, if appropriate and time allows, tell the reference some of the questions he might be asked. These might include the time he has known you, your relationship to each other, the title you worked under (be sure to remind your reference of promotions and title changes), your five or six most important duties, the key projects you worked on, your greatest strengths, your greatest weaknesses, your attitude toward your job, your attitude toward your peers, your attitude toward management, the timeliness, quality, and quantity of your work, your willingness to achieve above and beyond the call of duty (remind him of all those weekends you worked), whether he would rehire you (if company policy forbids rehiring, make sure your reference will mention this), your earnings, and any additional comments the reference would like to make.

When references are about to be checked for a specific job, get back to your chosen references, reacquaint them with any relevant areas the employer might wish to discuss, and tell them to expect a call. I have even known professionals who, with the approval of the potential employer, have their references call in with recommendations.

Some smart job hunters also take the precaution of having a friend do a dummy check on all references just to confirm what they will say when the occasion arises. This way you can distinguish the excellent references from the merely good. (For guaranteed peace of mind you could call Allison & Taylor at (248) 651-0286, and have them check your references for you. For a modest fee you'll know in advance just who will be your best spokespeople.)

ONLINE RESOURCE

Allison & Taylor, Inc.
http://www.allisontaylor.com
This firm will call your references for you to see just exactly what they're saying about you. This way, you'll be able to see who's making you look good, and who's making you look bad before your potential employers do. This site contains a company overview and general contact information.

5. College Placement Offices and Alumni/ae Associations

College Placement Offices. If you are leaving school or college, take advantage of this resource. Remember that the college placement office is not a substitute for your mother; it is not there to provide for you or hand you job offers. Rather, you will find there a wealth of experience that will accelerate the process and aid you in finding your own job.

Placement offices and their staffs are horrendously overworked, and merely keeping pace with the Herculean task of providing assistance to the student body as a whole is more than a full-time job. Take the time to make yourself known here and stress your sincerity and willingness to listen to good advice. Act on it; then, when you come back for more, you will have earned the placement director's respect and as such will begin to earn yourself that extra bit of attention and guidance that winners always manage for themselves.

Don't wait until the last minute, especially if you are hoping to gain your foothold on the ladder of success from on-campus recruiters who represent the big corporations. These recruiters go to society and association meetings on campus all year long. Take an active part in campus affairs and you may well find them coming after you. I know of one campus recruiter for a major accounting firm who swears she has selected all her prime choices before the campus recruiting season even opens. How do such campus recruiters pick the winners from the also-rans? Simple. They all maintain very close working relationships with the placement office, so an endorsement at the right time can mean an important introduction rather than a closed door.

Alumni/ae Associations. Even when your school days are in the misty distant past, this isn't the time to forget the people of the old school tie. People hire people like themselves, people with whom they share something in common. Your school or college alumni/ae association is a complete and valuable network just waiting for you.

As a member of the alumni/ae association you are likely to have access to a membership listing. Additionally, many of the larger schools have alumni/ae placement networks, so you may want to check with the alma mater and tap into the old-boy and -girl network.

6. Professional Associations

Professional associations provide excellent networks for your benefit. Almost all committed professionals are members of at least one or two professional networks. Their membership is based on:

a) Commitment to the profession
b) The knowledge that people who know people know where the opportunities are hidden

If you never got around to joining, or your membership has lapsed, it is time to visit the library and check out the *Encyclopedia of Associations* (published by Bowker). It tells you about all known associations for your profession and provides contact information and other relevant data.

You might also check out another important resource: *The Directory of Directories*. This reference work lists all the available directories in the country and details their content. For example, if you are an oil and gas geologist, you'll learn that there is a directory of geologists with 11,000 plus entries that includes full biographical and contact data. *The Directory of Directories* can be a major lead generator and significant professional networking resource for almost anybody.

Some professions have multiple associations, all of which could be of value to the serious job hunter. For example, if you happen to be in retail, you will find thirty national associations and fifty state associations. Together these associations represent one and a half million retailers who provide employment for over fourteen million people. And these are just retail associations that are members of the American Retail Federation. You may well discover even more.

There are two ways to make memberships in professional organizations work. The first is the membership directory, which provides you with a direct networking resource for direct verbal contact and mail campaigns. All associations supply their members with a directory of contact information for all other members. Additionally, all associations schedule regular meetings, which provide further opportunities to mingle with your professional peers on an informal basis, as well as opportunities to get involved on a volunteer basis with organizing such meetings or speaking at a meeting. Networking at the meetings and using an association's directory for contacts are wise and accepted uses of membership.

Professional associations all have newsletters. In addition to using the help-wanted section, you will be able to utilize them in other ways by following the advice on trade and business publications later in this chapter.

It is often one's active membership in professional associations that leads other disgruntled job hunters to mutter, "It's not what you know, it's who you know." (Membership in professional associations is also an excellent way to maintain long-term career stability.)

7. Job Fairs

Job fairs and career days are occasions where local or regional companies that are actively hiring get together, usually under the auspices of a job fair promoter or local employment agency, to attract large numbers of potential employees.

There aren't many of these occasions, so they won't be taking much of your time, but you shouldn't miss them when they do occur. They are always advertised in the local newspapers and frequently on the radio. Many also appear in the *National Business Employment Weekly*'s events calendar.

When the job fair is organized by a promoter, entrance is either free or nominal. When it is organized by a local employment service, it helps to be on their mailing list.

In addition to the exhibit hall, there are likely to be formal group presentations by employers. As all speakers love to get feedback, move in when the crush of presenter groupies has died down; you'll get more time and closer attention. You will also have additional knowledge of the company and the chance to spend a few minutes customizing the emphasis of your skills to meet the stated needs and interests of the employer in question.

When you attend job fairs, go prepared. Take:

- Business cards. (If employed, remember to request the courtesy of confidentiality in calls to the workplace.)
- Resumes—as many as there are exhibitors times two. You'll need one to leave at the exhibit booth and an additional copy for anyone you have a meaningful conversation with.
- Note pad and pen, preferably in a folder.

Go with specific objectives in mind:

- Visit every booth, not just the ones with the flashing lights and professional models stopping traffic.
- Talk to someone at every booth. Since they are the ones who are selling, you have a slight advantage. You can walk up and ask questions about the

company, who they are, and what they are doing, before you talk about yourself. This allows you to present yourself in the most relevant light.

- Collect business cards from everyone you speak to so that you can follow up with a letter and a call when they are not so harried. Very few people actually get hired at job fairs. For most companies the exercise is usually one of collecting resumes so that meaningful meetings can take place in the ensuing weeks. But be "on" in case someone wants to sit down and give you a serious interview on the spot. This is most likely to happen when you least expect it, so be prepared.
- Collect company brochures and collateral materials.
- Arrange times and dates to follow up with each employer. "Ms. Jones, I realize you are very busy today, and I would like to speak to you further. Your company sounds very exciting. I should like to set up a time when we could meet to talk further or perhaps set a time to call you in the next few days."
- Dress for business. You may be meeting your new boss, and you don't want the first impression to be less than professional.

Job fairs provide opportunity for administrative, professional, and technical people up to the middle management ranks. However, this doesn't mean that the senior executive should feel such an event beneath her. The opportunity still exists to have meaningful conversations with tens or hundreds of employers in a single day, from which may come further fruitful conversations.

On leaving each booth, and at the end of the day, go through your notes while everything is still fresh in your mind. Review each company and what possibilities it holds for you. Then review all the companies as a whole to see what you might glean about industry needs or marketplace shifts and long-term staffing needs. Make notes.

8. Trade and Business Magazines

This resource includes professional association periodicals, trade magazines, and the general business press. They can all be utilized in a similar fashion: by contacting the individuals and companies mentioned and using the article to begin discussion.

In these publications you may find the following:

- Focus articles about interesting companies, which can alert you to specific growth opportunities.

- Industry overviews and market development pieces, which can tip you off to subtle shifts in your professional marketplace and thereby alert you to opportunities—and provide you with the chance to customize your letters, calls, and resume for specific targets.
- Quotations. "The art of press writing demands frequent quotes, and by necessity, attributions," says Peregrine McCoy, senior partner of Connem, Covertrax and Splitt. Contacting the person quoted is flattering and shows that you have your finger on the pulse of your profession.
- Articles by industry professionals. When contacting the author of an article, you might include how much you agree with what was said, a little additional information on the subject, or words to the effect that "It's about time someone told it like it is." Never say anything in the vein of, "Hey, the article is great but you missed . . ."
- Opportunities to write the editors of the publication. The editors themselves are always on the lookout for quotable letters, so a flattering note about an article with a line or two about your background in the field may get you some valuable free publicity down the line.
- Columns on promotions, executive moves, and obituaries. If someone has just received a promotion, there are reasonable odds that somewhere in the chain is an opening. If executive A has moved to company B, it could mean the first company is looking for someone. The same applies to obituaries.
- Help-wanted sections. Many employers will give the general newspapers only token attention when it comes to filling hard-to-find professional and trade positions. They will concentrate their advertising budgets instead on the trade press.
- Advertisements for new products can tell you about companies that are making things happen, and that need people who can make things happen.

In all of the above instances it is advisable to clip and keep, in retrievable fashion, all the items that generate leads. There are two reasons for this: You can send a copy to the person you intend to approach, and you will have a copy on file to refresh your memory before any direct communication.

In short, just about every page of your average trade journal holds a valuable job lead. You just need to know how and where to look. Then having found something, you need to take action.

9. Networking

People frequently think networking means annoying the hell out of your friends until they stop taking your calls. What it should mean is using others to assist in your job search. You will find it surprising how willing friends, colleagues, and even strangers are to help you.

The bad news is that networks need nurturing and development. Networking is more than calling your relatives and waiting for them to call back with job offers. People know people, not just in your home town but all over the country and sometimes the world.

I used the word *networks*, not *network*. We all have a number of networks, any of which may produce that all-important job offer. Here are the typical networks we can all tap into:

- Family and relatives. This includes your spouse's family and relatives.
- Friends. This includes neighbors and casual acquaintances.
- Coworkers. This includes professional colleagues past and present. You will especially want to ask about headhunters they know or might hear from, and professional affiliations they have found valuable.
- Managers, past and present. A manager's success depends on tapping good talent. Even if a particular manager can't use you, a judicious referral to a colleague can gain goodwill for the future.
- Service industry acquaintances. This includes your banker, lawyer, insurance agent, realtor, doctors, and dentist.
- Other job hunters.
- Other professionals in your field.

Over a period of a few days you need to develop the most extensive lists you can in each of these categories. Start lists and add to them every day. The experienced professional should be able to come up with a minimum of twenty names for, say, the service industry network list, and upward of a couple of hundred professional colleagues.

Here are some tips for writing networking letters or making calls asking for assistance:

- Establish connectivity. Recall the last memorable contact you had or mention someone you both knew whom you have spoken to recently.

- Tell why you are writing or calling: "It's time for me to make a move. I just got laid off with one thousand others, and I'm taking a couple of days to catch up with old friends."
- Ask for advice and guidance about your tactics, what the happening companies are, and whether the person can take a look at your resume—because you really need an objective opinion and have always respected his viewpoint. Don't ask specifically, "Can you or your company hire me?" If there is some action available, he will let you know.
- Don't rely on a contact with a particular company to get you into that company. Mount and execute your own plan of attack. No one is as interested as you are in putting bread on your table.
- Let contacts know what you are open for. They will usually want to help, but you have to give them a framework within which to target their efforts.
- Discuss the profession, the industry, the areas of opportunity, and the people worthwhile to contact. If you comport yourself in a professional manner most fellow professionals will come up with a lead. If they can't think of a person, back off and ask them about companies. Everyone can think of a company. If they come up with a company, respond, "Hey, that's a great idea. I never thought of those people," even if you have just spoken to that outfit. Then after a suitable pause, ask for another company. When people see that their advice is appreciated, they will often come up with more. When you have gathered two or three company names, backtrack with, "Do you know of anyone I could speak to at _____ [company A, B, C]?" Every time you get a referral be sure to ask whether you can use your contact's name as an introduction. The answer will invariably be yes, but asking demonstrates professionalism and will encourage your contact to come up with more leads.

  Remember to ask for information about and specific leads from your targeted companies.
- At the end of the call make sure the contact knows how to get in touch with you. I find the nicest and most effective way of doing this is to say something like, "Mack, I really appreciate your help. I'd like to leave you my name and number in the hope that one day in the future I can return the favor." Not only is this a supremely professional gesture, it ensures that your contact information is available to that individual should openings arise within his sphere of influence. Say that you hope you'll get to see each other again soon, and that you look forward to doing something together. Invite the contact over for drinks, dinner, or a barbecue.

- When you do get help, say thank you. And if you get it verbally, follow it up in writing. The impression is indelible and just might get you another lead. Include a copy of your resume with the thank-you letter.
- Keep an open mind. You never know who your friends are. You will be surprised at how someone you always regarded as a real pal won't give you the time of day and how someone you never thought of as a friend will go above and beyond the call of duty for you.
- Whether your contacts help you or not, let them know when you get a job and maintain contact at least once a year. A career is a long time. It might be next week or a decade from now when a group of managers (including one from your personal network) are talking about filling a new position and the first thing they'll do is ask "Who do we know?" That could be you.

Networking is more than one call or letter to each person on your list. Once the first conversation is in the bag, another call in a couple of months won't be taken amiss. For examples of networking cover letters, see the book *Cover Letters That Knock 'em Dead.*

When you get referrals as a result of your networking, use your source as an introduction: "Jane, my name is Martin Yate. Our mutual friend George Smith suggested I call, so before I go any further I must pass on George's regards."

10. The Job Hunter's Network

In your job hunt you will invariably find that companies are looking for everyone but you. The recent graduate is told to come back when she has experience, the experienced professional is told that only entry-level people are being hired. That's the luck of the draw, but one person's problem is another's opportunity.

The solution is to join or create a support group and job hunting network of your own with people in the same situation as you are.

Existing Support Groups. In many communities these are sponsored by church or other social organizations. They meet, usually on a weekly basis, to discuss ideas, exchange tips and job leads, and provide encouragement and the opportunity to support and be supported by others in the same situation.

One national organization is known as the 40 Plus Club. The only requirements for membership are that you be a mature professional in your field. The 40 Plus Club has chapters around the country. You can find a comprehensive listing of these, other support groups, and networking opportunities in the weekly edition of the *National Business Employment Weekly*.

Creating Your Own Support Group. All this takes is finding someone in the same situation as yourself. Among your neighbors and friends someone probably knows someone who has the same needs as you do; all it takes is two. Your goals are quite simple: You meet on a regular basis to exchange ideas and tips; review each other's resumes, letters, and verbal presentations; and check on each other's progress. This means that if I tell you that in the last five days I've sent out only three resumes and made only two follow-up calls, you are obliged to get on my case. The purpose of such a group is to provide the pressure to perform that you experience at work.

You can advertise for members in your local penny saver. The paper might even be talked into running the ad for free as a community service.

Once you are involved in a group, you will meet others with different skill levels and areas of expertise. Then when an employer tells you she is hiring only accountants this month, you can offer a referral to the employer or give the lead to your accountant friend. In turn the accountant will be turning up leads in your field. If these openings don't make themselves known during your conversations, you can tag on a question of your own when the conversation is winding down: "John, I'm a member of an informal job hunting network. If you don't have a need for someone with my background right now, perhaps one of my colleagues could be just what you are looking for. What needs do you have at present and in the forseeable future?"

Becoming an active member in an existing group or creating one of your own can get you leads and provide a forum for you to discuss your fears and hopes with others who understand your concerns.

With all of this chapter's networks working for you, you will have maximum coverage and will have minimized the chances of your exhausting any one member or network through overworking their good will and patience. Do it. You have nothing to lose and everything to gain.

11. The Electronic Job Hunt

There's a new weapon in your arsenal.

You can use your modem and personal computer to access important job information. Savvy job hunters can now tap into huge reservoirs of online data before launching a search in earnest or going on an interview. This approach is a new one that may well help you gain an edge over your competition.

There have been many changes recently in the world of online information. Gale's *Directory of Databases* indicates that there continues to be strong growth in the database industry; the totals for databases, records, online searches, database entries, database producers, and vendors are all up. The industry is showing no signs of leveling off; nor do consumers appear to be at a loss when it comes to finding new ways to use the information available. Using an online service is a little like walking into the biggest library in the world and being able to get anything you want without having to walk anywhere (and without having to wait in line). Some services even offer affordable practice forums for developing online skills.

The flexibility of online services makes them extremely valuable. Through one of the new online database services, you can request a list of all the companies in a certain geographic region; you can specify that you want to see only companies in a certain area that do business in your field of choice; you can further narrow the list by asking to see a list that highlights only firms with a sales level of x dollars or more. It's all up to you. If you need to get a list of all the hospitals in Kansas with five hundred beds or more that boast a state-of-the-art magnetic resonance imaging system, all you have to do is punch in your requirements or explain them to a database representative. The data is all there waiting for you, in over a dozen established business information databases; you'll probably be able to secure names and contact information for key company executives as well.

Many libraries provide walk-in use of online fee-based services. Additionally, most will conduct searches for you based on your specific needs. So, if you're a computerphobe, you can get all the benefits without ever touching a keyboard. If your local library doesn't have these services, explain your needs and ask for information on how to contact a library or other database access point that does.

Of course, there is no guarantee that your nearest database access point has the information you want to find. Enter the *Directory of Fee-Based Information Services*, an invaluable resource listing around 440 U.S. and Canadian library systems. This book will provide the details of which library will allow you to access what; you can ask for it at the library or order it direct from the American Library Association at 800-545-2433. Many of the libraries listed in this directory will either conduct a company search for you or provide a full-service business library where you can run your own search for the price of a few photocopies. The retail cost of the most recent edition is $65.00.

Conducting Your Own Search

Online searching is a tricky task, but one that can open the doors to the employment world in seconds. Even with all the excitement you may feel at the prospect of entering the computer age with your job search, however, a few caveats are in order before you plunge in.

First and foremost, I would issue the warning that time is money when you're online; many job seekers, of course, are in short supply of both. If you're one of them, and if you aren't familiar with the sometimes perplexing world of online computer searching, *don't take on the job of cruising this ocean of information yourself.* Either have the search conducted for you by a computer-friendly navigator, or use your local library.

If you *are* familiar with both computer procedures and the online world, get ready for some exciting news about CompuServe. (And if you aren't, get ready to pass this part of the book on to your navigator.) The Knowledge Index available through CompuServe, offered from 6:00 P.M. to 6:00 A.M., contains over a hundred databases—featuring full text, abstracts, or summaries—for only forty cents a minute. Like most databases, this one is word-oriented, but managing the database with CompuServe's menu-assisted windows is pretty easy. This database does *not* charge a "per page" surcharge for the pages of text downloaded. It offers a variety of useful information, including a full-text Standard and Poor's directory of company information, a full-text newspaper database, a full-text *Who's Who* directory, and addresses, phone numbers, and information about key employees of the companies you're searching for. Add to this plenty of data on subsidiaries, financial performance, and any number of other important topics, and you have an avalanche of information that will help you distinguish yourself from the competition.

If you've worked up a little experience with this sort of thing, the average company search will run approximately five minutes online. That's just $2.00 in database charges per lead. For an additional eighteen minutes of online time (costing about $7.20), we were able to find and download over a hundred recent news articles about our target company using our modem. In short, we got a small library of invaluable interview-preparation information for under ten bucks. Not a bad value, eh?

Through its BIZ FILE option, CompuServe also offers access to consumer and business phone directories for just twenty-five cents a minute. We searched for the word "resume" and the database prompted us with "resume services." We then asked for a listing of all such companies in twenty major cities across the United States. In about an hour, we had downloaded a fifty-page booklet of names, addresses, and phone numbers; some of the cities had over two hundred resume companies each. Similarly, if you're searching for all the divisions of, say, Ford Motor Company operating in Southern California, you can conduct the same search by going into BIZ FILE and asking the computer to search for all Ford divisions in the applicable regions.

CompuServe, of course, is not the only operation offering such services. Many services do, and there is a bewildering array of access requirements and charges. A good number of the databases are cheaper in the evening; be sure to doublecheck the rates you are quoted for this feature. Some online databases are designed to keep professional people informed of developments in their field. These are usually cheaper than other services; typically, they are offered at nonpeak hours and are not always available in full-text format. If you find an entry abstract (rather than the material itself) online through one of these sources, you can usually do one of two things: build up a bibliography of articles and pop into the full-text index for the article you want, or head to the library, find the right copy of the publication in question, and make a copy of the article for five or ten cents a sheet on the library photocopier. The second option takes more time, but then again, the premium rate for printing an article in some online magazine or newspaper databases can run as high as $1.50 per page, plus online time and surcharges. Experts may (or may not) be able to make the longer searches for articles cost-effective; newcomers are once again advised to avoid paying for a costly—and, often, frustrating—learning-curve experience.

Classifieds on Your Screen

Among the most exciting developments in electronic databases has been E-Span, through which employers are effectively screening out the dinosaurs of the corporate world and zeroing in on the successful professionals of today. E-Span is essentially a national classified help-wanted database; it is also a service tailored to those growth industries of the future where computer literacy is an unspoken requirement for any job.

The ads run from entry-level through senior executive positions, and cover sixteen major professional groupings ranging from accounting to sales. Each of these major groupings has subheadings: The sales grouping, for instance, includes separate sections for advertisings, communications/public relations, customer service, and of course straight sales positions.

A great plus for the job hunter in comparison with a "real" help-wanted section is E-Span's lack of a newspaper's space restrictions. I noticed advertisements running one to two pages in length that gave job requirements in incredible detail. This can give you a substantial edge; it allows you to customize paperwork and focus your expertise in the appropriate direction.

The ads are national in nature, and will not necessarily feature opportunities in your own backyard. By the same token, some of the larger firms may have unadvertised opportunities in your area that you can track through E-Span.

E-Span is available through a number of media, including CompuServe; call 800-682-2901 for more information. This service can be an invaluable aid to your job search. I was able to pick out an ad that profiled a certain company; I then did an article search (through a separate online service) to get the latest breaking news on that firm, and I discovered three recent deals it had signed. Finally, I was able to pull up a quarterly interim balance sheet and get a breakdown on the company's worldwide core businesses. I started with nothing, discovered a specific job opening not likely to be advertised in the mainstream press, and gathered eight pages of first-rate analysis of the company.

If you can't get access to a computer, you can still find out what's cooking on E-Span. When we last checked with the service, you could order a disk of the current ads, then take the disk to your local library or copy shop for printout. The last we heard, disks were updated every two weeks. Call the E-Span number above for more information. (Words to the wise: Be sure to specify the working environment in which the disks will be printed out—usually IBM or Macintosh—and the disk size required.)

Close Encounters

As you can see, using online research services can do much more than provide extensive contact lists for your mail or phone campaigns. In a tightly run job race, being able to ace the "What do you know about us?" question could make all the differences. Online services can often yield more detailed information about a specific company than you'd ever imagined possible.

Imagine for a moment that you're a corporate galley slave with an interview slated with 3M in Minneapolis for the day after tomorrow. You decide to call Nexis Express, a service of the Nexis/Lexis databases, both of which are divisions of Mead Data Central. You pick up the phone, dial 800-227-9597, and give them the specifics, asking them to fax the data to a local copy shop for you to pick up.

The total cost is quite reasonable, considering the purpose for which you'll be using the information. The most recent pricing schedules are as follows: $6.00 per minute of online search time, four cents per line printing charge, and twenty-five cents per page if the information is faxed to you. If you want the material sent to you by Federal Express, add another fifteen bucks. There is no charge for information sent to you via the U.S. Mail, but you may decide that receiving your data in this way defeats the purpose of *express service*, which is presumably what led you to call in the first place.

What you get for your money is truly remarkable: over fifteen pages of data providing a complete overview of 3M from its inception to the present day, including contact information, officers and directors, the number of employees, subsidiaries of the company, corporate product lines and services, stock performance records, earnings and finances, and more. And you got it in no time flat. How's that for an advantage to carry into the heat of battle?

But you don't stop there. You call again to take advantage of the service's extensive article search capabilities. You ask for all the business articles run in the past year that featured 3M as the main topic and receive fourteen and a half more pages of material. (If you'd asked for everything about 3M, period, with no restrictions, you could have accessed literally thousands of articles, but you're pressed for time.) The entire process took ninety seconds on the phone and a few minutes of transmission time to your corner copy shop. The total cost for the article search and delivery is the same as for your company search; you can expect to pay $40.00 or a little more for each. Add it all up and you're cruising toward the hundred-dollar line, which is probably a little steep for that practice interview at Last Chance Electronics (where you don't want to work anyway), but may be perfectly appropriate for the Big Interview You've Been Waiting For at 3M.

Within ten minutes the company representative was inviting me in for an interview—and two hours earlier, I could have fit all I knew about microchips on the back of a Doritos package! Imagine what this kind of additional data could do for you if you had some idea of what you were talking about in the first place; it would be blindingly obvious at the interview that you were twice as sharp as any other applicant. While this kind of edge is desirable at any level, the seeming omniscience that comes with doing better research than anyone else is all the more important when applying for executive positions. For job seekers at all levels, Nexis gets you what you need—and quick.

Similarly mindboggling is the service available through Standard and Poor's *Research Reports*, which provides in-depth analyses of specific publicly traded companies. I ran across a job opening at Reebok, the major sports shoe manufacturer, called Standard and Poor's to request a report, and received ten pages of great information guaranteed to knock the socks off any interviewer in the place. You can order through Standard and Poor's *Research Reports* by calling 800-642-2858. They offer a quick company report for $9.95, plus a $3.00 faxing charge. Within ninety minutes you'll have pages of information on your target company.

The New Resume Databases

Another revolutionary job hunting technology is emerging: the public resume database. Under this system, you pay a nominal amount (usually between $10 and

$30) to have your resume loaded onto a database. Access to this resume bank is then sold to corporations; they pay a few hundred to a few thousand dollars for unlimited access.

The employer logs on, detailing exactly what qualifications are being sought. If the company has asked for someone with four years of experience with Corel desktop publishing software, the computer searches the scanned-in resume text for words such as "Corel" and "four years." (This means that you should check with the database service on guidelines for composing your resume in such a way that it is properly retrieved!) The employer receives hard-copy resumes that exactly meet its criteria. No one in human resources has to scan five hundred resumes; your resume reaches the right person. Everyone benefits.

To the employer, the new system provides a brand-new, cost-effective recruiting and initial screening tool; to the job hunter, it provides yet another great way to get that resume under the noses of forward-thinking employers. Of course, there is the added benefit that all resumes generated from the search are already perceived to be good matches. Consequently, your candidacy is likely to receive more serious initial evaluation and consideration.

There are currently about a dozen resume database companies in operation. Most claim to be national; none of them really are, at least not by my standards. I don't feel comfortable endorsing any specific companies at this point, but considering the low dollar amounts involved you probably can't go wrong with this method unless you rely on it as your sole means of generating interviews. As one of your many resources, resume banks are certainly worth a shot.

That's the picture now. I predict that by the turn of the century, however, registering one's resume on at least one public database will be a standard component of any professional job search. The savviest job hunters will keep their resumes permanently registered, on the theory that you can only turn down an opportunity if you have heard about it.

For more assistance on electronic job searches, check out the *Adams Electronic Job Search Almanac 1999* by Adams Media Corporation (1-800-USA-JOBS). This comprehensive resource covers everything from posting an electronic resume to using career centers on the World Wide Web.

Getting the Word Out

So much for the eleven paths most likely to lead you to the hidden job market. Remember, there is no single approach to landing your dream job. Friends may tell you that the only effective way is the way that worked for them. Of course, we are all different people, and some things will be harder for you than others.

Although each of these techniques has proven effective, no single one is guaranteed for any one individual. Your plan of attack must be balanced and comprehensive. It should include elements of every technique discussed in this section. A man who goes fishing and puts one hook in the water has but one chance of catching any one of the millions of fish in the sea; a man with two hooks in the water has double the chances of getting a bite. At this stage of the game you are looking for bites. The more hooks you have in the water, the better your chances.

In the end, of course, you will want to know how to contact the companies you learn about through your various types of research. You have two basic approaches to choose from: the verbal approach, usually by telephone, and the written approach, usually including a letter and resume.

One of these is likely to appeal to you more than the other. However, in execution you will see that they both simply become different steps in the same process. When you send out letters and resumes, you will invariably find yourself following up with phone calls. When you make phone contact, you will inevitably be following up with letters and resumes. Your program needs to maintain a delicate balance between the two, so that your calls force you to follow up in writing and your resumes and letters force you to follow up with phone calls.

The trick is not to overemphasize the approach that is easiest for you (say, networking with friends and colleagues) at the expense of other approaches (say, direct research calls). Now while ultimately it is the conversations, not the letters, that get you interviews, I recommend that you begin your campaign by researching contacts in every single category I have discussed; then begin with a combination of mailings and direct calls, because every letter and every resume and every call is another hook in the water. We will examine the written part of the campaign now; initial phone calls will be the topic of the next few chapters.

Letters

Must you send out hundreds or even thousands of letters in the coming weeks? Yes and no. The goal is to mail as much as you need in your field and no more. Two employer contacts a week will not get you accelerating along that career path again. Only if you approach and establish communication with every possible employer will you create the maximum opportunity for yourself. *Two contacts a week is the behavior of the long-term unemployed.*

On the other hand, I am not recommending that you immediately make up a list of seven hundred companies and mail letters to them today. That isn't the answer either. Your campaign needs strategy. While every job hunting campaign is unique, you will want to maintain a balance between the *number* of letters you send out on a daily and weekly basis and the *types* of letters you send out. Start off with balanced mailings and your phone contacts will maintain equilibrium, too.

The key is to send out a balanced mailing representing all the different types of leads, and to send them out regularly and in a volume that will allow you to make follow-up calls. Many headhunters manage their time so well that they average over fifty calls per day, year in and year out. While you may aim at building your call volume up to this number, I recommend that you start out with more modest goals. Send five to ten letters per day in each of the following areas:

- In response to newspaper advertisements
- To friends
- To professional colleagues
- To research contacts from reference works, newspapers, etc.
- To headhunters

With adequate research and the resources I have mentioned, there are literally thousands of contacts waiting to be made. So this breakdown of contacts is a daily quota. If it seems a bit steep to begin with, scale down the numbers until they are achievable and gradually build up the volume. But remember, the lower the volume, the longer the job search.

Do you need to write more than one letter? Almost certainly. There is a case to be made for having letters and resumes in more than one format. There is no need to waste precious time crafting your written communication entirely from scratch when templates exist. The key is to do each variation once and to do it right. This means doing your work on a computer if possible and keeping it comprehensively backed up on disk. This way you'll be loaded for bear regardless of when opportunity comes knocking on your door. More information on creating and managing an effective direct-mail campaign can be found in *Cover Letters That Knock 'em Dead.*

Multiple Submissions

You may sometimes find it valuable to send half a dozen contact letters to a given company, to assure that all the important players know of your existence. Let's say you are a young engineer who wants to work for Last Chance Electronics. It is well within the bounds of reason to mail cover or broadcast letters to any or all of the following people (each addressed by name so the letter doesn't end up in the trash): the company president, the vice president of engineering, the chief engineer, the engineering manager, the vice president of human resources, the technical engineering recruitment manager, and the technical recruiter.

A professionally organized and conducted campaign will proceed on two fronts.

Front One. A carefully targeted rifle approach to a select group of companies. You will have first identified these super-desirable places to work when you researched your long list of potential employers. You will continue to add to this primary target list as you unearth fresh opportunities in your day-to-day research efforts.

In this instance you have two choices:

1. Mail to everyone at once, remembering that the letters have to be personalized and followed up.
2. Start your mailings off with one to a line manager and one to a contact in human resources. Follow up in a few days and repeat the process to other names on your list.

Front Two. A carpet bombing approach to every possible employer in the area. After all, you won't know what opportunities exist unless you go find out.

Here you will begin with a mailing to one or two contacts within the company and then repeat the mailings to other contacts when your initial follow-up calls result in referrals or dead ends. Remember, just because Harry in engineering says there are no openings in the company doesn't necessarily make it so. Besides, any one of the additional contacts you make could well be the person *who knows the person* who is just dying to meet you.

Once your campaign is in motion and you have received some responses to your mailings and scheduled some interviews from your calls (how to make the calls is covered in the next chapter), your emphasis will change. Those contacts and interviews will require follow-up letters and conversation. You will be spending time preparing for the interviews.

This is exactly the point at which most job hunts stall. We get so excited about the interview activity that we convince ourselves that "This will be the offer." Experienced headhunters know that the offer that can't fail always will. The offer doesn't materialize, and we are left sitting with absolutely no interview activity. We let the interview funnel empty itself.

The more letters you send out, the more follow-up calls you can make to schedule interviews. The more direct calls you make, the more interviews you will schedule and the more leads you will generate. The more interviews you get, the better you feel and the better you get at interviewing. The better you get at interviewing, the better the offers you get—and the *more* offers you get.

So no matter how good things look, you must continue the campaign. While you have to maintain activity with those companies you are negotiating with, you must also make yourself maintain your daily marketing schedule. Write letters in *each* of the following areas:

- In response to newspaper ads
- To associations, alumni/ae, colleagues
- To direct research contacts
- To headhunters
- Follow-up letters

Small but consistent mailings have many benefits. The balance you maintain is important because most job hunters are tempted to send the easy letters and make the easy calls (networking with old friends). But this will knock you out of balance and kick you into a tailspin.

Don't stop searching even when an offer is pending, and your potential boss says, "Robin, you've got the job and we're glad you can start on Monday. The offer letter is in the mail." Never accept any "yes" until you have it in writing, you have started work, and the first paycheck has cleared at the bank! Until then keep your momentum building: It is the professional and circumspect thing to do.

It is no use mailing tens or even hundreds of resumes without following up on your efforts. If you are not getting a response with one resume format, you might want to redo it; try changing from a chronological to a functional or combination format, just as you would change the bait if the fish weren't taking what you had on the hook.

Keep things in perspective. Although your 224th contact may not have an opening for you, with a few polite and judicious questions she may well have a good lead. You will learn how to do this in the chapter entitled "Getting Live Leads from Dead Ends."

In the job hunt there are only two "yeses": Their "yes-I-want-you-to-work-for-us" and your "yes-I-can-start-on-Monday." Every "no" brings you closer to the big "yes." Never take rejections of your resume or your phone call as rejections of yourself; just as every job is not for you, you aren't right for every job.

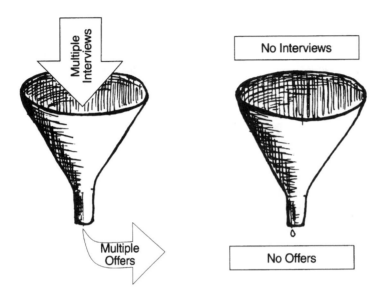

Stacking the Odds in Your Favor

We all have 168 hours a week to become bagmen or billionaires and to make our lives as fulfilling as they can be. For some of us this means a better job, for others it means getting back to work to keep a roof over our heads.

How we manage these hours will determine our success. These job hunting Commandments will see you successfully through the job change process or career transition:

- Those in the professional employment field reckon an average of seven hundred fresh contacts is required per job placement. You should anticipate at least this number. In a forty-hour week these professionals average approximately thirty-five to fifty contacts per day. Build to this momentum.
- Work at getting a new job. Work at least forty hours per week at it. Divide your time between contacting potential employers and generating new leads. Never stop the research and job hunting process until you have a written job offer in hand and you have accepted that job in writing with an agreed-upon start date.

- Research the companies you contact. In a tightly run job race the candidate who is most knowledgeable about the employer has a distinct advantage.
- Contact and recontact your job leads. Follow up on the resumes you send out. Resubmit your resume after six weeks. Change the format of your resume and resubmit yet again. (See my book *Resumes That Knock 'em Dead* for specific ideas on how to do this.)
- Stay in regular telephone contact with your job leads on a monthly basis to maintain top-of-the-mind awareness.
- Take off the blinkers. We all have two specific skills: our professional/technical skills—say, computer programming—and our industry skills—say, banking. Professional/technical skills can be transferable to other industries—say, manufacturing; and industry skills can open up other opportunities in your industry—say, as a technical trainer for programmers and/or technophobes.
- Develop examples of the personality traits that make you special—say, determination. Rehearse building these examples into your interview responses. (See chapter 14.)
- Send follow-up notes with relevant news clippings, cartoons, and so on to those in your networks.
- Work on your self-image. Use this time to get physically fit. Studies show that unfit, overweight people take longer to find suitable work. The more you do today the better you will feel about yourself.
- Maintain a professional demeanor during the work week (clothing, posture, personal hygiene).
- Use regular business hours for making contacts. Use the early morning, lunch time, after 5 P.M., and Saturday for doing the on-going research to maintain momentum.
- Don't feel guilty about taking time off from your job hunting job. Just do it conscientiously. If you regularly spend Saturday morning in the library doing research, you can take Wednesday afternoon off.
- Maintain records of your contacts. They will benefit not only this job search but maybe those in the future, too.
- Remember: It's all up to you. There are many excuses not to make calls or send resumes on any given day. There are many excuses to get up later or knock off earlier. There are many excuses to back off because this one's in the bag. There are no real reasons. There are no jobs out there for those who won't look. There are countless opportunities for those who assiduously turn over the stones.

Contact Trackers

Job hunting requires multiple contacts with employers and others. You should call an employer and schedule a follow-up conversation for a specific time and date next week, or you should send a resume today and should schedule a follow-up call four to eight days later. When you get up to speed, important opportunities will fall through the cracks unless you maintain a contact tracker like the one on page 62.

How to Use the Contact Tracker

I recommend you make 365 copies of the contact tracker, date each one, and put them in a ring binder. Once you have been going a couple of weeks, your days will plan themselves. Of course you probably won't use anywhere near all 365, but as we say in New York, "such a problem I should have."

Before making a day's mailing, fill out the contact tracker with the company name, telephone number, and contact name. This will help you structure your job hunting days. A mailing today will allow you to have a follow-up plan set and ready to go at the appropriate time. As a rule of thumb, a mailing today is ripe for follow-up four to eight days later. Much sooner and you can't guarantee the mail has arrived; much later and it will already be lost in an in-box or passed on.

You will know that you are on track when you are filling out one of these every day as a result of a mailing, and filling out a second one as a result of your follow-up calls.

Every month I hear from people who use these techniques effectively. Just last week I had a gentleman speak to me on a radio show in Texas who explained that he had been out of work for six months. He said he had bought the *Knock 'em Dead* books just five weeks earlier, had followed my advice to the letter, and had since generated four job offers. Follow my advice in letter and spirit and the same good fortune can be yours.

Network Index Sheets

As you develop your multiple networks, they too will become unwieldy and you will need some form of record keeping. Network index sheets like the one on page 63 will help you stay on top of the problem. The sheets should be developed on every good contact you make.

Good contacts from the contact tracker will be forwarded to a future date for follow-up; then, as you develop a history on that person, on a network index sheet you can add a memory jogger to the contact tracker.

Follow-up: The Key Ingredient

In theory the perfect letters you send cold or as a result of phone calls will receive a response rate of one hundred percent. Unfortunately there is no perfect letter or call in this less-than-perfect world. If you sit there like some fat Buddha waiting for the world to beat a path to your door, you may wait a long time.

While I was writing this chapter, a pal of mine advertised for a programmer analyst, a two-line ad in the local paper. By Wednesday of the following week he had over one hundred responses. Ten days later he was still plowing through them when he received a follow-up call (the only one he received) from one of the respondents. The job hunter was in the office within two hours, returned the following morning, and was hired before lunchtime.

The story? The candidate's paperwork was simply languishing there in the pile, waiting to be discovered. The follow-up phone call got it discovered. The call made the interviewer sort through the enormous pile of paper, pull out the letter and resume, and act on it. Follow-up calls, and follow-up calls on the follow-up calls, do work.

The best managers maintain a private file of great professionals whom they can't use today but want to keep available. I know of someone who got a top job as a result of being in these files. She got an interview and job offer from a broadcast letter she had sent *three years earlier.*

Grant yourself, with this approach, the right to pick and choose among many job offers. Because you are in control, it is possible to set your multiple interviews close together. This way your interviewing skills improve from one meeting to the next. And soon, instead of scheduling multiple interviews, you can be weighing multiple job offers.

Date: _____

CONTACT TRACKER

	Company	Tel #	Contact Name	Result	F/U Date	Sent Resume
1.						
2.						
3.						
4.						
5.						
6.						
7.						
8.						
9.						
10.						
11.						
12.						
13.						
14.						
15.						
16.						
17.						
18.						
19.						
20.						

NETWORK INDEX SHEET

Name: _____

Relationship: _____

How known: _____

Time known: _____

People in common: _____

_____

Telephone: (H) _____, (O) _____

Home address: _____

_____

Office address: _____

_____

Secretary: _____

Leads given: _____

_____

_____

BIOGRAPHICAL INFORMATION

Spouse: _____

Children: _____

Interests: _____

_____

Affiliations: _____

_____

Professional experience: _____

_____

_____

Date last contacted: _____

Result: _____

_____

_____

Part II | Getting to Square One

With the grunt work completed, you are prepared to set up multiple interviews with just a few phone calls. Ready?

With the grunt work completed, you are loaded for bear and ready to knock 'em dead. So how do you begin?

It bears repeating that you must take the initiative when it comes to finding a job. You must do so in a distinctive way. What is your first instinct when you must "go look for a job"? Read the want ads? Everybody else does. Apply for jobs listed with the unemployment office? Everybody else does. Send resumes to companies on the off-chance they have a job that fits your resume? Everybody else does. Or, of course, you can wait for someone to call you. Employ those tactics as your main thrust for hunting down the best jobs in town, and you will fail, as do millions of others who fall into the trap of using such outdated job hunting techniques.

Today's business marketplace demands a different approach. Your career does not take care of itself—you must go out and grab the opportunities.

"Hello, Mr. Smith? My name is Martin Yate. I am an experienced training specialist. . . ."

It's as easy as that.

Guide your destiny by speaking directly to the professionals who make their living in the same way you do. A few minutes spent calling different companies from your research dossier, and you will have an interview. When you get one interview from making a few calls, how many do you think could be arranged with a day's concerted effort?

5 | Paint the Perfect Picture on the Phone

**When you call the company representative, you must have four goals: get attention, generate interest, create a desire to know more about you, and make the company representative take action. Here are three easy steps that will get you closer to landing the interview.
Also: the care and feeding of pesky corporate gatekeepers.**

Before making that first nerve-wracking telephone call, you must be prepared to achieve one of these three goals. They are listed in order of priority.

- I will arrange a meeting.
- I will arrange a time to talk further on the phone.
- I will ask for a lead on a promising job opening elsewhere.

Always keep these goals in mind. By the time you finish the next four chapters, you'll be able to achieve any one of these goals quickly and easily.

To make the initial phone call a success, all you need to do is paint a convincing word picture of yourself. To start, remember the old saying: "No one really listens; we are all just waiting for our turn to speak." With this in mind, you shouldn't expect to hold anyone's attention for an extended period, so the picture you create needs to be brief yet thorough. Most of all, it should be specifically vague: specific enough to arouse interest, to make the company representative prick up his ears, and yet vague enough to encourage questions, to make him pursue you. The aim is to paint a representation of your skills in broad brush strokes with examples of the money-making, money-saving, or time-saving accomplishments all companies like to hear about.

A presentation made over the telephone must possess four characteristics to be successful. These can best be remembered by an old acronym from the advertising world: *AIDA*.

A—You must get the company representative's Attention.
I—You must get the company representative's Interest.
D—You must create a Desire to know more about you.
A—You must encourage the company representative to take Action.

With AIDA you get noticed. The interest you generate will be displayed by the questions that are being asked: "How much are you making?" "Do you have a degree?" "How much experience do you have?" By giving the appropriate answers to these and other questions (which I will discuss in detail), you will change interest into a desire to know more and then parlay that desire into an interview.

The types of questions you are asked also enable you to identify the company's specific needs, and once they are identified, you can gear the ongoing conversation toward those needs.

Here are the steps in building your AIDA presentation:

Step One:

This covers who you are and what you do. It is planned to get the company representative's attention, to give the person a reason to stay on the phone. This introduction will include your job title and a brief generalized description of your duties and responsibilities. Use a nonspecific job title, as you did for your resume. Remember, getting a foot in the door with a generalized title can provide the occasion to sell your superior skills.

Tell just enough about yourself to whet the company's appetite and cause the representative to start asking questions. Again, keep your description a little vague. For example, if you describe yourself simply as experienced, the company representative must try to qualify your statement with a question: "How much experience do you have?" You have established a level of interest. But if you describe yourself as having four years of experience, while the company is looking for seven, you are likely to be ruled out before you are even aware a job exists. Never specify exact experience or list all your accomplishments during the initial presentation. Your aim is just to open a dialogue.

EXAMPLE:

"Good morning, Mr. Smith. My name is Joan Jones. I am an experienced office equipment salesperson with an in-depth knowledge of the office products industry. Have I caught you at a good time?"

Never ever ask if you have caught someone at a bad time. You are offering your contact an excuse to say "yes." By the same token, asking whether you have caught someone at a good time will usually get you a "yes." Then you can go directly into the rest of your presentation.

Step Two:

Now you are ready to generate interest, and from that, desire; it's time to sell one or two of your accomplishments. You already should have identified these during earlier resume-building exercises. Pull out no more than two items and follow your introductory sentence with them. Keep them brief and to the point, without embellishments.

EXAMPLE:

"As the #3 salesperson in my company, I increased sales in my territory 15 percent to over $1 million. In the last six months, I won three major accounts from my competitors."

Step Three:

You have made the company representative want to know more about you, so now you can make him take action. Include the reason for your call and a request to meet. It should be carefully constructed to finish with a question that will bring a positive response, which will launch the two of you into a nuts-and-bolts discussion.

EXAMPLE:

"The reason I'm calling, Mr. Smith, is that I'm looking for a new challenge, and having researched your company, I felt we might have some areas for discussion. Are these the types of skills and accomplishments you look for in your staff?"

Your presentation ends with a question that guarantees a positive response, and the conversation gets moving.

☐　　☐　　☐

Your task before calling is to write out a presentation using these guidelines and your work experience. Knowing exactly what you are going to say and what you wish to achieve is the only way to generate multiple interviews and multiple job offers. When your presentation is prepared and written, read it aloud to yourself, and imagine the faceless company representative on the other end of the line. Practice with a friend or spouse, or use a tape recorder to critique yourself.

After you make the actual presentation on the phone, you'll really begin to work on arranging a meeting, another phone conversation, or establishing a referral. There will likely be a silence on the other end after your initial pitch. Be patient. The company representative needs time to digest your words. If you feel tempted to break the silence, resist; you do not want to break the person's train of thought, nor do you want the ball back in your court.

This contemplative silence may last as long as twenty seconds, but when the company representative responds, only three things can happen.

1. The company representative can agree with you and arrange a meeting.
2. The company representative can ask questions that show interest: "Do you have a degree?" "How much are you earning?" (Any question, because it denotes interest, is considered a buy signal. Handled properly, it will enable you to arrange a meeting.)
3. The company representative can raise an objection: "I don't need anyone like that now." "Send me a resume."

These objections, when handled properly, will also result in an interview with the company, or at least a referral to someone else who has job openings. In fact, you will frequently find that objections prove to be terrific opportunities.

□   □   □

I hope you can handle the first option, "I'd like to meet with you," with little assistance; for obvious reasons, it doesn't get its own chapter.

It will sometimes happen that an overly officious receptionist or secretary will try to thwart you in your efforts to present your credentials directly to a potential employer. At least it appears that way to you.

In fact, it is very rare that these corporate gatekeepers, as they are known, are specifically directed to screen calls from professionals seeking employment, as to do so can only increase employment costs to the company. What they are there to do is to screen the nuisance calls from salespeople and the like.

However, to arm you for the occasional objectionable gatekeeper standing between you and making a living, you might try the following techniques used by investigative reporters, private eyes, and headhunters.

Go up the Ladder

If you can't get through to the person you want to speak to, say the accounting manager, go up the ladder to the controller or the vice president of finance.

Interestingly enough, the higher you go, the more accessible people are. In this instance the senior manager may well not schedule an interview with you but instead refer you back down to the appropriate level. Which means that to the pesky gatekeeper you can now say, "Mr. Bigshot, your divisional vice president of finance, asked me to call your Mr. Jones. Is he there?" Or if you didn't get through, and Bigshot's secretary referred you down the ladder, you say, "Mr. Bigshot's office recommended . . ." Then the conversation with your target can begin with your standard introduction, but be sure to mention first that so-and-so suggested you call.

Preempt

Most gatekeepers are trained at most to find out your name and the nature of your business. But when they are asking the questions, they control the conversation. You can remain in control by preempting their standard script. "Hi, I'm Mr. Yate [always use your surname for the intimidation value]. I need to speak to Ms. Jones about an accounting matter. Is she there?" Should a truly obnoxious gatekeeper ask snidely, "Perhaps I can help you?" you can effectively utilize any of the following options: "Thank you, but I'd rather discuss it with Ms. Jones." "It's personal." (Well, it's your livelihood isn't it?) Or you can blind them with science. "Yes, if you can talk to me about the finer points of release 6.2 of Lotus 1-2-3," which invariably they can't, so you're in like Flynn.

When you are clear about who you want to speak to and can predict possible screening devices, you are usually assured of getting through. When you don't have the name, try these techniques.

Explain to gatekeepers that you need to send a letter to [whatever the title is] and ask for the correct spelling of the name. There is usually more than one person worth speaking to at any company, so ask for more than one name and title. In the finance area, and depending on your title, any or all of the following could provide useful contacts: the accounting supervisor, the accounting manager, the assistant controller, the controller, the vice president of finance, the executive vice president, the COO, the CEO, and the chairman.

Anyone who will give you one name will invariably give you more. Some years ago in Colorado I sat with a job hunter using this technique who gathered 142 names in one hour!

In companies where security is at a premium, the gatekeepers are expressly forbidden to give out names and titles. In this case use some of my blind-siding techniques: There are certain people in every company who by the very nature of their jobs have contacts with people at all levels of the company, and who are not given the responsibility to screen calls. These include people in the mail room and in the gate house, guards, shipping and receiving employees, second-, third-, and fourth- shift employees, new or temporary employees, advertising and public relations people, sales and marketing people, and travel center, Q/A, or customer service employees.

Automatic Phone Systems

Automatic phone systems are on the increase. If the techniques I've mentioned don't turn the trick for you, these will. When the recorded voice tells you to enter the extension key, keep keying until you hit one that is on the money. It doesn't matter who answers as long as someone does. The conversation goes like this:

"Jack speaking."

"Jack, this is Martin Yate. I'm calling from outside and I'm lost on this damn telephone system." This usually gets a smile. "I'm trying to get hold of [whatever the title is]. Could you check who that would be for me?"

or

"Jack, this is Martin Yate. I'm lost on this damn telephone system. I need some help. Can you spare me a minute?"

Whichever technique you use, be sensitive to the person in a rush and don't leave numerous messages. Try to get the extension of the person you want, rather than letting yourself be transferred.

6 | Responding to Buy Signals

When you are on the phone, certain questions will tell you that the company representative is interested in you. Learn how to respond correctly to keep the interest alive.

With just a touch of nervous excitement you finish your presentation: "Are these the types of skills and accomplishments you look for in your staff?" There is silence on the other end. It is broken by a question. You breathe a sigh of relief because you remember that any question denotes interest and is a buy signal.

Now, conversation is a two-way street, and you are most likely to win an interview when you take responsibility for your half. Just as the employer's questions show interest in you, your questions should show your interest in the work done at the company. By asking questions of your own in the normal course of conversation—questions usually tagged on to the end of one of your answers—you will forward the conversation. Also, such questions help you find out what particular skills and qualities are important to the employer. Inquisitiveness will increase your knowledge of the opportunity at hand, and that knowledge will give you the power to arrange a meeting.

The alternative is to leave all the interrogation to the employer. That will place you on the defensive, and at the end of the talk, you will be as ignorant of the real parameters of the job as you were at the start. And the employer will know less about you than you might want.

Applying the technique of giving a short answer and finishing that reply with a question will carry your call to its logical conclusion: The interviewer will tell you the job specifics, and as that happens, you will present the relevant skills or attributes. In any conversation, the person who asks the questions controls its outcome. You called the employer to get an interview as the first step in generating a job offer, so take control of your destiny by taking control of the conversation.

EXAMPLE:

Joan Jones: **"Good morning, Mr. Smith. My name is Joan Jones. I am an experienced office equipment salesperson with an in-depth knowledge of the office products industry. Have I caught you at a good time? . . . . As the #3** salesperson in my company, I increased sales in my territory 15 percent to over $1 million. In the last six months, I won three major accounts from my competitors. The reason I'm calling, Mr. Smith, is that I'm looking for a new challenge, and having researched your company, I felt we might have areas for discussion. Are these the types of skills and accomplishments you look for in your staff?"

[Pause.]

Mr. Smith: "Yes, they are. What type of equipment have you been selling?" *[Buy signal!]*

J: "My company carries a comprehensive range, and I sell both the top and bottom of the line, according to my customers' needs. I have been noticing a considerable interest in the latest fax and scanning equipment." *[You've made it a conversation; you further it with the following.]* "Has that been your experience recently?"

S: "Yes, especially in the color and acetate capability machines." *[Useful information for you.]* "Do you have a degree?" *[Buy signal!]*

J: "Yes, I do." *[Just enough information to keep the company representative chasing you.]* "I understand your company prefers degreed salespeople to deal with its more sophisticated clients." *[Your research is paying off.]*

S: "Our customer base is very sophisticated, and they expect a certain professionalism and competence from us." *[An inkling of the kind of person they want to hire.]* "How much experience do you have?" *[Buy signal!]*

J: "Well, I've worked in both operations and sales, so I have a wide experience base." *[General but thorough.]* "How many years of experience are you looking for?" *[Turning it around, but furthering the conversation.]*

S: "Ideally, four or five for the position I have in mind." *[More good information.]* "How many do you have?" *[Buy signal!]*

J: "I have two with this company, and one and a half before that. I fit right in with your needs, don't you agree?" *[How can Mr. Smith say "no"?]*

S: "Uhmmm . . . What's your territory?" *[Buy signal!]*

J: "I cover the metropolitan area. Mr. Smith, it really does sound as if we might have something to talk about." *[Remember, your first goal is the face-to-face interview.]* "I am planning to take Thursday and Friday off at the end of the

week. Can we meet then?" *[Make Mr. Smith decide what day he can see you, rather than whether he will see you at all.]* **"Which would be best for you?"**

S: "How about Friday morning? Can you bring a resume?"

Your conversation should proceed with that kind of give-and-take. Your questions show interest, carry the conversation forward, and teach you more about the company's needs. By the end of the conversation you have an interview arranged and several key areas to promote when you arrive:

- The company sees growth in the latest fax and scanning equipment, especially those with color and acetate capabilities.
- They want business and personal sophistication.
- They ideally want four or five years' experience.
- They are interested in your metropolitan contacts.

The above is a fairly simple scenario, but even though it is constructive, it doesn't show you the tricky buy signals that can spell disaster in your job hunt. These are questions that appear to be simple buy signals, yet in reality are a part of every interviewer's arsenal called "knock-out" questions—questions that can save the interviewer time by quickly ruling out certain types of candidates. Although these questions most frequently arise during the initial telephone conversation, they can crop up at the face-to-face interview; the answering techniques are applicable throughout the interview cycle.

Note: We all come from different backgrounds and geographical areas. So understand that while my answers cover correct approaches and responses, they do not attempt to capture the regional and personal flavor of conversation. You and I will never talk alike, so don't learn the example answers parrot-fashion. Instead, you should take the essence of the responses and personalize them until the words fall easily from your lips.

Buy Signal
"How much are you making/do you want?"
This is a direct question looking for a direct answer, yet it is a knock-out question. Earning either too little or too much could ruin your chances before you're given the opportunity to shine in person. There are a number of options that could serve you better than a direct answer. First, you must understand that questions about money at this point in the conversation are being used to screen you in or screen you out of the "ballpark"—the answers you give now should be geared

specifically toward getting you in the door and into a face-to-face meeting. (Handling the serious salary negotiations that are attached to a job offer are covered extensively in chapter 23, "Negotiating the Offer.") For now, your main options are as follows:

☐ **Put yourself above the money**: "I'm looking for a job and a company to call home. If I am the right person for you, I'm sure you'll make me a fair offer. What is the salary range for the position?"

☐ **Give a vague answer**: "The most important things to me are the job itself and the company. What is the salary range for the position?"

☐ **Or you could answer a question with a question:** "How much does the job pay?"

When you are pressed a second time for an exact dollar figure, be as honest and forthright as circumstances permit. Some people (often, unfortunately, women) are underpaid for their jobs when their work is compared with that of others in similar positions. It is not a question of perception; these women in fact make less money than they should. If you have the skills for the job and you are concerned that your current low salary will eliminate you before you have the chance to show your worth, you might want to add into your base salary the dollar value of your benefits. If it turns out to be too much, you can then simply explain that you were including the value of your benefits. Or, you could say, "Mr. Smith, my previous employers felt I am well worth the money I earn due to my skills, dedication, and honesty. Were we to meet, I'm sure I could demonstrate my value and my ability to contribute to your department. You'd like an opportunity to make that evaluation, wouldn't you?"

Notice the "wouldn't you?" at the end of the reply. A reflexive question such as this is a great conversation-forwarding technique because it encourages a positive response. Conservative use of reflexive questions can really help you move things along. Watch the sound of your voice, though. A reflexive question can sound pleasantly conversational or pointed and accusatory; it's not really what you say, but how you say it.

Such questions are easy to create. Just conclude with "wouldn't you?" "didn't you?" "won't you?" "couldn't you?" "shouldn't you?" or "don't you?" as appropriate at the end of virtually any statement, and the interviewer will almost always answer "yes." You have kept the conversation alive, and moved it closer to your goal. Repeat the reflexive questions to yourself. They have a certain rhythm that will help you remember them.

Buy Signal

"Do you have a degree?"

Always answer the exact question; beware of giving unrequested (and possibly excessive) information. For example, if you have a bachelor's degree in fine arts from New York University, your answer is "Yes," not "Yes, I have a bachelor's degree in fine arts from NYU." Perhaps the company wants an architecture degree. Perhaps the company representative has bad feelings about NYU graduates. You don't want to be knocked out before you've been given the chance to prove yourself.

"Yes, I have a degree. What background are you looking for?" Or, you can always answer a question with a question: "I have a diverse educational background. Ideally, what are you looking for?"

When a degree is perceived as mandatory and you barely scraped through grade school, don't be intimidated. As Calvin Coolidge used to say, "The world is full of educated layabouts." You may want to use the "Life University" answer. For instance: "My education was cut short by the necessity of earning a living at an early age. My past managers have found that my life experience and responsible attitude is a valuable asset to the department. Also, I intend to return to school to continue my education."

A small proportion of the more sensitive employers are verifying educational credentials, and if yours are checked it means the employer takes such matters seriously, so an untruth or an exaggeration could cost you a job. Think hard and long before inflating your educational background.

Buy Signal

"How much experience do you have?"

Too much or too little could easily rule you out. Be careful how you answer and try to gain time. It is a vague question, and you have a right to ask for qualifications.

"Could you help me with that question?" or, "Are you looking for overall experience or in some specific areas?" or, "Which areas are most important to you?" Again, you answer a question with a question. The employer's response, while gaining you time, tells you what it takes to do the job and therefore what you have to say to get it, so take mental notes—you can even write them down, if you have time. Then give an appropriate response.

You might want to retain control of the conversation by asking another question, for example: "The areas of expertise you require sound very interesting, and it sounds as if you have some exciting projects at hand. Exactly what projects would I be involved with in the first few months?"

After one or two buy-signal questions are asked, ask for a meeting. Apart from those just outlined, questions asked over the phone tend not to contain traps. If you simply ask, "Would you like to meet me?" there are only two possible responses: "yes" or "no." Your chances of success are greatly decreased. When you intimate, however, that you will be in the area on a particular date or dates—"I'm going to be in town on Thursday and Friday, Mr. Smith. Which would be better for you?"—you have asked a question that moves the conversation along dramatically. Your question gives the company representative the choice of meeting you on Thursday or Friday, rather than meeting you or not meeting you. By presuming the "yes," you reduce the chances of hearing a negative, and increase the possibility of a face-to-face meeting.

7 | Responding to Objections

Being stonewalled? This chapter shows you how to turn flat statements of no interest into opportunity.

Even with the most convincing word picture, the silence may be broken not by a buy signal, but by an objection. An objection is usually a statement, not a question: "Send me a resume," or, "I don't have time to see you," or, "You are earning too much," or, "You'll have to talk to personnel," or, "I don't need anyone like you right now."

Although these seem like brush-off lines, often they are really disguised opportunities to get yourself a job offer—handled properly, almost all objections can be parlayed into interviews. This section will teach you to seize hidden opportunities successfully; notice that all your responses have a commonality with buy-signal responses. They all end with a question, one that will enable you to learn more about the reason for the objection, overcome it, and once again lead the conversation toward a face-to-face interview.

In dealing with objections, as with differences of opinion, nothing is gained by confrontation, though much is to be gained by appreciation of the other's viewpoint. Most objections you hear are best handled by first demonstrating your understanding of the other's viewpoint. Always start your response with "I understand," or, "I can appreciate your position," or, "I see your point," or, "Of course," followed by, "However," or, "Also consider," or a similar line that puts you back into consideration.

Remember, these responses should not be learned merely to be repeated. You need only to understand and implement their meaning, to understand their concept and put the answers in your own words. Personalize all the suggestions to your character and style of speech.

□ □ □

Objection:

"Why don't you send me a resume?"

Danger here. The company representative may be genuinely interested in seeing your resume as a first step in the interview cycle; or it may be a polite way of getting you off the phone. You should identify what the real reason is without causing antagonism. At the same time, you want to open up the conversation. A good reply would be: "Of course, Mr. Smith. Would you give me your exact title and the full address? . . . Thank you. So that I can be sure that my qualifications fit your needs, what skills are you looking for in this position?"

Notice the steps:

- Apparent agreement to start
- A show of consideration
- A question to further the conversation

Answering in that fashion will open up the conversation. Mr. Smith will relay the aspects of the job that are important to him, and with this knowledge, you can sell Smith on your skills over the phone. Also, you will be able to use the information to draw attention to your skills in the future, in:

- Following conversations
- The cover letter to your resume
- Your executive briefing
- Your face-to-face meeting
- Your follow-up after the meeting

The information you glean will give you power and will increase your chances of receiving a job offer.

□   □   □

Objection:

"I don't have time to see you."

If the employer is too busy to see you, he or she has a problem, and by recognizing that, perhaps you can show yourself as the one to solve it. You should avoid confrontation, however—it is important that you demonstrate empathy for the speaker. Agree, empathize, and ask a question that moves the conversation forward.

"I understand how busy you must be; it sounds like a competent, dedicated, and efficient professional [whatever your title is] could be of some assistance.

Perhaps I could call you back at a better time, to discuss how I might make you some time. When are you least busy, in the morning or afternoon?"

The company representative will either make time to talk now, or will arrange a better time for the two of you to talk further.

Here are some other ideas you could use to phrase the same objection: "Since you are so busy, what is the best time of day for you? First thing in the morning, or is the afternoon a quieter time?" or, "I will be in your area tomorrow, so why don't I come by and see you?"

Of course, you can combine the two: "I'm going to be in your part of town tomorrow, and I could drop by and see you. What is your quietest time, morning or afternoon?" By presuming the invitation for a meeting, you make it harder for the company representative to object. And if he or she is truly busy, your consideration will be appreciated and will still make it hard to object.

☐   ☐   ☐

Objection:

"You are earning too much."

You should not have brought up salary in the first place. Go straight to jail. If the company representative brought up the matter, that's a buy signal, which was discussed in the last chapter. If the job really doesn't pay enough, you got (as the carnival barker says) close, but no cigar! How to make a success of this seeming dead end is handled in the next chapter. You may also refer to helpful information covered in chapter 23, "Negotiating the Offer."

☐   ☐   ☐

Objection:

"We only promote from within."

Your response could be: "I realize that, Mr. Smith. Your development of employees is a major reason I want to get in! I am bright, conscientious, and motivated. When you do hire from the outside, what assets are you looking for?"

The response finishes with a question designed to carry the conversation forward, and to give you a new opportunity to sell yourself. Notice that the response assumes that the company is hiring from the outside, even though the company representative has said otherwise. You have called his bluff, but in a professional, inoffensive manner.

□   □   □

Objection:

"You'll have to talk to personnel."

Your reply is: "Of course, Mr. Smith. Whom should I speak to in personnel, and what specific position should I mention?"

You cover a good deal of ground with that response. You establish whether there is a job there or whether you are being fobbed off to personnel to waste their time and your own. Also, you move the conversation forward again while changing the thrust of it to your advantage. Develop a specific job-related question to ask while the company representative is answering the first question. It can open a fruitful line for you to pursue. If you receive a nonspecific reply, probe a little deeper. A simple phrase like, "That's interesting, please tell me more," or, "Why's that?" will usually do the trick.

Or you can ask: "When I speak to personnel, will it be about a specific job you have, or is it to see whether I might fill a position elsewhere in the company?"

Armed with the resulting information, you can talk to personnel about your conversation with Mr. Smith. Remember to get the name of a specific person with whom to speak, and to quote the company representative.

EXAMPLE:

"Good morning, Mr. Johnson. Mr. Smith, the regional sales manager, suggested we should speak to arrange an interview."

That way, you will show personnel that you are not a waste of time; because you know someone in the company, you won't be regarded as one of the frequent "blind" calls they get every day. As the most overworked, understaffed department in a company, they will appreciate that. Most important, you will stand out, and be noticed.

Don't look at the personnel department as a roadblock; it may contain a host of opportunities for you. Because a large company may have many different departments that can use your talents, personnel is likely to be the only department that knows all the openings. You might be able to arrange three or four interviews with the same company for three or four different positions!

□   □   □

Objection:

"I really wanted someone with a degree."

You could respond to this by saying: "Mr. Smith, I appreciate your position. It was necessary that I start earning a living early in life. If we meet, I am certain you would recognize the value of my additional practical experience."

You might then wish to ask what the company policy is for support and encouragement of employees taking night classes or continuing-education courses, and will naturally explain how you are hoping to find an employer who encourages employees to further their education. Your response will end with: "If we were to meet, I am certain you would recognize the value of my practical experience. I am going to be in your area next week. When would be the best time of day to get together?"

☐   ☐   ☐

Objection:

"I don't need anyone like you now."

Short of suggesting that the employer fire someone to make room for you (which, incidentally, has been done successfully on a few occasions), chances of getting an interview with this particular company are slim. With the right question, however, that person will give you a personal introduction to someone else who could use your talents. Asking that right question or series of questions is what networking and the next chapter are all about. So on the occasions when the techniques for answering buy signals or rebutting objections do not get you a meeting, "Getting Live Leads from Dead Ends" will!

8 | Getting Live Leads from Dead Ends

Not every company has an opening for you. It's up to you to create leads, though, and here are nine questions you can ask that will steer you to opportunity elsewhere.

There will be times when you have said all the right things on the phone, but hear, "I can't use anyone like you right now." Not every company has a job opening for you, nor are you right for every job. Sometimes you must accept a temporary setback and understand that the rejection is not one of you as a human being. By using these special interview development questions, though, you will be able to turn those setbacks into job interviews.

The company representative is a professional and knows other professionals in his or her field, in other departments, subsidiaries, and even other companies. If you approach the phone presentation in a professional manner, he or she, as a fellow professional, will be glad to advise you on who is looking for someone with your skills. Nearly everyone you call will be pleased to point you in the right direction, but only if you *ask*! And you'll be able to ask as many questions as you wish, because you will be recognized as a colleague intelligently using the professional network. The company representative also knows that his good turn in referring you to a colleague at another company will be returned in the future. And, as a general rule, companies prefer candidates to be referred this way over any other method.

But do not expect people to be clairvoyant. There are two sayings: "You get what you ask for," and "If you don't ask, you don't get." Each is pertinent here.

When you are sure that no job openings exist within a particular department, ask one of these questions:

- "Who else in the company might need someone with my qualifications?"
- "Does your company have any other divisions or subsidiaries that might need someone with my attributes?"
- "Whom do you know in the business community who might have a lead for me?"
- "Which are the most rapidly growing companies in the area?"
- "Whom should I speak to there?"

- "Do you know anyone at the ABC Electronics Company?"
- "When do you anticipate an opening in your company?"
- "Are you planning any expansion or new projects that might create an opening?"
- "When do you anticipate change in your manpower needs?"

Each one of those interview-development questions can gain you an introduction or lead to a fresh opportunity. The questions have not been put in any order of importance—that is for you to do. Take a sheet of paper and, looking at the list, figure out what question you would ask if you had time to ask only one. Write it down. Do that with the remaining questions on the list. As you advance, you will develop a comfortable set of prioritized questions. Add questions of your own. For instance, the type of computer or word-processing equipment a company has might be important to some professions, but not to others, and a company representative might be able to lead you to companies that have your machines. Be sure that any question you add to your list is specific and leads to a job opening. Avoid questions like, "How's business these days?" Time is valuable, and time is money to both of you. When you're satisfied with your list of interview development questions, put them on a fresh sheet of paper and store it safely with your telephone presentation and resume.

Those interview development questions will lead you to a substantial number of jobs in the hidden job market. You are getting referrals from the "in" crowd, who know who is hiring whom long before that news is generally circulated. By being in with the "in" crowd, you establish a very effective referral network.

When you get leads on companies and specific individuals to talk to, be sure to thank your benefactor and ask to use his or her name as an introduction. The answer, you will find, will always be "yes," but asking shows you to be someone with manners—in this day and age, that alone will set you apart.

You might also suggest to your contact that you leave your telephone number in case he or she runs into someone who can use you. You'll be surprised at how many people call back with a lead.

With personal permission to use someone's name on your next networking call, you have been given the greatest of job search gifts: a personal introduction. Your call will begin with something like: "Hello, Ms. Smith. My name is Jack Jones. Joseph McDonald recommended I give you a call. By the way, he sends his regards." [Pause for any response to this.] "He felt we might have something valuable to discuss."

Follow up on every lead you get. Too many people become elated at securing an interview for themselves and then cease all effort to generate additional interviews, believing a job offer is definitely on its way. Your goal is to have a choice of the best jobs in town, and without multiple interviews, there is no way you'll have that choice. Asking interview-development questions ensures that you are tapping all the secret recesses of the hidden job market.

Networking is a continuous cycle:

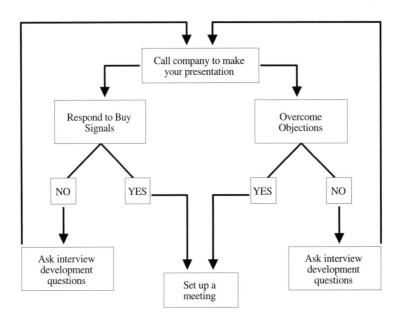

Make a commitment to sell yourself, to make telephone calls, to make a referral network, and to recognize buy signals and objections for what they really are— opportunities to shine. Make a commitment to ask interview development questions at every seeming dead end: They will lead you to all the jobs in town.

9 | The Telephone Interview

In this electronic age, interviewers use the telephone to weed out applicants. Your goal is a face-to-face meeting, and here are the methods you must use to get it.

In this glorious technological age, the first substantive contact with a potential employer is virtually always by telephone. It's the way business is done today.

It happens in one of three ways:

- You are networking, and the company representative goes into a screening process immediately because you have aroused his or her interest.
- A company calls unexpectedly as a result of a resume you have mailed and catches you off-guard.
- You or a headhunter who has agreed to take you on has set up a specific time for a telephone interview.

Whatever circumstance creates the telephone interview, you must be prepared to handle the questioning and use every means at your disposal to win the real thing—the face-to-face meeting. The telephone interview is the trial run for the face-to-face and is an opportunity you must not bumble; your happiness and prosperity may hinge on it.

This, the first contact with your future employer, will test your mental preparation. Remember: You can plant in your mind any thought, plan, desire, strategy, or purpose, and translate it into reality. Put your goal down on paper and read it aloud to yourself every day, because the constant reiteration will crystallize your aims, and clear goals provide the most solid base of preparation.

Being prepared for a telephone interview takes organization. You never know when a company is going to call once you have started networking and sending your resume out (the word gets around more quickly than you think if it's a resume that knocks 'em dead). Usually the call comes at the worst of times, such as 8 o'clock Monday morning when you are sleeping late, or 4:56 in the afternoon, just as you return from walking the dog. You can avoid being caught completely off-guard by keeping your resume and alphabetized company dossiers by the telephone.

The most obvious (and often most neglected) point to remember is this: During the interview, the company representative has only ears with which to judge you, and that is something you must overcome. Here are some tips.

- **Take a surprise call in stride.** If you receive a call as a result of a mailed resume or a telephone message you left, and you are unprepared, be calm. Sound positive, friendly, and collected: "Thank you for calling, Mr. Smith. Would you wait just a moment while I close the door?"

    Put the phone down, take three deep breaths to slow your heart down, pull out the appropriate company dossier and your resume, put a smile on your face (it improves the timbre of your voice), and pick up the phone again. Now you are in control of yourself and the situation.
- **Beware of over-familiarity.** You should always refer to the interviewer by his or her surname until invited to do otherwise.
- **Allow the company representative to do most of the talking**—to ask most (but not all) of the questions. Keep up your end of the conversation—this is, after all, a sales presentation, so be sure to ask a few questions of your own that will reveal you as an intelligent person and provide you the opportunity to promote your candidacy. For example, ask what immediate projects the interviewer's department is involved in, or the biggest challenges that are being tackled. When the interviewer answers your question, you will either have a clear picture of how to sell yourself, or you will ask a follow-up question for clarification.

    For example: "What specific skills and personality traits do you think are necessary for a person to succeed with those challenges?" Everyone hires a problem solver—find the problem and you are already halfway toward the offer.
- **Beware of giving yes/no answers.** They give no real information about your abilities.
- **Be factual in your answers.** You should be brief yet thorough.
- **Speak directly into the telephone.** Keep the mouthpiece about one inch from your mouth. Do not smoke or eat while on the phone. Numbered among the mystical properties of our telephone system is its excellence at picking up and amplifying background music and voices, especially young ones. That is excelled only by its power to transmit the sounds of food or gum being chewed or smoke being inhaled or exhaled. Smokers, take note: There are no laws about discriminating against smokers, and therefore, all nonsmokers naturally discriminate. They will assume that even if you don't actually light up at the interview, you'll have been chain-smoking beforehand and will

carry the smell with you as long as you are around. Taking no chances, they probably won't even give you a chance to get through the door once they hear you puffing away over the phone.

- **Take notes.** They will be invaluable to you in preparing for the face-to-face meeting. Were it not for the recent furor over the clandestine use of tape recorders, I would have recommended that you buy a cheap tape recorder and a phone attachment from your local electronics store and tape the whole conversation.

    If, for any reason, the company representative is interrupted, jot down the topic under discussion. When he or she gets back on the line, you can helpfully recap: "We were just discussing . . ." That will be appreciated and will set you apart from the others.

The company representative may talk about the corporation, and from the dossier in front of you, you will also know facts about the outfit. A little flattery goes a long way: Admire the company's achievements and you are, in fact, admiring the interviewer. Likewise, if any areas of common interest arise, comment on them, and agree with the interviewer when possible—people hire people like themselves.

If the interviewer does not give you the openings you need to sell yourself, be ready to salvage the situation and turn it to your advantage. Have a few work-related questions prepared—for example, "What exactly will be the three major responsibilities in this job?" or "What will be the first job I get my teeth into?" While you are getting the explanation, wait for a pause so that you can tell the interviewer your appropriate skills: "Would it be of value if I described my experience in the area of office management?" or "Then my experience in word processing should be a great help to you," or "I recently completed an accounting project just like that."

Under no circumstances, though, should you ask about the money you want, or benefits and vacation time; that comes later.

Remember that your single objective at this point is to sell yourself and your skills; if you don't do that, you may never get the face-to-face interview.

The telephone interview has come to an end when you are asked whether you have any questions. Ask any more questions that will improve your understanding of the job requirements. If you haven't asked before, now is the time to establish what projects you would be working on in the first six months. By discovering them now, you will have time before the face-to-face meeting to package your skills to the needs at hand, and to create the appropriate Executive Briefing.

And if you have not already asked or been invited to meet the interviewer, now is the time. Take the initiative.

"It sounds like a very interesting opportunity, Ms. Smith, and a situation where I could definitely make a contribution. The most pressing question I have now is, when can we get together?" (*Note:* Even though the emphasis throughout has been on putting things in your own words, do use "make a contribution." It shows pride in your work—a key personal trait.)

Once the details are confirmed, finish with this request: "If I need any additional information before the interview, I would like to feel free to get back to you." The company representative will naturally agree. No matter how many questions you get answered in the initial conversation, there will always be something you forgot. This allows you to call again to satisfy any curiosity—it will also enable you to increase rapport. Don't take too much advantage of it, though: One well-placed phone call that contains two or three considered questions will be appreciated; four or five phone calls will not.

Taking care to ascertain the correct spelling and pronunciation of the interviewer's name shows your concern for the small but important things in life—it will be noticed. This is also a good time to establish who else will be interviewing you, their titles, and how long the meeting is expected to last.

Follow with a casual inquiry as to what direction the meeting will take. You might ask, "Would you tell me some of the critical areas we will discuss on Thursday?" The knowledge gained will help you to package and present yourself, and will allow you time to bone up on any weak or rusty areas.

It is difficult to evaluate an opportunity properly over the telephone. Even if the job doesn't sound right, go to the interview. It will give you practice, and the job may look better when you have more facts. You might even discover a more suitable opening elsewhere within the company when you go to the face-to-face interview.

10 | Dressing for Interview Success

Unless you look the part, don't expect an offer. Here are guidelines for men's and women's suits, shirts, shoes, neckwear, accessories, jewelry, overcoats, makeup, and personal hygiene.

The moment we set eyes on someone, our minds make evaluations and judgments with lightning speed. The same is true for the potential employers who must assess us.

"What you see is what you get!"

"If a candidate can't put himself together in a professional manner, why should you assume he can put it all together on the job? Unless you look the part, don't expect an offer!" It may sound harsh, but that's an accurate summary of most employers' feelings on this issue. It's a fair estimate that nine out of ten of today's employers will reject an unsuitably dressed applicant without a second thought. Similarly dispiriting odds confront those who expect promotions but wear less than appropriate attire on the job. Like it or not, your outward image, your attitude, your confidence level, and your overall delivery are all affected by the clothes you wear.

The respect you receive at the interview is in direct proportion to the respect your visual image earns for you before you have the chance to say a word. If you wear clothes that are generally associated with leisure activities, you may be telling those who see you that you do not take your career seriously, and therefore are not committed to your work. By the same token, if you report for work the first day on a new job wearing clothes that undercut your perceived effectiveness, personal skills, and professionalism, it will be hard for you to be seen as a major contributor—no matter what you do between nine and five.

Employers rarely make overt statements about acceptable dress codes to their employees, much less to interviewees; more often there is an unspoken dictum that those who wish to climb the professional career ladder will dress appropriately and those who don't, won't.

There are some areas of employment where on-the-job dress (as opposed to interview dress) is somewhat less conservative than in the mainstream: Fashion, entertainment, and advertising are three examples. In these and a few other fields, there is a good deal of leeway with regard to personal expression in workplace attire. But for most of us, our jobs and our employers require a certain minimal level of professionalism in our dress. Interviewees must exceed these standards. That is not to say that you must dress like the chairman of the board (although that probably won't hurt), but you should be aware that dressing for the Friday night Macarena party (or even "dress down Friday") on the day of your interview is not in your best professional interests. For the interview, it is generally accepted that you should dress one or two levels up from the job you are applying for, while remaining consistent with the type occupation it is within.

Dressing Sharp: Your Interviewing Advantage

Our appearance tells people how we feel about ourselves as applicants, as well as how we feel about the interviewer(s), the company, and the process of interviewing itself. By dressing professionally, we tell people that we understand the niceties of corporate life, and we send a subtle "reinforcing" message that we can, for example, be relied on to deal one-on-one with members of a company's prized client base.

More to the point, the correct image at an interview will give you a real edge over your competition. In fact, your overall appearance and presentation may even leave a more tangible impression than the words you say, since memory is rooted most strongly in pictures and impressions. At the very least, you can expect what you say to be strongly influenced in the mind of your interviewer by the way you present yourself.

Of course, the act of taking time to present an attractive professional image before your interview will add to your own sense of self-esteem and confidence. That is perhaps the greatest advantage of all. Therefore, it is important that your professional dress code matches your own personal flavor. You must feel comfortable and "yourself" in what you wear in order to present a confidence image. As G. Bruce Boyer, fashion editor for *GQ* and *Esquire* magazines so aptly puts it, "The whole idea of individualized clothing is devoted to personal comfort. But what we have always been conscious of is that individuality and comfort are not the enemies of propriety and appropriateness. In the end the clothes that make sense are the ones that bring together the public and private person. Individuality, propriety, and comfort can be nicely brought together in a good-fitting, well-made suit.

The Look

The safest look for both men and women at interviews is traditional and conservative. Look at investing in a "good-fitting, well-made" suit as your first step to a successful new career. Up until recent years, this was fairly easy for men, as their professional fashions tended not to change much from year to year. These days, men's fashions are experiencing a metamorphosis, with high fashion designers offering affordable lines of updated, yet professionally acceptable looks. However, a man can always interview with confidence and poise in his three-year-old Brooks Brothers suit, provided that it isn't worn to a shine.

For women, the matter is a little more complicated. Appropriate female attire for the interview should ideally reflect the current fashion if the applicant is to be taken seriously. Moreover, in selecting her current professional look the female applicant must walk a fine line, combining elements of both conformity (to show she belongs) and panache (to show a measure of individuality and style).

The key for both sexes is to dress for the position you want, not the one you have. This means that the upwardly mobile professional might need to invest in the clothes that project the desired image. The employee who dresses like one of the corporate walking wounded is unlikely to move to Mahogany Row. Positions of responsibility are awarded to those who demonstrate that they are able to shoulder the burden. Looking capable will inspire others with the confidence to give you the most visible challenges.

The correct appearance alone probably won't get you a job offer, but it will go a long way toward winning attention and respect. When you know you look right, you can stop worrying about the impression your clothes are making and concentrate on communicating your message.

To be sure, every interview and every interviewer is different; because of this, it isn't possible to set down rigid guidelines for exactly what to wear in each situation. There is, however, relevant broadly based counsel that will help you make the right decision for your interview.

As we have seen, much of what we believe about others is based on our perception of their appearance; this chapter will help you ensure that you are perceived as practical, well-mannered, competent, ethical, and professional.

General Guidelines

Appropriate attire, as we have noted, varies from industry to industry. The college professor can sport tweed jackets with elbow patches on the job, but is nevertheless likely to wear a suit to an interview. The advertising executive may wear wild ties as a badge of creativity (that is what he is being paid for), but he too is likely to dress more conservatively for an interview. In all instances, our clothes are sending a message about our image, and the image we want to convey is one of reliability, trustworthiness, and attention to detail.

Most of us are far more adept at recognizing the dress mistakes of others than at spotting our own sartorial failings. When we do look for a second opinion, we often make the mistake of asking only a loved one. It's not that spouses, lovers, and parents lack taste; these people are, however, more in tune with our positive qualities than the rest of the world, and frequently they do not recognize how essential it is to reflect those qualities in our dress. Better candidates for evaluation of your interview attire are trusted friends who have proved their objectivity in such matters, or even a colleague at work.

Whenever possible, find out the dress code of the company you are visiting. For example, if you are an engineer applying for a job at a high-tech company, a blue three-piece suit might be overpowering. It is perfectly acceptable to ask someone in personnel about the dress code (written or informal) of the company. You may even want to make an anonymous visit to get a sense of the corporate style of the company. In the above example, you might be perfectly comfortable showing up *for work* in a sports coat or blazer; nevertheless, you are advised to wear a suit for at least the first interview.

You may simply decide to change your look somewhat after learning of a more informal atmosphere with regard to dress at the firm you visit. If you are told that everyone works in shirt-sleeves and that there is never a tie in sight, a prudent and completely acceptable approach is to opt for your less formal brown or beige suit, rather than blues, grays, or pinstripes. One final piece of advice: Be wary of 100 percent synthetic garments. Their sheen can make them unattractive and they often retain body odor despite many washings.

Men

Following are the best current dress guidelines for men preparing for a professional interview.

Men's Suits

The most acceptable colors for men's suits are navy through medium blue and charcoal through light gray, followed by brown and at some distance, beige (except in summer when a lightweight beige suit is fine, especially at second or third interviews). Preferably, the fabric should be 100 percent wool; wool looks and wears better than any other material. The darker the suit, the more authority it carries (but beware: A man should *not* wear a black suit to an interview unless applying for an undertaker's job). Pinstripes are acceptable, so long as the stripes themselves are muted and very narrow. Of the solids, dark gray, navy, or medium blue are equally acceptable. In fact many feel that a dark solid suit is the best option, because it gives authority to the wearer and is less intimidating than a pinstripe suit. Equally as important, the color of your suit should complement your own coloring and should be one *you* feel comfortable wearing.

Wearing a three-piece suit to an interview is no longer necessary. In fact a well-fitted, two-piece suit is preferable; more refined, less showy. In most cases, double-breasted jackets should be avoided (unless it is an important part of your self-image, for instance to add "bulk" to the appearance of those of you lucky enough to be skin & bones only). A three-button single-breasted jacket is quite acceptable, but the standard two-button suit jacket remains the perennial favorite.

Above all, it's the quality and fit of your suit that matters. Current fashions favor a slimmer cut, particularly in the trousers. However, the fit and cut must complement your own build. The leaner, tapered look elongates your appearance, the looser cuts add bulk. There should be no pull at the jacket shoulders, no gape at the back, the cuffs should break just at your wrists. Your trousers should fit comfortably at the waist, a flat front is most flattering (unless, once again, you are enviably scrawny), and there should be only a slight break at the hemline, preferably uncuffed (a height enhancer).

Men's Shirts

The principles here are simple:

Rule One: Always wear a long-sleeved shirt.
Rule Two: Always wear a white, cream, or pale-blue shirt.
Rule Three: Never violate Rules One or Two.

By white, I do not mean to exclude, for instance, shirts with very thin red or blue pinstripes: These white shirts are acceptable, although not really first-rate. There is something about a solid white shirt that conveys honesty, intelligence, and stability; it should be your first choice. It is true that artists, writers, engineers, and other creative types are sometimes known to object to white shirts; for them pale blue may be the best option. Remember that the paler and more subtle the shade, the better the impression you will make. Pale colors draw attention, and your collar is right next to your face, which is where we want the interviewer to stay focused.

While monograms are common enough in this country, those who don't accept them usually feel strongly about the implied ostentation of stylized initials on clothing. If you can avoid it, don't take the chance of giving your interviewer the chance to find fault in this area. (On the other hand, if your choice is between wearing your monogrammed shirt or pulling out the old Motley Crue tee-shirt, then your choice should be clear, and so should your conscience.)

Cotton shirts look better and hold up under perspiration more impressively than their synthetic counterparts; if at all possible, opt for a cotton shirt that's been professionally cleaned and starched. A cotton and polyester blend can be an acceptable alternative, but keep in mind that the higher the cotton content, the better the shirt will look. While these blend shirts wrinkle less easily, you are advised to ignore the "wash-and-wear-no-need-to-iron" claims you'll read on the front of the package when you purchase them. Experience has shown that any shirt you wear to an interview must be ironed and starched.

Make sure your shirt fits properly; the collar should fit the neck properly, the sleeve cuff ends just at the wrist. Details such as frayed fabric and loose buttons will not go unnoticed when you are under professional scrutiny.

Men's Neckwear: Ties

While an expensive suit can be ruined by a cheap-looking tie, the right tie can do a lot to pull the less-than-perfect suit together for a professional look. When you can't afford a new suit for the interview, you can upgrade your whole look with the right tie.

A pure silk tie makes the most powerful professional impact, has the best finish and feel, and is easiest to tie well. Linen ties are too informal, wrinkle too easily, and may only be worn during warmer weather. (What's more, they can only be tied once between cleanings because they wrinkle so easily.) A wool tie is casual in appearance and has knot problems. Man-made fibers are shiny, make colors look harsh when you want them to look subtle, and may undercut your professional image. A pure silk tie, or a fifty-fifty wool and silk blend (which is almost wrinkle-proof) should be your choice for the interview.

The tie should complement your suit. This means that there should be a physical balance: The rule of thumb is that the width of your tie should approximate the width of your lapels. The prevailing standard, which has held good for over a decade now, is that ties can range in width between $2^3/_4$" and $3^1/_2$". Wearing anything wider may mark you as someone still trapped in the disco era.

While the tie should complement the suit, it should not *match* it. You would never, for instance, wear a navy blue tie with a navy blue suit. Choose an appropriate tie that neither vanishes into nor does battle with your suit pattern; the most popular and safest styles are found within the categories of solids, foulards, stripes, and paisleys.

Do not wear ties with large polka dots, pictures of animals such as leaping trout or soaring mallards, or sporting symbols such as golf clubs or (God forbid) little men on polo ponies. Avoid wearing any piece of apparel that has a manufacturer's symbol emblazoned on the front as part of the decoration.

Other considerations include the length of the tie (it should, when tied, extend to your trouser belt), the size of the knot (smaller is better), and whether you should wear a bow tie to an interview (you shouldn't).

Men's Shoes

Shoes should be either black leather or brown leather. Stay away from all other materials and colors: They are too risky.

Lace-up wing tips are the most conservative choice and are almost universally acceptable. Slightly less conservative, but equally appropriate, are slip-on dress shoes—not to be confused with boating shoes. The slip-on, with its low, plain vamp or tassel is versatile enough to be used for both day and evening business wear. (The lace-up wing tip can look a bit cloddish at dinner.)

In certain areas of the South, Southwest, and West, heeled cowboy boots are not at all unusual for business wear, and neither are those Grand Ole Opry versions of the business suit. But beware: Outside of such specifically defined areas, you will attract only puzzled stares—and few, if any, professional career opportunities—with these wardrobe selections.

Men's Socks

Socks should complement the suit; accordingly, should be blue, black, gray, or brown. They should also be long enough for you to cross your legs without showing off lots of bare skin, and should not fall in a bunch toward the ankle as you move. Elastic-reinforced, over-the-calf socks are your best bet.

Men's Accessories

The right accessories can enhance the professional image of any applicant, male or female; the wrong accessories can destroy it.

The guiding principle here is to include nothing that could conceivably be misconstrued or leave a bad impression. Never, for instance, should you wear religious or political insignias in the form of rings, ties, or pins. If you would not initiate a conversation about such topics at a job interview (and you shouldn't), why send smoke signals asking your interviewer to do so? The watch you wear should be simple and plain. This means Mickey Mouse is out, as are sports-oriented and Swatch-style watches. No one is impressed by digital watches these days; don't be afraid to wear a simple analog model with a leather strap. (Besides, you don't want people wondering whether you can really tell time, do you?) Avoid cheap-looking pseudo-gold watchbands at all costs.

Your briefcase, if you carry one, can make a strong professional statement about you. Leather makes the best impression, while all other materials follow far behind. Brown and burgundy are the colors of choice. The case itself should be plain, although some very expensive models offer a host of embellishments that only detract from the effect you want.

A cotton or linen handkerchief should be part of every job hunter's wardrobe. Plain white is best. Your handkerchief can also be used to relieve the clammy-hands syndrome so common before the interview. Anything to avoid the infamous "wet fish" handshake!

(By the way, avoid the matching tie-and-pocket-square look at all costs. It's hideous and inappropriate for a professional interview.)

Belts should match or complement the shoes you select. Accordingly, a blue, black, or gray suit will require a black belt and black shoes, while brown, tan, or beige suits call for brown. With regard to materials, stick with plain leather. The most common mistake made with belts is the buckle: An interview is not the place for your favorite Harley Davidson, Grateful Dead, or Bart Simpson buckle. Select a small, simple buckle that doesn't overwhelm the rest of your look.

Men's Jewelry

Men may wear a wedding band, if applicable, and a small pair of subdued cuff links (if wearing French cuffs, of course). Anything more is dangerous. Even fraternity rings—much less bracelets, neck chains, earrings, or medallions—can send the wrong message. Tie tack and clips are passé.

Men's Overcoats

The safest and most utilitarian colors for overcoats are beige and blue; stick to these two exclusively. If you can avoid wearing an overcoat, do so (it's an encumbrance and adds to clutter).

Men's Makeup

It is inadvisable for a man to wear makeup to an interview or at any other time during his professional life.

Women

Following are the best current dress guidelines for women preparing for a professional interview.

Women's Suits

You have more room for creativity in this area than men do, but also more room for mistakes. Until recent years, your professional fashion creativity had to remain within certain accepted guidelines created not by the fashion industry, but by the consensus of the business world which, alas, tends to trail behind the rest of us. And while there are still the limits of good taste and necessary conservatism for the interviewee, the fashion designers have worked hard to create workable professional alternatives for the ever growing female work force. One such designer, Sharon McCollick, formed a fashion company, "Essential Suits," to specifically address this starving market. Her clothing line is available through JC Penney, and a growing number of chains.

A woman's business wardrobe need no longer be simply a pseudo-male selection of drab gray skirts and blouses. (Recent advice that women should avoid pinstripes or ties is dated. With the right cuts, pinstripes and ties can look both stylish and professional.)

Wool and linen are both accepted as the right look for professional women's suits, but there is a problem. Linen wrinkles so quickly that you may feel as though you leave the house dressed for success and arrive at your destination destined for bag-ladyhood. Cotton-polyester blends are great for warm climates: They look like linen but lack the "wrinklability" factor. Combinations of synthetics and natural fabrics do have their advantages: suits made of such material will certainly retain their shape better. The eye trained to pay attention to detail, however (read: your interviewer's), may well detect the type of fabric, say, a cheap polyester blend, and draw unwarranted conclusions about your personality and taste. The choice is up to you; if you do opt for natural fabrics, you will probably want to stay with wool. It provides the smartest look of all, and is most versatile and rugged. There are wonderful ultra light wool gaberdines available now that will take you through the toughest interview on the hottest summer day.

While men are usually limited to either solid or pinstripe suits, a woman can add to this list the varied category of plaids. The Prince of Wales plaid, for instance, is attractive and is utterly acceptable for businesswomen (no doubt because of its regal namesake). A solid skirt with a coordinating subtle plaid jacket is also acceptable, but make sure there is not too much contrast or it will detract from the focus of your meeting: the interview. Colors most suitable for interview suits include charcoal, medium gray, steel gray, black, and navy blue. Of all these looks, the cleanest and most professional is the simple solid navy or gray suit with a white blouse.

Jackets should be simple, well-tailored and stylish, but not stylized. This is probably not the time to wear a peplum style jacket; a standard length that falls just at the hips is preferable; the cut and style should flatter your build and reflect your personal style, without detracting from what you have to say. Attention to details such as smooth seams, even hemlines, correctly hanging linings, and well-sewn buttons are essential.

How long a skirt should you wear? Any hard-and-fast rule I could offer here would be in danger of being outdated almost immediately, as the fashion industry demands dramatically different looks every season in order to fuel sales. (After all, keeping the same hemlines would mean that last season's clothes could last another season or two.) It should go without saying that you don't want to sport something that soars to the upper thigh if you want to be taken seriously as an applicant. Your best bet is to dress somewhat more conservatively than you would if you were simply showing up for work at the organization in question. Hemlines come and go, and while there is some leeway as to what is appropriate for everyday wear on the job, the safest bet is usually to select something that falls just at or no more than 2" above the knee.

Increasingly popular is the one-piece business dress with a matching jacket. This outfit is particularly useful for the "business day into evening crowd," but can be perfectly suitable for interviews if it is impeccably styled and fitted. It is particularly important to stick with subtle solid colors for this look.

Blouses

With regard to blouses, long sleeves will project the authoritative, professional look you desire. Three-quarter-length sleeves are less desirable, and they are followed in turn by short sleeves. Never wear a sleeveless blouse to an interview. (You may be confident that there is absolutely no chance that you will be required to remove your jacket, but why take the risk?)

Solid colors and natural fabrics (particularly cotton and silk) are the best selections for blouses. Combinations of natural and synthetic fabrics, while wrinkle-resistant, do not absorb moisture well.

The acceptable color spectrum is wider for blouses than for men's shirts, but it is not limitless. The most prudent choices are still white or cream; these offer a universal professional appeal. Pale pink, soft yellow, or light blue can also work, but should be worn only if it fully blends into your overall look. Light colors are "friendly" and draw attention to your face, yet will not distract the interviewer from what you have to say. The blouse with a front-tie bow has become dated, a classic softened shirt collar works best with a suit. The button-down collar always looks great, particularly if you are interviewing with a conservative company or industry.

Women's Neckwear: Scarves

While a woman might choose to wear a string of pearls instead of a scarf to an interview, the scarf can still serve as a powerful status symbol. A good outfit can be ruined by a cheap-looking scarf. Opting to wear a scarf means that the scarf will be saying something dramatic about you: Make sure it's something dramatically positive. A pure silk scarf will offer a conservative look, a good finish, and ease in tying. Some of the better synthetic blends achieve an overall effect that is almost as good. While some books on women's clothing will recommend buying blouses that have matching scarves attached to the collar, there is an increasingly vocal lobby of stylish businesswomen who feel this is the equivalent of mandating that a man wear a clip-on bow tie. As with men's ties, the objective is to complement the outfit, not match it. Avoid overly flamboyant styles, and stick with the basics: solids, foulards, small polka dots, or paisleys, and always in subtle colors that will complement, not compete with your outfit or your conversation.

Women's Shoes

Female applicants have a greater color selection in footwear than do their male counterparts. The shoes should preferably be leather, but in addition to brown and black, a woman is safe in wearing navy, burgundy, forest green, or even, if circumstances warrant, red. The color of your shoes should always be the same or a darker tone than your skirt.

It is safest to stay away from faddish or multicolored shoes (even such classics as two-toned oxfords). There are two reasons for this: First, all fashion is transitory, and even if you are up-to-date, you cannot assume that your interviewer is; second, many interviewers are male and thus likely to exhibit an inability to appreciate vivid color combinations. As with the rest of your wardrobe, stay away from radical choices and opt for the easily comprehensible professional look.

Heel height is important, as well. Flats are fine; a shoe with a heel of up to about $2^1/_2$" is perfectly acceptable. Stay away from high heels: At best you will wobble slightly, and at worst you will walk at an angle. The pump or court shoe, with its closed toe and heel, is perhaps the safest and most conservative look. A closed heel with a slightly open toe is acceptable, too, as is the sling-back shoe with a closed toe. The toe on any style should not be overly pointed.

Stockings or Pantyhose

These should not make a statement of their own. Neutral skintones are the safest, most conservative choice, though you are perfectly within the realm of professional etiquette when wearing a sheer white or cream if it complements your blouse or dress. You may be an exception if you are interviewing for a job in the fashion industry, in which case you might coordinate colors with your outfit, but be very sure of the company standard already in place. Even in such an instance, avoid loud or glitzy looks. A bold black, of course, is out entirely.

Pantyhose and stockings are prone to developing runs at the worst possible moment. Keep an extra pair in your purse or briefcase.

Women's Accessories

Because a briefcase is a symbol of authority, it is an excellent choice for the female applicant. Do not, however, bring both your purse and a briefcase to the interview. (You'll look awkward juggling them around.) Instead, transfer essential items to a small clutch bag you can store in the case. In addition to brown and burgundy (recommended colors for the men), you may include navy and black as possible colors for your case, which should be free of expensive and distracting embellishments.

With regard to belts, the advice given for men holds for women as well. Belts should match or complement the shoes you select; a black or gray suit will require a black belt and black shoes, while brown, tan, or beige suits will call for brown, and navy looks best with navy or burgundy accessories. In addition, women may wear snakeskin, lizard, and the like (though beware of offending the animal rights activists). Remember that the belt is a functional item; if it is instantly noticeable, it is wrong.

Women's Jewelry

As far as jewelry goes, less is more. A woman should restrict rings to engagement or wedding bands if these are applicable, but she can wear a necklace and earrings, as long as these are subdued and professional-looking. (I should note that some men are put off by earrings of any description in the workplace, so if you wear them keep them small, discreet, and in good taste. Avoid fake or strangely colored pearls, anything with your name or initials on it, and earrings that dangle or jangle.) In addition, a single bracelet on the woman's wrist is acceptable; anything around the ankle is not. Remember, too much of the wrong kind of jewelry can keep a woman from receiving an offer she might otherwise receive, or inhibit her promotional opportunities once on the team.

Women's Makeup

Take care never to appear overly made-up. Natural is the key word; eye makeup should be subtle, so as not to overwhelm the rest of the face. As a general rule, I advise very little lipstick at an interview because it can cause negative reactions in some interviewers, and because it can smudge and wear off, as the hours wear on. (Who can say, going in, how long the meeting will last?) However, as women advance into their thirties and beyond, the natural pinkness of the lips can fade; you might feel you look pale and washed out without lipstick. So if you feel "undressed" without your lipstick, use some; but apply it sparingly and carefully, using a subdued color.

For Men and Women: A Note on Personal Hygiene

It should go without saying that bad breath, dandruff, body odor, and dirty, unmanicured nails have the potential to undo all your efforts at putting across a good first impression. These and related problems denote an underlying professional slovenliness, which an interviewer will feel is likely to reflect itself in your work. You want to show yourself to be appealing, self-respecting, and enjoyable to be around. You can't do that if the people you meet with have to call on exceptional powers of self-control in order to stay in the same room with you.

Don't ask yourself whether any friend or colleague has actually come out and suggested that you pay more attention to these matters; ask yourself how you felt the last time you had to conduct business of any sort with a person who had a hygiene problem. Then resolve never to leave that kind of impression.

11 | Body Language

Learn to control negative body movements and employ positive ones. Discover the seven guidelines for good body language during your interview.

Given the choice of going blind or going deaf, which would you choose?

If you are like nine out of ten other people, you would choose to go deaf. The vast majority of us rely to a remarkable degree on our ability to gather information visually. This really is not all that surprising: While speech is a comparatively recent development, humans have been sending and receiving nonverbal signals from the dawn of the species.

In fact, body language is one of the earliest methods of communication we learn after birth. We master the spoken word later in life, and in so doing we forget the importance of nonverbal cues. But the signals are still sent and received (usually at a subconscious level), even if most of us discount their importance.

It is common to hear people say of the body language they use, "Take me or leave me as I am." This is all very well if you have no concern for what others think of you. For those seeking professional employment, however, it is of paramount importance that the correct body language be utilized. If your mouth says "Hire me," but your body says something quite different, you are likely to leave the interviewer confused. "Well," he or she will think, "the right answers all came out, but there was something about that candidate that just rubbed me the wrong way." Such misgivings are generally sufficient to keep any candidate from making the short list.

When we are in stressful situations (and a job interview is certainly right there in Stress Hell), our bodies react accordingly. The way they react can send unintentional negative messages. The interviewer may or may not be aware of what causes the concern, but the messages will be sent, and our cause will suffer.

Of course, interviewers can be expected to listen carefully to what we say, too. When our body language doesn't contradict our statements, we will generally be given credence. When our body language complements our verbal statements, our message will gain a great deal of impact. But when our body language *contradicts* what we say, it is human nature for the interviewer to be skeptical. In short, learning to control negative body movements during an interview—and learning to use positive body signals—will greatly increase the chances for job interview success.

Under the Microscope

What is the interviewer watching us for during the interview? The answer is: clues. The mystery for the interviewer is what kind of an employee would we make. It is incumbent on us to provide not just any old clues but the ones most likely to prompt a decision to hire.

Let's begin at the beginning. When we are invited in to an interview, we are probably safe in assuming that our interviewer believes we meet certain minimum standards, and could conceivably be hired. (Otherwise, why take the time to interview?) Once in the door, we can assume that we will be scrutinized in three main areas:

- Ability (Can we do the job?)
- Willingness (Will we do the job?)
- Manageability (Will we be a pleasure or a pain to have around?)

Appropriate control and use of our gestures can help us emphasize positive features of our personality in these key areas—and also project integrity, honesty, attention to detail, and the like.

The adage that actions speak louder than words appears to be something we should take quite literally. Studies done at the University of Chicago found that over 50 percent of all effective communication relies on body language. Since we can expect interviewers to respond to the body language we employ at the interview, it is up to us to decide what messages we want them to receive.

There are also studies that suggest that the impression we create in the first few minutes of the interview is the most lasting. Since the first few minutes after we meet the interviewer is a time when he or she is doing the vast majority of the talking, we have very little control over the impression we create with our words: We can't say much of anything! It is up to our bodies, then, to do the job for us.

The Greeting

Giving a "dead fish" handshake will not advance one's candidacy; neither will the opposite extreme, the iron-man bonecrusher grip.

The ideal handshake starts before the meeting actually occurs. Creating the right impression with the handshake is a three-step process. Be sure that:

1. Your hands are clean and adequately manicured.
2. Your hands are warm and reasonably free of perspiration. (There are a number of ways to ensure this, including washing hands in warm water at the interview site, holding one's hand close to the cheek for a few seconds, and even applying a little talcum powder.)
3. The handshake itself is executed professionally and politely, with a firm grip and a warm smile.

Remember that if you initiate the handshake, you may send the message that you have a desire to dominate the interview; this is not a good impression to leave with one's potential boss. Better to wait a moment and allow the interviewer to initiate the shake. (If for any reason you do find yourself initiating the handshake, do not pull back; if you do, you will appear indecisive. Instead, make the best of it, smile confidently, and make good eye contact.)

The handshake should signal cooperation and friendliness. Match the pressure extended by the interviewer—never exceed it. Ideally, the handshake should last for between three and five seconds, and should "pump" for no more than six times. (The parting handshake may last a little longer. Smile and lean forward very slightly as you shake hands before departing.)

Certain cultural and professional differences should be considered with regard to handshakes, as well. Many doctors, artists, and others who do delicate work with their hands can and do give less enthusiastic handshakes than other people. Similarly, the English handshake is considerably less firm than the American, while the German variety is more firm.

Use only one hand; always shake vertically. Do not extend your hand parallel to the floor, with the palm up, as this conveys submissiveness. By the same token, you may be seen as being too aggressive if you extend your flat hand outward with the palm facing down.

Taking Your Seat

> *Some thirty inches from my nose*
> *The frontier of my person goes.*
> *Beware of rudely crossing it;*
> *I have no gun, but I can spit.*
> (With apologies to W. H. Auden)

Encroaching on another's "personal zone" is a bad idea in any business situation, but it is particularly dangerous in an interview. The thirty-inch standard is a good one to follow: It is the distance that allows you to extend your hand comfortably for a handshake. Maintain this distance throughout the interview, and be particularly watchful of intrusions during the early stages when you meet, greet, and take a seat.

Applying this principle may seem simple enough, but how often have you found yourself dodging awkwardly in front of someone to take a seat before it has been offered? A person's office is an extension of sorts of his personal zone; this is why it is not only polite but also sound business sense to wait until the interviewer offers you a seat.

It is not uncommon to meet with an interviewer in a conference room or other supposedly "neutral" site. Again, wait for the interviewer to motion you to a spot, or, if you feel uncomfortable doing this, tactfully ask the interviewer to take the initiative: "Where would you like me to sit?"

Facial/Head Signals

Once you take your seat, you can expect the interviewer to do most of the talking. You can also probably expect your nervousness to be at its height. Accordingly, you must be particularly careful about the nonverbal messages you send at this stage.

Now, while all parts of the body are capable of sending positive and negative signals, the head (including the eyes and mouth) is under closest scrutiny. Most good interviewers will make an effort to establish and maintain eye contact, and thus you should expect that whatever messages you are sending from the facial region will be picked up, at least on a subliminal level.

Our language is full of expressions testifying to the powerful influence of facial signals. When we say that someone is shifty-eyed, is tight-lipped, has a furrowed brow, flashes bedroom eyes, stares into space, or grins like a Cheshire cat, we are speaking in a kind of shorthand, and using a set of stereotypes that enables us to make judgments—consciously or unconsciously—about the person's abilities and qualities. Those judgments may not be accurate, but they are usually difficult to reverse.

Tight smiles and tension in the facial muscles often bespeak an inability to handle stress; little eye contact can communicate a desire to hide something; pursed lips are often associated with a secretive nature; and frowning, looking sideways, or peering over one's glasses can send signals of haughtiness and arrogance. Hardly the stuff of which winning interviews are made!

The Eyes

Looking at someone means showing interest in that person, and showing interest is a giant step forward in making the right impression. (Remember, each of us is our own favorite subject!)

Your aim should be to stay with a calm, steady, and nonthreatening gaze. It is easy to mismanage this, and so you may have to practice a bit to overcome the common hurdles in this area. Looking away from the interviewer for long periods while he is talking, closing your eyes while being addressed, and repeatedly shifting focus from the subject to some other point are likely to leave the wrong impression.

Of course, there is a big difference between looking and staring at someone! Rather than looking at the speaker straight-on at all times, create a mental triangle incorporating both eyes and the mouth; your eyes will follow a natural, continuous path along the three points. Maintain this approach for roughly three-quarters of the time; you can break your gaze to look at the interviewer's hands as points are emphasized, or to refer to your note pad. These techniques will allow you to leave the impression that you are attentive, sincere, and committed. Staring will only send the message that you are aggressive or belligerent.

Be wary of breaking eye contact too abruptly, and of shifting your focus in ways that will disrupt the atmosphere of professionalism. Examining the interviewer below the head and shoulders, for instance, is a sign of overfamiliarity. (This is an especially important point to keep in mind when being interviewed by someone of the opposite sex.)

The eyebrows send messages as well. Under stress, one's brows may wrinkle; as we have seen, this sends a negative signal about our ability to handle challenges in the business world. The best advice on this score is simply to take a deep breath and collect yourself. Most of the tension that people feel at interviews has to do with anxiety about how to respond to what the interviewer will ask. As a reader of *Knock 'em Dead*, you will be prepared with credible responses for even the toughest queries. Relax.

The Head

Rapidly nodding your head can leave the impression that you are impatient and eager to add something to the conversation—if only the interviewer would let you. Slower nodding, on the other hand, emphasizes interest, shows that you are validating the comments of your interviewer, and subtly encourages him to continue. Tilting the head slightly, when combined with eye contact and a natural smile, demonstrates friendliness and approachability. The tilt should be momentary and not exaggerated, almost like a bob of the head to one side. (Do not overuse this technique!)

The Mouth

One guiding principle of good body language is to turn upward rather than downward. Look at two boxers after a fight: The loser is slumped forward, brows knit and eyes downcast, while the winner's smiling face is thrust upward and outward. The victor's arms are raised high, his back is straight, his shoulders are square. In the first instance the signals we receive are those of anger, frustration, belligerence, and defeat; in the second, happiness, openness, warmth, and confidence.

Your smile is one of the most powerful positive body signals in your arsenal; it best exemplifies the up-is-best principle, as well. Offer an unforced, confident smile as frequently as opportunity and circumstances dictate. *Avoid at all costs* the technique some applicants use: grinning idiotically for the length of the interview, no matter what. This will only communicate that you are either insincere or not quite on the right track.

It's worth remembering that the mouth provides a seemingly limitless supply of opportunities to convey weakness. This may be done by touching the mouth frequently (and, typically, unconsciously); "faking" a cough when confronted with a difficult question; and/or gnawing on one's lips absentmindedly. Employing any of these "insincerity signs" when you are asked about, say, why you lost your last job, will confirm or instill suspicions about your honesty and effectiveness.

Glasses

Those who wear glasses sometimes leave them off when going on an interview in an attempt to project a more favorable image. There are difficulties with this approach. The first is that farsighted people who don't wear their glasses will (unwittingly) seem to stare long and hard at the people they converse with, and this, as we have seen, is a negative signal. The second problem is that peering over the top of your glasses—even if you wear reading glasses and have been handed something to read and subsequently asked a question—carries professorial connotations that are frequently interpreted as critical. (If you wear glasses for reading, you should remove them when conversing, replacing them only when appropriate.)

Wearing dark glasses to an interview will paint you as secretive, cold, and devious. Even if your prescription glasses are tinted, the effect will be the same. Try to obtain nontinted glasses for your interview; if you are unable to do so, contacts may be preferable to eyeglasses.

If you are concerned about wearing glasses to an interview, why not pick up a pair of contact lenses. Modern contacts are far more comfortable and affordable than they used to be. You'll look good and feel confident; and won't have the embarrassment of having left your glasses in the personnel office as you are handed blueprints for comments in the boardroom.

Body Signal Barricades

Folding or crossing the arms, or holding things in front of the body, is a wonderful way to send negative messages to the interviewer. The signal is, essentially, "I know you're there, but you can't come in. I'm nervous and closed for business."

It is bad enough to feel this way, but worse to express it with blatant signals. Don't fold your arms or "protect" your chest with hands, clipboard, briefcase, or anything else during the interview. (These positions, in fact, should be avoided in any and every business situation.)

Hands

As we have seen, a confident and positive handshake breaks the ice and gets the interview moving in the right direction. Proper use of the hands throughout the rest of the interview will help to convey an above-board, "nothing-to-hide" message.

Watch out for hands and fingers that take on a life of their own, fidgeting with themselves or other objects such as pens, paper, or your hair. Pen tapping is interpreted as the action of an impatient person; this is an example of an otherwise trivial habit that can take on immense significance in an interview situation. (Rarely will an interviewer ask you to stop doing something annoying; instead, he'll simply make a mental note that you are an annoying person, and congratulate himself for picking this up before making the mistake of hiring you.)

Negative hand messages are legion. Some of the most dangerous are listed below:

- You can demonstrate smugness and superiority by clasping your hands behind your head. (You'll also expose any perspiration marks that are under your arms.)
- A man can show insecurity by simply adjusting his tie, and that's not the worst of it: When interviewing with a woman, his gesture will show something other than a businesslike interest in the interviewer.
- Slouching in your chair, with hands in pockets or thumbs in belt, can brand you as insolent and aggressive—and when this error is made in the presence of an interviewer of the opposite sex, it carries sexually aggressive overtones

as well. (Beware, too, of sending these signals while you are walking on a tour of the facility.)

- Pulling your collar away from your neck for a moment may seem like an innocent enough reaction to the heat of the day, but the interviewer might assume that you are tense and/or masking an untruth. (The same goes for scratching the neck during, before, or after your response to a question.)

- Moving the hands toward a feature one perceives as deficient is a common unconscious reaction to stress. A man with thinning hair, for example, may thoughtlessly put his hand to his forehead when pondering how to respond to the query, "Why aren't you earning more at your age?" This habit may be extremely difficult for you to detect in the first place, much less reverse, but make the effort. Such protective movements are likely to be perceived—if only on a subliminal level—as acknowledgments of low status.

- Picking at invisible bits of fluff on one's suit looks like what it is: a nervous tic. Keep your focus on the interviewer. (If you do have some bit of lint somewhere on your clothing, the best advice is usually to ignore it rather than call attention to it by brushing it away.)

By contrast, employing the hands in a positive way can further your candidacy. Here are some of the best techniques:

- Subtly exposing your palms now and then as you speak can help to demonstrate that you are open, friendly, and have nothing to hide. (The technique is used to great effect by many politicians and television talk show hosts; watch for it.)

- When considering a question, it can sometimes be beneficial to "steeple" your fingers for a few seconds as you think and when you first start to talk. Unless you hold the gesture for long periods of time, it will be perceived as a neutral demonstration of your thoughtfulness. (Of course, if you overuse this or hold the position for too long, you may be taken as condescending.) Steepling will also give you something constructive to do with your hands; it offers a change from holding your pad and pen.

Seating

The signals you send with your body during an interview can be affected by the type of chair you sit in. If you have a choice, go with an upright chair with arms. Deep armchairs can restrict your ability to send certain positive signals, and encourage the likelihood of negative ones. (They're best suited for watching television, not for projecting the image of a competent professional.)

There is only one way to sit during an interview: bottom well back in the chair and back straight. Slouching, of course, is out, but a slight forward leaning posture will show interest and friendliness toward the interviewer. Keep your hands on the sides of the chair; if there are no arms on the chair, keep your hands in your lap or on your pad of paper.

Crossed legs, in all their many forms, send a mixture of signals; most of them are negative:

- Crossing one ankle over the other knee can show a certain stubborn and recalcitrant outlook (as well as the bottom of your shoe, which is not always a pretty sight). The negative signal is intensified when you grasp the horizontally crossed leg or—worst of all—cross your arms across your chest.
- Crossed ankles have often been assumed to indicate that the person doing the crossing is withholding information. However, some dress fashions encourage decorous ankle crossing. Of course, since the majority of interviews take place across a desk, crossed ankles will often be virtually unnoticeable. The best advice on this body signal is that it is probably the most permissible barrier you can erect; if you must allow yourself one body language vice, this is the one to choose.
- When sitting in armchairs or on sofas, crossing the legs may be necessary to create some stability amid all the plush upholstery. In this instance, the signals you send by crossing your legs will be neutral, as long as your crossed legs point toward, rather than away from, the interviewer.

Feet

Some foot signals can have negative connotations. Women and men wearing slip-on shoes should beware of dangling the loose shoe from the toes; this can be quite distracting and, as it is a gesture often used to signal physical attraction, it has no place in a job interview. Likewise, avoid compulsive jabbing of floor, desk, or chair with your foot; this can be perceived as a hostile and angry motion, and is likely to annoy the interviewer.

Walking

Many interviews will require that you walk from point A to point B with the interviewer, either on a guided tour of facilities or to move from one office to another. (Of course, if you are interviewing in a restaurant, you will have to walk with your interviewer to and from the dining facility.) How long these walks last is not as important as how you use them to reinforce positive traits and impressions.

Posture is the first concern. Keep your shoulders back, maintain an erect posture, smile, and make eye contact when appropriate. Avoid fidgeting with your feet as you move, rubbing one shoe against the other, or kicking absentmindedly at the ground as you stand: These signals will lead others to believe that you are anxious and/or insecure. Crossing your arms or legs while standing carries the same negative connotations as it does when you are sitting. Putting your hands in your pockets is less offensive—assuming you don't jangle keys or coins—but men must be careful not to employ the hands-on-hips or thumbs-in-belt postures discussed earlier. These send messages that you are aggressive and dominating.

Seven Signals for Success

So far we have focused primarily on the pitfalls to avoid; but what messages *should* be sent, and how? Here are seven general suggestions on good body language for the interview.

1. Walk slowly, deliberately, and tall upon entering the room.
2. On greeting your interviewer, give (and, hopefully, receive) a friendly "eyebrow flash": that brief, slight raising of the brows that calls attention to the face, encourages eye contact, and (when accompanied by a natural smile) sends a strong positive signal that that interview has gotten off to a good start.
3. Use mirroring techniques. In other words, make an effort—subtly!—to reproduce the positive signals your interviewer sends. (Of course, you should never mirror negative body signals.) Say the interviewer leans forward to make a point; a few moments later, you lean forward slightly in order to hear better. Say the interviewer leans back and laughs; you "laugh beneath" the interviewer's laughter, taking care not to overwhelm your partner by using an inappropriate volume level. This technique may seem contrived at first, but you will learn that it is far from that, if only you experiment a little.
4. Maintain a naturally alert head position; keep your head up and your eyes front at all times.
5. Remember to avert your gaze from time to time so as to avoid the impression that you are staring; when you do so, look confidently and calmly to the right or to the left; never look down.

6. Do not hurry any movement.
7. Relax with every breath.

Putting It All Together

We have discussed the individual gestures that can either improve or diminish your chances of success at the interview. Working in our favor is the fact that positive signals reinforce one another; employing them in combination yields an overwhelming positive message that is truly greater than the sum of its parts. Now it is time to look at how to combine the various positive elements to send a message of competence and professionalism.

Here is the best posture to aim for during the interview:

* Sit well back in the chair; allow the back of it to support you and help you sit upright. Increase the impression of openness ("I have nothing to hide!") by unbuttoning your jacket as you sit down. Keep your head up. Maintain eye contact a good portion of the time, especially when the interviewer begins to speak and when you reply. Smile naturally whenever the opportunity arises. Avoid folding your arms; it is better to keep them on the arms of your chair. Remember to show one or both of your palms occasionally as you make points, but do not overuse this gesture.

Open for Business

The more open your body movements during the interview, the more you will be perceived as open yourself. Understanding and directing your body language will give you added power to turn interviews into cooperative exchanges between two professionals.

Just as you interpret the body language of others, both positive and negative, so your body language makes an indelible impression on those you meet. It tells them whether you like and have confidence in yourself, whether or not you are pleasant to be around, and whether you are more likely to be honest or deceitful. Like it or not, our bodies carry these messages for the world to see.

Job interviews are reliable in one constant: They bring out insecurities in those who must undergo them. All the more reason to consciously manage the impressions the body sends!

12 | The Curtain Goes Up

First impressions are the strongest. Here are the small preparations you can make before you walk into the interviewer's office.

Backstage in the theater, the announcement "Places, please" is made five minutes before the curtain goes up. It's the performers' signal to psych themselves up, complete final costume adjustments, and make time to reach the stage. They are getting ready to go on stage and knock 'em dead. You should go through a similar process.

Winning that job offer depends not only on the things you do well but also on the absence of things you do poorly. As the interview date approaches, settle down with your resume and the exercises you performed in building it. Immerse yourself in your past successes and strengths. This is a time for building confidence. A little nervousness is perfectly natural and healthy, but channel the extra energy in a positive direction by beginning your physical and mental preparations.

First, you should assemble your interview kit:

- **The company dossier.**
- **Two or three copies of your resume and executive briefing, one for you and one or two for the interviewer.** It is perfectly all right to have your resume in front of you at the interview; it shows that you are organized. It also makes a great cheat sheet (after all, the interviewer is using it for that reason)—you can keep it on your lap during the interview with pad and pencil. It is not unusual to hear, "Mr. Jones wasn't hired because he didn't pay attention to detail and could not even remember his employment dates." And those are just the kinds of things you are likely to forget in the heat of the moment.
- **A pad of paper and writing instruments.** These articles have a twofold purpose. They demonstrate your organization and interest in the job and they give you something constructive to do with your hands during the interview. Bring along a blue or black ballpoint pen for filling out applications.
- **Contact telephone numbers.** If you get detained on the way to the interview, you can call and let the company representative know.
- **Reference letters.** Take the sensible precaution of gathering these from your employers, on the off-chance they are requested.

- **A list of job-related questions.** During the interview is the time when you gather information to evaluate a job (the actual evaluation comes when you have an offer in hand). At the end of the interview, you will be given the opportunity to ask additional questions. Develop some that help you understand the job's parameters and potential.

    You might ask: "Why is the job open?" "Where does the job lead?" "What is the job's relationship to other departments?" "How do the job and the department relate to the corporate mission?"

For a longer list of questions that might be valuable to ask along those lines, see chapter 23, "Negotiating the Offer." Understand, though, that some of those will obviously only be appropriate in the context of a serious negotiation talk. You can also find good questions to ask in the answer to "Do you have any questions?" at the end of chapter 14, "How to Knock 'em Dead."

- **Any additional information you have about the company or the job.** If time permits, ask the interviewer's secretary to send you some company literature. Absorb whatever you can.

ONLINE RESOURCES

Infoseek
http://www.infoseek.com
For information on finding corporate websites, click on the Business subhead at this directory. Then choose Companies in the websites section. This path will bring up many sites that can help you find corporate websites.

Companies Online
http://www.companiesonline.com
To find a particular company's website, you can search this database by company name, city, state, industry, or stock ticker symbol. Your search will bring up complete contact information including the website if there is one available for that company.

Comfind
http://www.comfind.com
Another useful site for finding corporate websites if they're available, Comfind allows you to search its database by business category, product, or service; company name; or community area by area code or city. This last search method can be extremely useful when you want to find websites for companies in your area.

- **Directions to the interview.** Decide on your form of transportation and finalize your time of departure. Check the route, distance, and travel time. Write it all down legibly and put it with the rest of your interview kit. If you forget to verify date, time, and place (including floor and suite number), you might not even arrive at the right place, or on the right day, for your interview.

☐   ☐   ☐

First impressions are the strongest you make, and they are based on your appearance. There is only one way to dress for the first meeting: clean-cut and conservative. You may or may not see yourself that way, but how you see yourself is not important now—your only concern is how others see you. As you could be asked to appear for an interview at a scant couple of hours notice, you must be in a constant state of readiness. Keep your best two suits of clothing freshly cleaned, your shirts or blouses wrinkle-free, and your shoes polished. Never wear these outfits unless you are interviewing.

Here are some more tips:

- Regardless of sex or hairstyle, take it to the lawn doctor once a month.
- While a shower or bath prior to an interview is most desirable, and the use of an unscented deodorant advisable, the wearing of after-shave or perfume should be avoided. You are trying to get hired, not dated.
- You should never drink alcohol the day before an interview. It affects eyes, skin color, and your wits.
- Nails should be trimmed and manicured at all times, even if you work with your hands.

To arrive at an interview too early indicates overanxiousness; to arrive late is inconsiderate. The only sensible solution is to arrive at the interview on time, but at the location early. That allows you time to visit the restroom and make the necessary adjustments to your appearance. Take a couple of minutes in this temporary sanctuary to perform your final mental preparations:

- Review the company dossier.
- Recall the positive things you will say about past employers.
- Breathe deeply and slowly for a minute. This will dispel your natural physical tension.
- Repeat to yourself that the interview will be a success and that afterward the company representatives will wonder how they ever managed without you.
- Smile and head for the interview.

Under no circumstances back out because you do not like the receptionist or the look of the office—that would be allowing interview nerves to get the better of you. As you are shown into the office, you are on!

This potential new employer wants an aggressive and dynamic employee, but someone who is less aggressive and dynamic than he or she is, so take your lead from the interviewer.

Do:
- Give a firm handshake—one shake is enough.
- Make eye contact and smile. Say, "Hello, Ms. Smith. I am John Jones. I have been looking forward to meeting you."

Do not:
- Use first names (unless asked).
- Smoke (even if invited).
- Sit down (until invited).
- Show anxiety or boredom.
- Look at your watch.
- Discuss equal rights, sex, race, national origin, religion, or age.
- Show samples of your work (unless requested).
- Ask about benefits, salary, or vacation.
- Assume a submissive role. Treat the interviewer with respect, but as an equal.

Now you are ready for anything—except for the tough questions that are going to be thrown at you next.

Part III | Great Answers to Tough Interview Questions

This section tells you not only what to answer but also how to answer. It provides the real preparation for getting the job you want and deserve.

"Like being on trial for your life" is how many people look at a job interview. They are probably right. With the interviewer as judge and jury, you are at least on trial for your livelihood. Therefore, you must lay the foundation for a winning defense. F. Lee Bailey, America's most celebrated defense attorney, attributes his success in the courtroom to preparation. He likens himself to a magician going into court with fifty rabbits in his hat, not knowing which one he'll really need, but ready to pull out any single one. Bailey is successful because he is ready for any eventuality. He takes the time to analyze every situation and every possible option. He never underestimates his opposition. He is always prepared. F. Lee Bailey usually wins.

Another famous attorney, Louis Nizer, successfully defended all of his fifty-plus capital offense clients. When lauded as the greatest courtroom performer of his day, Nizer denied the accolade. He claimed for himself the distinction of being the *best prepared*.

You won't win your day in court just based on your skills. As competition for the best jobs increases, employers are comparing more and more applicants for every opening and asking more and more questions. To win against stiff competition, you need more than just your merits. When the race is close, the final winner is often as not picked for a comparative lack of negatives when ranged against the other contenders. Like Bailey and Nizer, you can prove to yourself that the prize always goes to the best prepared.

During an interview, employers ask you dozens of searching questions—questions that test your confidence, poise, and desirable personality traits. Questions that trick you into contradicting yourself. Questions that probe your quick thinking and job skills. They are all designed so that the interviewer can make decisions in some critical areas:

- Can you do the job?
- Will you complement or disrupt the department?
- Are you willing to take the extra step?
- Are you manageable?
- Is the money right?

Notice that only one of the critical areas has anything to do with your actual job skills. Being able to do the job is only a small part of getting an offer. Whether you will fit in and make a contribution, and whether you are manageable, are just as important to the interviewer. Those traits the company probes for during the interview are the same that will mark a person for professional growth when on board. In this era of high unemployment and high specialization, companies become more critical in the selection process and look more actively for certain traits, some of which cannot be ascertained by a direct question or answer. Consequently, the interviewer will seek a pattern in your replies that shows your possession of such traits—I discuss them in detail in the next chapter.

The time spent in "court" on trial for your livelihood contains four deadly traps:

- Your failure to listen to the question
- Annoying the interviewer by answering a question that was not asked
- Providing superfluous information (you should keep answers brief, thorough, and to the point); attempting to interview without preparation

The effect of those blunders is cumulative, and each reduces your chances of receiving a job offer.

The number of offers you win in your search for the ideal job depends on your ability to answer a staggering array of questions in terms that have value and relevance to the employer: "Why do you want to work here?" "What are your biggest accomplishments?" "How long will it take you to make a contribution?" "Why should I hire you?" "What can you do for us that someone else cannot do?" "What is your greatest weakness?" "Why aren't you earning more?" and "What interests you least about this job?" are just some of the questions you will be asked.

The example answers in the following chapters come from across the job spectrum. Though the example answer might come from the mouth of an administrator, while you are a scientist or in one of the service industries, the commonality of all job functions in contributing to the bottom line will help you draw the parallel to your job.

You will also notice that each of the example answers teaches a small yet valuable lesson in good business behavior—something you can use both to get the job and to make a good impression when you are on board.

And remember, the answers provided in the following chapters should not be repeated word for word, exactly as they come off the page. You have your own style of speech (not to mention your own kind of business experience), so try to put the answers in your own words.

13 | The Five Secrets of the Hire

Knowing how an interviewer thinks is a critical element of the job search that is too frequently overlooked.

Before we examine the "dos and don'ts" advice on interviewing contained in the next chapter, it's a good idea to review the interview process from the employer's perspective. As we have observed, there is a fallacy that all that is necessary for success at the interview is for you to show that you have what it takes to do the job. There's a lot more to it than that.

The First Secret: Ability and Suitability

Saying, "Hey, I can do this job—give me a shot and I'll prove it to you" is not enough anymore. Today you have to *prove* ability and suitability.

Every working professional has a combination of skills that broadly define his or her ability and suitability. How well you program that computer, service that client, or sew up that appendix is part of the picture; knowing the steps involved well enough *to be able to explain them clearly and simply to others* is another part.

Itemize your technical/professional skills as they parallel the requirements of the job. Then recall an incident to illustrate each of those skills. When you have done this, and not before, you will be in a position to begin justifying your ability and suitability to an employer.

If you are applying for a job in an industry with which you are familiar, you should also consider highlighting your industry sensibilities. Industry sensibilities means knowing "how we do it here." For example, a good computer programmer working in a bank has technical and professional skills; that is, the ability to program a computer is required by the employer. That same programmer has knowledge of how to get things done *in the industry in which he or she operates*; that is, the ability to work well with bankers, which is quite different than being able to work well with, say, public television fundraisers.

Demonstrating both professional/technical and industry skills will set you apart from the vast majority of candidates. Show that you understand these combinations and you will stand out from the pack.

The Second Secret: Willingness

Ten years ago, if a woman were asked during an interview whether she would be willing to make coffee, she might have experienced some awkwardness in answering. Nowadays that awkwardness is less common, as she is likely to know that she is within her rights in asking whether the duties were part of her job description. But in doing so, she might be losing an opportunity to demonstrate her readiness to pitch in at any task. This question is being used more and more by potential employers who want to gauge *willingness*—and have no intention of sending applicants off to brew the perfect cup of Good Morning America. Male applicants, too, are well advised to consider an answer along the lines of "Yes, and how would you like your eggs?"

Today, the issue isn't whether you are prepared to do demeaning tasks. It is whether you are the kind of person who is prepared to do whatever it takes to help the team survive and prosper. Can you take the rough with the smooth? Are you prepared to go that extra mile? You are? Great. Think of a time when you did. Figure out how your doing so helped the company. Now rehearse the story until you can tell it in about ninety seconds.

The Third Secret: Manageability and Teamwork

There isn't a manager in the world who enjoys a sleepless night caused by an unmanageable employee. Avoiding such nights is a major concern for managers, who develop, over time, a remarkable sixth sense when it comes to spotting and cutting out mavericks.

Manageability is defined in different ways: the ability to work alone; the ability to work with others; the ability to take direction and criticism when it is carefully and considerately given; and, perhaps dearest to the manager's heart, the ability to take direction when it *isn't* carefully and considerately given, often because of a crisis. Also crucial is a willingness to work with others regardless of their sex, age, religion, physical appearance, abilities or disabilities, skin color, or national origin.

Such "manageability" considerations make a job interview tricky. Yes, you should certainly state your strongly held convictions—after all, you don't want to appear wishy-washy—but you should do so *only as long as they are professional in nature and relate to the job at hand.*

Let me give you an example of what I mean. A number of people have asked me about what they perceive as discrimination as a result of their being born-again Christians. However, each discussion invariably ends in the conclusion that a job interview is simply no place to bring up personal beliefs. Today's managers will usually go well out of their way to avoid even the perception of intolerance toward sincerely held spiritual beliefs. Yet, by the same token, they are deeply suspicious of any strident religious rhetoric that surfaces in a professional setting. (This also holds true of political, ethnic, or other inappropriate issues raised by a candidate during an interview.) The potential employer's caution in these circumstances, far from representing discrimination, is a sign of concern that the candidate might not be tolerant of the views of others—and might thereby become an obstacle to a harmonious work group.

The rules here are simple. Don't bring up religious, political, or racial matters during the job interview. Even a casual reference to such topics can put a potential employer on the spot, since he or she could subject the company to a lawsuit if a racial or religious topic is perceived as having influenced a hiring decision. The interview is a potential paycheck; don't mess with it.

You're a team player, someone who gets along well with others and has no problem tolerating other opinions or beliefs. Demonstrate that with your every word and action.

The Fourth Secret: Professional Behavior

I emphasize *professional* behavior throughout this book because, to a large extent, the traits that are most desirable to employers are learned and developed as a result of our experiences in the workplace.

As you will see in the next chapter, there are twenty universally admired behavioral traits common to successful people in all fields. Once you review them, you will no doubt find that they are important to you, too, since just understanding what they are will give you up to twenty unique points to make about your candidacy. But understanding the traits is only part of the secret.

Harry works in Shipping and Receiving. He reads the list of traits, comes across the category labeled "Determination," and thinks, "Yeah, that's me. I'm a determined guy." On its own, though, he knows this is not enough. Then Harry recalls the time he came in over the weekend to clear the warehouse in time to make room for the twenty-ton press due in Monday morning at seven. When he tells this story to the interviewer, he gets a lot further than he would if he simply said, "Hire me; I'm determined." The interviewer, instead of a bland, unsubstantiated claim that would be forgotten almost the instant it left Harry's mouth, gets a mental movie of the event that's hard to forget: Harry coming in on the weekend to make room for that press. Actually, the interviewer *really* sees something much more important, namely, Harry applying the same level of determination and extra effort on behalf of the interviewer's company.

Simple statements don't leave any lasting impression on employers. Anecdotes that prove a point do.

The Fifth Secret: Everyone Hires for the Same Job

Surprised? Here's another, related news flash: No one in the history of industry and commerce has ever been added to a payroll for the love of mankind.

Regardless of job or profession, we are all, at some level, *problem solvers*. That's the first and most important part of the job description for anyone who has ever been hired for any job, at any level, in any organization, anywhere in the world. This fifth secret is absolutely key to job hunting and career success in any field.

Think of your profession in terms of its problem-solving responsibilities. Once you have identified the particular problem-solving business you are in, you will have gone a long way toward isolating what the interviewer will want to talk about. Identify and list for yourself the typical problems you tackle for employers on a daily basis. Come up with plenty of specific examples. Then move on to the *biggest and dirtiest* problems you've been faced with. Again, recall specifically how you solved them.

Here's a technique used by corporate outplacement professionals to help people develop examples of their problem-solving skills and the resultant achievements:

1. *State the problem.* What was the situation? Was it typical of your job, or had something gone wrong? If the latter, be leery of apportioning blame.
2. *Isolate relevant background information.* What special knowledge or education were you armed with to tackle this dilemma?

3. *List your key qualities.* What professional skills and personal behavior traits did you bring into play to solve the problem?
4. *Recall the solution.* How did things turn out in the end? (If the problem did not have a successful resolution, do not use it as an example.)
5. *Determine what the solution was worth.* Quantify the solution in terms of money earned, money saved, or time saved. Specify your role as a team member or as a lone gun, as the facts demand.

With an improved understanding of what employers seek in employees, you will have a better understanding of yourself and what you have to offer in the way of specific problem-solving abilities. If you follow the steps outlined above, you will develop a series of illustrative stories for each key area. Remember, stories help interviewers visualize you solving *their* problems—as a paid member of the team.

Here's a story for you. It's based on a real-life interview pattern, although the names are fictional.

Mr. Wanton Grabbit, eighty-year-old senior partner at the revered Washington law firm of Sue, Grabbit, and Runne, ran a help-wanted advertisement in the *Washington Post* for a word processing specialist. He was looking for someone with five years of experience in W.P. and the same amount working in a legal environment. He also wanted someone with experience in using the office computer system, a Bambleweeney 5000.

Grabbit interviewed ten candidates with exactly the experience the advertisement demanded. Each of them came away from the interview convinced that a job offer was imminent. None of them got the job. The person who did get the job had *three* years of experience and had *never before set foot* inside a law office.

Sue Sharp, the successful candidate, understood the fifth secret and asked a few intelligent questions of her own during the interview. Specifically, she asked, "What are the first projects I will be involved with?" This led Mr. Grabbit to launch into a long discourse on his desire to see the law firm rush headlong into the 21st century by the year 2001. The first project, he explained, would be to load the firm's approximately 4,000 manual files onto the Bambleweeney.

Now, although Sue had never worked in a law firm before, she had, on her last job, automated a cumbersome manual filing system. Having faced the *problem* before, even though she had done so in the "wrong" setting, she was able to demonstrate an understanding of the challenges the position presented. Furthermore, she was able to tell the illustrative stories from her last job that enabled Mr. Grabbit to see her, in his mind's eye, tackling and solving his immediate, specific, short-term problems successfully.

We get two very special benefits when we understand and apply the fifth secret. First, we show that we possess the problem-solving abilities of a first-rate professional in the field. Second, when we ask about the problems, challenges, projects, deadlines, and pressure points that will be tackled in the early months, we show that we will be able to hit the ground running on those first critical projects.

□   □   □

Integrate the five secrets of the hire as you read the rest of this section. You will reap the rewards—while your competition must resign themselves to harvesting sour grapes.

14 | How to Knock 'em Dead

The basics of interviewing are found in the basics of business, and each question is asked to find out whether you have the right stuff. Discover the twenty key personality traits of the most successful businesspeople, and how to convey them.

- "Describe a situation where your work or an idea was criticized."
- "Have you done the best work you are capable of doing?"
- "What problems do you have getting along with others?"
- "How long will you stay with the company?"
- "I'm not sure you're suitable for the job."
- "Tell me about something you are not very proud of."
- "What are some of the things your supervisor did that you disliked?"
- "What aspects of your job do you consider most crucial?"

Can you answer all these questions off the top of your head? Can you do it in a way that will set your worth above the other job candidates? I doubt it—they were *designed* to catch you off-guard. But they won't after you have read the rest of *Knock 'em Dead*.

Even if you could answer some of them, it would not be enough to assure you of victory: The employer is looking for certain intangible assets as well. Think back to your last job for a moment. Can you recall someone with fewer skills, less professionalism, and less dedication who somehow leveraged his or her career into a position of superiority to you? He or she was able to do that only by cleverly projecting a series of personality traits that are universally sought by all successful companies. Building those key traits into your answers to the interviewer's questions will win you any job and set the stage for your career growth at the new company.

There are twenty universally admired key personality traits; they are your passport to success at any interview. Use them for reference as you customize your answers to the tough questions in the following chapters.

Personal Profile:

The interviewer searches for personal profile keys to determine what type of person you really are. The presence of these keys in your answers tells the company representative how you feel about yourself, your chosen career, and what you would be like to work with. Few of them will arise from direct questions—your future employer will search for them in your answers to specific job-performance probes. The following words and phrases are those you will project as part of your successful, healthy personal profile.

- **Drive:** A desire to get things done. Goal-oriented.
- **Motivation:** Enthusiasm and a willingness to ask questions. A company realizes that a motivated person accepts added challenges and does that little bit extra on every job.
- **Communication Skills:** More than ever, the ability to talk and write effectively to people at all levels in a company is a key to success.
- **Chemistry:** The company representative is looking for someone who does not get rattled, wears a smile, is confident without self-importance, gets along with others—who is, in short, a team player.
- **Energy:** Someone who always gives that extra effort in the little things as well as important matters.
- **Determination:** Someone who does not back off when a problem or situation gets tough.
- **Confidence:** Not braggadocio. Poise. Friendly, honest, and open to employees high or low. Not intimidated by the big enchiladas, nor overly familiar.

Professional Profile:

All companies seek employees who respect their profession and employer. Projecting these professional traits will identify you as loyal, reliable, and trustworthy.

- **Reliability:** Following up on yourself, not relying on anyone else to ensure the job is well done, and keeping management informed every step of the way.
- **Honesty/Integrity:** Taking responsibility for your actions, both good and bad. Always making decisions in the best interests of the company, never on whim or personal preference.

- **Pride:** Pride in a job well done. Always taking the extra step to make sure the job is done to the best of your ability. Paying attention to the details.
- **Dedication:** Whatever it takes in time and effort to see a project through to completion, on deadline.
- **Analytical Skills:** Weighing the pros and cons. Not jumping at the first solution to a problem that presents itself. Weighing the short- and long-term benefits of a solution against all its possible negatives.
- **Listening Skills:** Listening and understanding, as opposed to waiting your turn to speak.

Achievement Profile:

Earlier, I discussed that companies have very limited interests: making money, saving money (the same as making money), and saving time (which does both). Projecting your achievement profile, in however humble a fashion, is the key to winning any job.

- **Money Saved:** Every penny saved by your thought and efficiency is a penny earned for the company.
- **Time Saved:** Every moment saved by your thought and efficiency enables your company to save money and make more in the additional time available. Double bonus.
- **Money Earned:** Generating revenue is the goal of every company.

Business Profile:

Projecting your business profile is important on those occasions when you cannot demonstrate ways you have made money, saved money, or saved time for previous employers. These keys demonstrate you are always on the lookout for opportunities to contribute, and that you keep your boss informed when an opportunity arises.

- **Efficiency:** Always keeping an eye open for wastage of time, effort, resources, and money.
- **Economy:** Most problems have two solutions: an expensive one, and one the company would prefer to implement.

- **Procedures:** Procedures exist to keep the company profitable. Don't work around them. That also means keeping your boss informed. You tell your boss about problems or good ideas, not his or her boss. Follow the chain of command. Do not implement your own "improved" procedures or organize others to do so.
- **Profit:** All the above traits are universally admired in the business world because they relate to profit.

□   □   □

As the requirements of the job are unfolded for you at the interview, meet them point by point with your qualifications. If your experience is limited, stress the appropriate key profile traits (such as energy, determination, motivation), your relevant interests, and your desire to learn. If you are weak in just one particular area, keep your mouth shut—perhaps that dimension will not arise. If the area is probed, be prepared to handle and overcome the negative by stressing skills that compensate and/or demonstrate that you will experience a fast learning curve.

Do not show discouragement if the interview appears to be going poorly. You have nothing to gain by showing defeat, and it could merely be a stress interview tactic to test your self-confidence.

If for any reason you get flustered or lost, keep a straight face and posture; gain time to marshal your thoughts by asking, "Could you help me with that?" or "Would you run that by me again?" or "That's a good question; I want to be sure I understand. Could you please explain it again?"

□   □   □

Now it is time for you to study the tough questions. Use the examples and explanations to build answers that reflect your background and promote your skills and attributes.

"What are the reasons for your success in this profession?"

With this question, the interviewer is not so much interested in examples of your success—he or she wants to know what makes you tick. Keep your answers short, general, and to the point. Using your work experience, personalize and use value keys from your personal, professional, and business profiles. For example: "I attribute my success to three reasons: First, I've always received support from coworkers, which encourages me to be cooperative and look at my specific job in terms of what we as a department are trying to achieve. That gives me great pride in my work and its contribution to the department's efforts, which is the second factor. Finally, I find that every job has its problems, and while there's always a costly solution, there's usually an economical one as well, whether it's in terms of time or money." Then give an example from your experience that illustrates those points.

"What is your energy level like? Describe a typical day."

You must demonstrate good use of your time, that you believe in planning your day beforehand, and that when it is over, you review your own performance to make sure you are reaching the desired goals. No one wants a part-time employee, so you should sell your energy level. For example, your answer might end with: "At the end of the day when I'm ready to go home, I make a rule always to type one more letter [make one more call, etc.] and clear my desk for the next day."

"Why do you want to work here?"

To answer this question, you must have researched the company and built a dossier. Your research work from chapter 1 is now rewarded. Reply with the company's attributes as you see them. Cap your answer with reference to your belief that the company can provide you with a stable and happy work environment—the company has that reputation—and that such an atmosphere would encourage your best work.

"I'm not looking for just another paycheck. I enjoy my work and am proud of my profession. Your company produces a superior product/provides a superior service. I share the values that make this possible, which should enable me to fit in and complement the team."

"What kind of experience do you have for this job?"

This is a golden opportunity to sell yourself, but before you do, be sure you know what is most critical to the interviewer. The interviewer is not just looking for a competent engineer, typist, or what-have-you—he or she is looking for someone who can contribute quickly to the current projects. When interviewing, companies invariably give everyone a broad picture of the job, but the person they hire will be a problem solver, someone who can contribute to the specific projects in the first six months. Only by asking will you identify the areas of your interviewer's greatest urgency and therefore interest.

If you do not know the projects you will be involved with in the first six months, you must ask. Level-headedness and analytical ability are respected, and the information you get will naturally let you answer the question more appropriately. For example, a company experiencing shipping problems might appreciate this answer: "My high-speed machining background and familiarity with your equipment will allow me to contribute quickly. I understand deadlines, delivery schedules, and the importance of getting the product shipped. Finally, my awareness of economy and profit has always kept reject parts to a bare minimum."

"What are the broad responsibilities of a [e.g.] systems analyst?"

This is suddenly becoming a very popular question with interviewers, and rightly so. There are three layers to it. First, it acknowledges that all employees nowadays are required to be more efficiency- and profit-conscious, and need to know how individual responsibilities fit into the big picture. Second, the answer provides some idea of how much you will have to be taught or reoriented if and when you join the company. Third, it is a very effective knock-out question—if you lack a comprehensive understanding of your job, that's it! You'll be knocked out then and there.

While your answer must reflect an understanding of the responsibilities, be wary of falling afoul of differing corporate jargon. A systems analyst in one company, for instance, may be only a programmer trainee in another. With that in mind, you may wish to preface your answer with, "While the responsibilities of my job title vary somewhat from company to company, at my current/last job, my responsibilities included . . ." Then, in case your background isn't an exact match, ask, "Which areas of relevant expertise haven't I covered?" That will give you the opportunity to recoup.

"Describe how your job relates to the overall goals of your department and company."

This not only probes your understanding of department and corporate missions but also obliquely checks into your ability to function as a team member to get the work done. Consequently, whatever the specifics of your answer, include words to this effect: "The quality of my work directly affects the ability of others to do their work properly. As a team member, one has to be aware of the other players."

"What aspects of your job do you consider most crucial?"

A wrong answer can knock you out of the running in short order. The executive who describes expense reports as the job's most crucial aspect is a case in point. The question is designed to determine time management, prioritization skills, and any inclination for task avoidance.

"Are you willing to go where the company sends you?"

Unfortunately with this one, you are, as the saying goes, damned if you do and damned if you don't. What is the real question? Do they want you to relocate or just travel on business? If you simply answer "no," you will not get the job offer, but if you answer "yes," you could end up in Monkey's Eyebrow, Kentucky. So play for time and ask, "Are you talking about business travel, or is the company relocating?" In the final analysis, your answer should be "yes." You don't have to accept the job, but without the offer you have no decision to make. Your single goal at an interview is to sell yourself and win a job offer. Never forget, only when you have the offer is there a decision to make about that particular job.

"What did you like/dislike about your last job?"

The interviewer is looking for incompatibilities. If a trial lawyer says he or she dislikes arguing a point with colleagues, such a statement will only weaken—if not immediately destroy—his or her candidacy.

Most interviews start with a preamble by the interviewer about the company. Pay attention: That information will help you answer the question. In fact, any statement the interviewer makes about the job or corporation can be used to your advantage.

So, in answer, you liked everything about your last job. You might even say your company taught you the importance of certain keys from the business, achievement, or professional profile. Criticizing a prior employer is a warning flag that you could be a problem employee. No one intentionally hires trouble, and that's what's behind the question. Keep your answer short and positive. You are allowed only one negative about past employers, and then only if your interviewer has a "hot button" about his or her department or company; if so, you will have written it down on your notepad. For example, the only thing your past employer could not offer might be something like "the ability to contribute more in different areas in the smaller environment you have here." You might continue with, "I really liked everything about the job. The reason I want to leave it is to find a position where I can make a greater contribution. You see, I work for a large company that encourages specialization of skills. The smaller environment you have here will, as I said, allow me to contribute far more in different areas." Tell them what they want to hear—replay the hot button.

Of course, if you interview with a large company, turn it around. "I work for a small company and don't get the time to specialize in one or two major areas." Then replay the hot button.

"What is the least relevant job you have held?"

If your least relevant job is not on your resume, it shouldn't be mentioned. Some people skip over those six months between jobs when they worked as soda jerks just to pay the bills, and would rather not talk about it, until they hear a question like this one. But a mention of a job that, according to all chronological records, you never had, will throw your integrity into question and your candidacy out the door.

Apart from that, no job in your profession has been a waste of time if it increases your knowledge about how the business works and makes money. Your answer will include: "Every job I've held has given me new insights into my profession, and the higher one climbs, the more important the understanding of the lower-level, more menial jobs. They all play a role in making the company profitable. And anyway, it's certainly easier to schedule and plan work when you have first-hand knowledge of what others will have to do to complete their tasks."

"What have you learned from jobs you have held?"

Tie your answer to your business and professional profile. The interviewer needs to understand that you seek and can accept constructive advice, and that your business decisions are based on the ultimate good of the company, not your personal whim or preference. "More than anything, I have learned that what is good for the company is good for me. So I listen very carefully to directions and always keep my boss informed of my actions."

"How do you feel about your progress to date?"

This question is not geared solely to rate your progress; it also rates your self-esteem (personal profile keys). Be positive, yet do not give the impression you have already done your best work. Make the interviewer believe you see each day as an opportunity to learn and contribute, and that you see the environment at this company as conducive to your best efforts.

"Given the parameters of my job, my progress has been excellent. I know the work, and I am just reaching that point in my career when I can make significant contributions."

"Have you done the best work you are capable of doing?"

Say "yes," and the interviewer will think you're a has-been. As with all these questions, personalize your work history. For this particular question, include the essence of this reply: "I'm proud of my professional achievements to date, especially [give an example]. But I believe the best is yet to come. I am always motivated to give my best efforts, and in this job there are always opportunities to contribute when you stay alert."

"How long would you stay with the company?"

The interviewer might be thinking of offering you a job. So you must encourage him or her to sell you on the job. With a tricky question like this, end your answer with a question of your own that really puts the ball back in the interviewer's court. Your reply might be: "I would really like to settle down with this company. I take direction well and love to learn. As long as I am growing professionally, there is no reason for me to make a move. How long do you think I would be challenged here?"

"How long would it take you to make a contribution to our company?"

Again, be sure to qualify the question: In what area does the interviewer need rapid contributions? You are best advised to answer this with a question: "That is an excellent question. To help me answer, what do you anticipate my responsibilities will be for the first six or seven months?" or "What are your greatest areas of need right now?" You give yourself time to think while the interviewer concentrates on images of you working for the company. When your time comes to answer, start with: "Let's say I started on Monday the seventeenth. It will take me a few weeks to settle down and learn the ropes. I'll be earning my keep very quickly, but making a real contribution . . . [give a hesitant pause] Do you have a special project in mind you will want me to get involved with?" That response could lead directly to a job offer, but if not, you already have the interviewer thinking of you as an employee.

"What would you like to be doing five years from now?"

The safest answer contains a desire to be regarded as a true professional and team player. As far as promotion, that depends on finding a manager with whom you can grow. Of course, you will ask what opportunities exist within the company before being any more specific: "From my research and what you have told me about the growth here, it seems that operations is where the heavy emphasis is going to be. It seems that's where you need the effort and where I could contribute toward the company's goals." Or, "I have always felt that first-hand knowledge and experience open up opportunities that one might never have considered, so while at this point in time I plan to be a part of [e.g.] operations, it is reasonable to expect that other exciting opportunities will crop up in the meantime."

"What are your qualifications?"

Be sure you don't answer the wrong question. Does the interviewer want job-related or academic job qualifications? Ask. If the question concerns job-related information, you need to know what problems must be tackled first before you can answer adequately. If you can determine this, you will also know what is causing the manager most concern. Then, if you can show yourself as someone who can contribute to the solution of those projects or problems, you have taken a dramatic step ahead in the race for the job offer. Ask for clarification, then use appropriate value keys from all four categories tied in with relevant skills and achievements. You might say: "I can give you a general answer, but I feel my answer might be more valuable if you could tell me about specific work assignments in the early months."

Or: "If the major task right now is to automate the filing system, I should tell you that in my last job I was responsible for creating a computerized database for a previously uncomputerized firm."

"What are your biggest accomplishments?"

Keep your answers job related; from earlier exercises, a number of achievements should spring to mind. If you exaggerate contributions to major projects, you will be accused of suffering from "coffee-machine syndrome," the affliction of a junior clerk who claimed success for an Apollo space mission based on his relationships with certain scientists, established at the coffee machine. You might begin your reply with: "Although I feel my biggest achievements are still ahead of me, I am proud of my involvement with . . . I made my contribution as part of that team and learned a lot in the process. We did it with hard work, concentration, and an eye for the bottom line."

"How do you organize and plan for major projects?"

Effective planning requires both forward thinking ("Who and what am I going to need to get this job done?") and backward thinking ("If this job must be completed by the twentieth, what steps must be made, and at what time, to achieve it?"). Effective planning also includes contingencies and budgets for time and cost overruns. Show that you cover all the bases.

"How many hours a week do you find it necessary to work to get your job done?"

No absolutely correct answer here, so again, you have to cover all the bases. Some managers pride themselves on working nights and weekends, or on never taking their full vacation quota. Others pride themselves on their excellent planning and time management that allows them never to work more than regular office hours. You must pick the best of both worlds: "I try to plan my time effectively and usually can. Our business always has its rushes, though, so I put in whatever effort it takes to get the job finished." It is rare that the interviewer will then come back and ask for a specific number of hours. If that does happen, turn the question around: "It depends on the projects. What is typical in your department?" The answer will give you the right cue, of course.

"Tell me how you moved up through the organization."

A fast-track question, the answer to which tells a lot about your personality, your goals, your past, your future, and whether you still have any steam left in you. The answer might be long, but try to avoid rambling. Include a fair sprinkling of your key personality traits in your stories (because this is the perfect time to do it). As well as listing the promotions, you will want to demonstrate that they came as a result of dedicated, long-term effort, substantial contributions, and flashes of genius.

"Can you work under pressure?"

You might be tempted to give a simple "yes" or "no" answer, but don't. It reveals nothing, and you lose the opportunity to sell your skills and value profiles. Actually, this common question often comes from an unskilled interviewer, because it is closed-ended. (How to handle different types of interviewers is covered in chapter 16, "The Other Side of the Desk.") As such, the question does not give you the chance to elaborate. Whenever you are asked a closed-ended question, mentally add: "Please give me a brief yet comprehensive answer." Do that, and you will give the information requested and seize an opportunity to sell yourself. For example, you could say: "Yes, I usually find it stimulating. However, I believe in planning and proper management of my time to reduce panic deadlines within my area of responsibility."

"What is your greatest strength?"

Isolate high points from your background and build in a couple of the key value profiles from different categories. You will want to demonstrate pride, reliability, and the ability to stick with a difficult task yet change course rapidly when required. You can rearrange the previous answer here. Your answer in part might be: "I believe in planning and proper management of my time. And yet I can still work under pressure."

"What are your outstanding qualities?"

This is essentially the same as an interviewer asking you what your greatest strengths are. While in the former question you might choose to pay attention to job-specific skills, this question asks you to talk about your personality profile. Now while you are fortunate enough to have a list of the business world's most desirable personality traits at the beginning of this chapter, try to do more than just list them. In fact, rather than offering a long "laundry list," you might consider picking out just two or three and giving an illustration of each.

"What interests you most about this job?"

Be straightforward, unless you haven't been given adequate information to determine an answer, in which case you should ask a question of your own to clarify. Perhaps you could say, "Before answering, could I ask you to tell me a little more about the role this job plays in the departmental goals?" or "Where is the biggest vacuum in your department at the moment?" or "Could you describe a typical day for me?" The additional information you gather with those questions provides the appropriate slant to your answer—that is, what is of greatest benefit to the department and to the company. Career-wise, that obviously has the greatest benefit to you, too. Your answer then displays the personality traits that support the existing need. Your answer in part might include, "I'm looking for a challenge and an opportunity to make a contribution, so if you feel the biggest challenge in the department is _____, I'm the one for the job." Then include the personality traits and experience that support your statements. Perhaps: "I like a challenge, my background demonstrates excellent problem-solving abilities [give some examples], and I always see a project through to the finish."

"What are you looking for in your next job?"

You want a company where your personal profile keys and professional profile keys will allow you to contribute to business value keys. Avoid saying what you want the company to give you; you must say what you want in terms of what you can give to your employer. The key word in the following example is "contribution": "My experience at the XYZ Corporation has shown me I have a talent for motivating people. That is demonstrated by my team's absenteeism dropping 20 percent, turnover steadying at 10 percent, and production increasing 12 percent. I am looking for an opportunity to continue that kind of contribution, and a company and supervisor who will help me develop in a professional manner."

"Why should I hire you?"

Your answer will be short and to the point. It will highlight areas from your background that relate to current needs and problems. Recap the interviewer's description of the job, meeting it point by point with your skills. Finish your answer with: "I have the qualifications you need [itemize them], I'm a team player, I take direction, and I have the desire to make a thorough success."

"What can you do for us that someone else cannot do?"

This question will come only after a full explanation of the job has been given. If not, qualify the question with: "What voids are you trying to eradicate when you fill this position?" Then recap the interviewer's job description, followed with: "I can bring to this job a determination to see projects through to a proper conclusion. I listen and take direction well. I am analytical and don't jump to conclusions. And finally, I understand we are in business to make a profit, so I keep an eye on cost and return." End with: "How do these qualifications fit your needs?" or "What else are you looking for?"

You finish with a question that asks for feedback or a powerful answer. If you haven't covered the interviewer's hot buttons, he or she will cover them now, and you can respond accordingly.

"Describe a difficult problem you've had to deal with."

This is a favorite tough question. It is not so much the difficult problem that's important—it's the approach you take to solving problems in general. It is designed to probe your professional profile; specifically, your analytical skills.

"Well, I always follow a five-step format with a difficult problem. One, I stand back and examine the problem. Two, I recognize the problem as the symptom of other, perhaps hidden, factors. Three, I make a list of possible solutions to the problem. Four, I weigh both the consequences and cost of each solution, and determine the best solution. And five, I go to my boss, outline the problem, make my recommendation, and ask for my superior's advice and approval."

Then give an example of a problem and your solution. Here is a thorough example: "When I joined my present company, I filled the shoes of a manager who had been fired. Turnover was very high. My job was to reduce turnover and increase performance. Sales of our new copier had slumped for the fourth quarter in a row, partly due to ineffective customer service. The new employer was very concerned, and he even gave me permission to clean house. The cause of the problem? The customer-service team never had any training. All my people needed was some intensive training. My boss gave me permission to join the American Society for Training and Development, which cost $120. With what I learned there, I turned the department around. Sales continued to slump in my first quarter. Then they skyrocketed. Management was pleased with the sales and felt my job in customer service had played a real part in the turnaround; my boss was pleased because the solution was effective and cheap. I only had to replace two customer-service people."

"What would your references say?"

You have nothing to lose by being positive. If you demonstrate how well you and your boss got along, the interviewer does not have to ask, "What do you dislike about your current manager?"

It is a good idea to ask past employers to give you a letter of recommendation. That way, you know what is being said. It reduces the chances of the company representative checking up on you, and if you are asked this question you can pull out a sheaf of rousing accolades and hand them over. If your references are checked by the company, it must by law have your written permission. That permission is usually included in the application form you sign. All that said, never offer references or written recommendations unless they are requested.

"Can we check your references?"

This question is frequently asked as a stress question to catch the too-smooth candidate off-guard. It is also one that occasionally is asked in the general course of events. Comparatively few managers or companies ever check references—that astounds me, yet it's a fact of life. On the other hand, the higher up the corporate ladder you go, the more likely it is that your references will be checked. There is only one answer to this question if you ever expect to get an offer: "Yes."

Your answer may include: "Yes, of course you can check my references. However, at present, I would like to keep matters confidential, until we have established a serious mutual interest [i.e., an offer]. At such time I will be pleased to furnish you with whatever references you need from prior employers. I would expect you to wait to check my current employer's references until you have extended an offer in writing, I have accepted, we have agreed upon a start date, and I have had the opportunity to resign in a professional manner." You are under no obligation to give references of a current employer until you have a written offer in hand. You are also well within your rights to request that reference checks of current employers wait until you have started your new job.

"What type of decisions did you make on your last job?"

Your answer should include reference to the fact that your decisions were all based on appropriate business profile keys. The interviewer may be searching to define your responsibilities, or he or she may want to know that you don't overstep yourself. It is also an opportunity, however humble your position, to show your achievement profile.

For example: "Being in charge of the mailroom, my job is to make sure people get information in a timely manner. The job is well defined, and my decisions aren't that difficult. I noticed a year or two ago that when I took the mail around at 10 A.M., everything stopped for twenty minutes. I had an idea and gave it to my boss. She got it cleared by the president, and ever since, we take the mail around just before lunch. Mr. Gray, the president, told me my idea improved productivity, saved time, and that he wished everyone was as conscientious."

"What was the last book you read (or movie you saw)? How did it affect you?"

It doesn't really matter what you say about the latest book or movie, just as long as you have read or seen it. Don't be like the interviewee who said the name of the first book that came to mind—*In Search of Excellence*—only to be caught by the follow-up, "To what extent do you agree with Peters' simultaneous loose/tight pronouncements?" Also, by naming such a well-known book, you have managed only to say that you are like millions of others, which doesn't make you stand out in the crowd. Better that you should name something less faddish—that helps to avoid nasty follow-up questions. And you needn't mention the most *recent* book or movie you've seen. Your answer must simply make a statement about you as a potential employee. Come up with a response that will set you apart and demonstrate your obvious superiority. Ideally you want to mention a work that in some way has helped you improve yourself; anything that has honed any of the twenty key personality traits will do.

"How do you handle tension?"

This question is different from "Can you handle pressure?"—it asks *how* you handle it. You could reply, "Tension is caused when you let things pile up. It is usually caused by letting other areas of responsibility slip by for an extended period. For instance, if you have a difficult presentation coming up, you may procrastinate in your preparations for it. I've seen lots of people do things like that—a task seems so overwhelming they don't know where to begin. I find that if you break those overwhelming tasks into little pieces, they aren't so overwhelming any more. So I suppose I don't so much handle tension as handle the causes of it, by not letting things slip in other areas that can give rise to it."

"How long have you been looking for another position?"

If you are employed, your answer isn't that important—a short or long time is irrelevant to you in any follow-up probes, because you are just looking for the right job, with the right people and outfit that offers you the right opportunities. If, on the other hand, you are unemployed at the time of the question, how you answer becomes more important. If you say, "Well, I've been looking for two years now," it isn't going to score you any points. The interviewer thinks, "Two years, huh? And no one else wanted him in that time. I certainly don't." So if you must talk of months or more be careful to add something like, "Well, I've been looking for about a year now. I've had a number of offers in that time, but I have determined that as I spend most of my waking hours at work, the job I take and the people I work with have got to be people with values I can identify with. I made the decision that I just wasn't going to suffer clock-watchers and work-to-rule specialists anymore."

"Have you ever been fired?"

Say "no" if you can; if not, act on the advice given to the next question.

"Why were you fired?"

If you were laid off as part of general work force reduction, be straightforward and move on to the next topic as quickly as possible. If you have been terminated with cause, however, this is a very difficult question to answer. Like it or not, termination with cause is usually justified, because the most loathed responsibility of any manager is to take away someone's livelihood. Virtually no one fires an employee for the heck of it.

Looking at that painful event objectively, you will probably find the cause of your dismissal rooted in the absence of one or more of the twenty profiles. Having been fired also creates instant doubt in the mind of the interviewer, and greatly increases the chances of your references being checked. So if you have been fired, the first thing to do is bite the bullet and call the person who fired you, find out why it happened, and learn what he or she would say about you today.

Your aim is to clear the air, so whatever you do, don't be antagonistic. Reintroduce yourself, explain that you are looking (or, if you have been unemployed for a while, say you are "still looking") for a new job. Say that you appreciate that the manager had to do what was done, and that you learned from the experience. Then ask, "If you were asked as part of a pre- or post-employment reference check, how would you describe my leaving the company? Would you say that I was fired or that I simply resigned? You see, every time I tell someone about my termination, whoosh, there goes another chance of getting another paycheck!" Most managers will plump for the latter option (describing your departure as a resignation). After all, even testy managers tend to be humane after the fact, and such a response saves them potential headaches and even lawsuits.

Whatever you do, don't advertise the fact you were fired. If you are asked, be honest, but make sure you have packaged the reason in the best light possible. Perhaps: "I'm sorry to say, but I deserved it. I was having some personal problems at the time, and I let them affect my work. I was late to work and lost my motivation. My supervisor (whom, by the way, I still speak to) had directions to trim the work force anyway, and as I was hired only a couple of years ago, I was one of the first to go."

If you can find out the employee turnover figures, voluntary or otherwise, you might add: "Fifteen other people have left so far this year." A combination answer of this nature minimizes the stigma. You have even managed to demonstrate that you take responsibility for your actions, which shows your analytical and listening skills. If one of your past managers will speak well of you, there is nothing to lose and everything to gain by finishing with: "Jill Johnson, at the company, would be a good person to check for a reference on what I have told you."

I would never advise you to be anything but honest in your answers to any interview question. If, however, you have been terminated by a manager who is still vindictive, take heart: Only about 10 percent of all successful job candidates ever get their references checked.

"Have you ever been asked to resign?"

When someone is asked to resign, it is a gesture on the part of the employer: "You can quit, or we will can you, so which do you want it to be?" Because you were given the option, though, that employer cannot later say, "I had to ask him to resign"—that is tantamount to firing and could lead to legal problems. In the final analysis, it is safe to answer "no."

"Were you ever dismissed from your job for a reason that seemed unjustified?"

Another sneaky way of asking, "Were you ever fired?" The sympathetic phrasing is geared to getting you to reveal all the sordid details. The cold hard facts are that hardly anyone is ever fired without cause, and you're kidding yourself if you think otherwise. With that in mind, you can quite honestly say, "No," and move on to the next topic.

"In your last job, what were some of the things you spent most of your time on, and why?"

Employees come in two categories: goal-oriented (those who want to get the job done), and task-oriented (those who believe in "busy" work). You must demonstrate good time management, and that you are, therefore, goal-oriented, for that is what this question probes.

You might reply: "I work on the telephone like a lot of businesspeople; meetings also take up a great deal of time. What is more important to me is effective time management. I find more gets achieved in a shorter time if a meeting is scheduled, say, immediately before lunch or at the close of business. I try to block my time in the morning. At four o'clock, I review what I've achieved, what went right or wrong, and plan adjustments and my main thrust of business for tomorrow."

"In what ways has your job prepared you to take on greater responsibility?"

This is one of the most important questions you will have to answer. The interviewer is looking for examples of your professional development, perhaps to judge your future growth potential, so you must tell a story that demonstrates it. The following example shows growth, listening skills, honesty, and adherence to procedures. Parts of it can be adapted to your personal experience. Notice the then-and-now aspect of the answer.

"When I first started my last job, my boss would brief me morning and evening. I made some mistakes, learned a lot, and got the jobs in on time. As time went by I took on greater responsibilities, [list some of them]. Nowadays, I meet with her every Monday for breakfast to discuss any major directional changes, so that she can keep management informed. I think that demonstrates not only my growth but also the confidence my management has in my judgment and ability to perform consistently above standard."

"In what ways has your job changed since you originally joined the company?"
You can use the same answer here as for the previous question.

"How does this job compare with others you have applied for?"
This is a variation of more direct questions, such as "How many other jobs have you applied for?" and "Who else have you applied to?" but it is a slightly more intelligent question and therefore more dangerous. It asks you to compare. Answer the question and sidestep at the same time.

"No two jobs are the same, and this one is certainly unlike any other I have applied for." If you are pressed further, say, "Well, to give you a more detailed answer, I would need to ask you a number of questions about the job and the company. Would now be a good time to do that or would it be better later in the interview process?"

"What makes this job different from your current/last one?"
If you don't have enough information to answer the question, say so, and ask some of your own. Behind the question is the interviewer's desire to uncover experience you are lacking—your answer could be used as evidence against you. Focus on the positive: "From what I know of the job, I seem to have all the experience required to make a thorough success. I would say that the major differences seem to be . . ." and here you play back the positive attributes of the department and company as the interviewer gave them to you, either in the course of the interview or in answer to your specific questions.

"Do you have any questions?"
A good question. Almost always, this is a sign that the interview is drawing to a close, and that you have one more chance to make an impression. Remember the

adage: People respect what you inspect, not what you expect. Create questions from any of the following:

- Find out why the job is open, who had it last, and what happened to him or her. Did he or she get promoted or fired? How many people have held this position in the last couple of years? What happened to them subsequently?
- Why did the interviewer join the company? How long has he or she been there? What is it about the company that keeps him or her there?
- To whom would you report? Will you get the opportunity to meet that person?
- Where is the job located? What are the travel requirements, if any?
- What type of training is required, and how long is it? What type of training is available?
- What would your first assignment be?
- What are the realistic chances for growth in the job? Where are the opportunities for greatest growth within the company?
- What are the skills and attributes most needed to get ahead in the company?
- Who will be the company's major competitor over the next few years? How does the interviewer feel the company stacks up against them?
- What has been the growth pattern of the company over the last five years? Is it profitable? How profitable? Is the company privately or publicly held?
- If there is a written job description, may you see it?
- How regularly do performance evaluations occur? What model do they follow?

15 | "What Kind of Person Are You Really, Mr. Jones?"

Learn the techniques an interviewer uses to find out whether you will fit into the company and the department, and most important, whether you are a good person to work with.

Will you reduce your new employer's life expectancy? The interviewer wants to know! If you are offered the job and accept, you will be working together fifty weeks of the year. Every employer wants to know whether you will fit in with the rest of the staff, whether you are a team player, and most of all: Are you manageable?

There are a number of questions the interviewer might use to probe this area. They will mainly be geared to your behavior and attitudes in the past. Remember: It is universally believed that your past actions predict your future behavior.

"How do you take direction?"

The interviewer wants to know whether you are open-minded and can be a team player. Can you follow directions or are you a difficult, high-maintenance employee? It is hoped that you are a low-maintenance professional who is motivated to ask clarifying questions about a project before beginning, and who then gets on with the job at hand, coming back to initiate requests for direction as circumstances dictate.

This particular question can also be defined as "How do you take direction?" and "How do you accept criticism?" Your answer should cover both points: "I take direction well and recognize that it can come in two varieties, depending on the circumstances. There is carefully explained direction, when my boss has time to lay things out for me in detail; then there are those times when, as a result of deadlines and other pressures, the direction might be brief and to the point. While I have seen some people get upset with that, personally I've always understood that there are probably other considerations I am not aware of. As such, I take the direction and get on with the job without taking offense, so my boss can get on with her job. It's the only way."

"Would you like to have your boss's job?"

It is a rare boss who wants his or her livelihood taken away. On my own very first job interview, my future boss said, "Mr. Yate, it has been a pleasure to meet you. However, until you walked in my door, I wasn't out on the street looking for a new job."

The interviewer wants to know if you are the type of person who will be confrontational, challenging, undermining, or too ambitious or arrogant. He also seeks to determine how goal-oriented and motivated you are in your work life—so you may also want to comment on your sense of direction. But remember that while ambition is admired, it is admired most by the ambitious. Be cautiously optimistic; perhaps, "Well, if my boss were promoted over the coming years, I would hope to have made a consistent enough contribution to warrant his recommendation. It is not that I am looking to take anyone's job; rather, I am looking for a manager who will help me develop my capabilities and grow with him."

"What do you think of your current/last boss?"

Short, sweet, and shut up. People who complain about their employers are recognized to be the same people who cause the most disruption in a department. This question means the interviewer has no desire to hire trouble. "I liked her as a person, respected her professionally, and appreciated her guidance." The question is often followed by one that tries to validate your answer.

"Describe a situation where your work or an idea was criticized."

A doubly dangerous question. You are being asked to say how you handle criticism and to detail your faults. If you are asked this question, describe a poor idea that was criticized, not poor work. Poor work can cost money and is a warning sign, obviously, to the interviewer.

One of the wonderful things about a new job is that you can leave the past entirely behind, so it does not matter how you handled criticism in the past. What does matter is how the interviewer would like you to handle criticism, if and when it becomes his or her unpleasant duty to dish it out; that's what the question is really about. So relate one of those it-seemed-like-a-good-idea-at-the-time ideas, and finish with how you handled the criticism. You could say: "I listened carefully and resisted the temptation to interrupt or defend myself. Then I fed back what I heard to make sure the facts were straight. I asked for advice, we bounced some ideas around, then I came back later and represented the idea in a more viable format. My supervisor's input was invaluable."

"Tell me about yourself."

This is not an invitation to ramble on. If the context isn't clear, you need to know more about the question before giving an answer. In such a situation, you could ask, "Is there a particular aspect of my background that would be most relevant to you?" This will enable the interviewer to help you find the appropriate focus and avoid discussing irrelevancies.

Whichever direction your answer ultimately takes, be sure that it has some relevance to the world of your professional endeavors. The tale you tell should demonstrate, or refer to, one or more of your key behavioral profiles in action—perhaps honesty, integrity, being a team player, or determination. If you choose "team player" (maybe you're the star player at first base on a community team), you can tell a story about yourself outside of work that also speaks volumes about you at work. In part, your answer should make the connection between the two, such as "I put my heart into everything I do, whether it be sports or work. I find that getting along with teammates—or professional peers—makes life more enjoyable and productive."

Or you might describe yourself as someone who is able to communicate with a variety of people, and give an example from your personal life that indicates an ability to communicate that would also apply at work.

This isn't a question that you can answer effectively off the cuff. Take some time in advance to think about yourself, and those aspects of your personality and/or background that you'd like to promote or feature for your interviewer.

"How do you get along with different kinds of people?"

You don't have to talk about respect for others, the need for diversity, or how it took you ten years to realize Jane was a different sex and Charley a different color, because that is not what this question is about. If you do respect others, then you will demonstrate this by explaining to your interviewer how you work in a team environment (because this is, in reality, a "team player" question), and how you solicit and accept input, ideas, and viewpoints from a variety of sources. If you can give a quick, honest, illustration of learning from a coworker who is obviously different from you in some way, it won't hurt.

"Rate yourself on a scale of one to ten."

A stupid question. That aside, bear in mind that this is meant to plumb the depths of your self-esteem. If you answer ten, you run the risk of portraying yourself as insufferable; on the other hand, if you say less than seven, you might as well get up and leave. You are probably best claiming to be an eight or nine, saying that you always give of your best, but that in doing so you always increase your skills and therefore always see room for improvement.

"What kinds of things do you worry about?"

Some questions, such as this one, can seem so off-the-wall that you might start treating the interviewer as a father confessor in no time flat. Your private phobias have nothing to do with your job, and revealing them can get you labeled as unbalanced. It is best to confine your answer to the sensible worries of a conscientious professional. "I worry about deadlines, staff turnover, tardiness, back-up plans for when the computer crashes, or that one of my auditors burns out or defects to the competition—just the normal stuff. It goes with the territory, so I don't let it get me down."

"What is the most difficult situation you have faced?"

The question looks for information on two fronts: How do you define difficult? and What was your handling of the situation? You must have a story ready for this one in which the situation both was tough and allowed you to show yourself in a good light. Avoid talking about problems that have to do with coworkers. You can talk about the difficult decision to fire someone, but emphasize that once you had examined the problem and reached a conclusion you acted quickly and professionally, with the best interests of the company at heart.

"What are some of the things that bother you?" "What are your pet hates?" "Tell me about the last time you felt anger on the job."

These questions are so similar that they can be treated as one. It is tremendously important that you show you can remain calm. Most of us have seen a colleague lose his or her cool on occasion—not a pretty sight and one that every sensible employer wants to avoid. This question comes up more and more often the higher up the corporate ladder you climb, and the more frequent your contact with clients and the general public. To answer it, find something that angers conscientious workers. "I enjoy my work and believe in giving value to my employer. Dealing with clock-watchers and the ones who regularly get sick on Mondays and Fridays really bothers me, but it's not something that gets me angry or anything like that." An answer of this nature will help you much more than the kind given by a California engineer, who went on for some minutes about how he hated the small-mindedness of people who don't like pet rabbits in the office.

"What have you done that shows initiative?"

The question probes whether you are a doer, someone who will look for ways to increase sales, save time, or save money—the kind of person who gives a manager a pleasant surprise once in a while, who makes life easier for coworkers. Be sure, however, that your example of initiative does not show a disregard for company policies and procedures.

"My boss has to organize a lot of meetings. That means developing agendas, letting employees around the country know the dates well in advance, getting materials printed, etc. Most people in my position would wait for the work to be given them. I don't. Every quarter, I sit down with my boss and find out the dates of all his meetings for the next six months. I immediately make the hotel and flight arrangements and then work backwards. I ask myself questions like, 'If the agenda for the July meeting is to reach the field at least six weeks before the meeting, when must it be finished by?' Then I come up with a deadline. I do that for all the major activities for all the meetings. I put the deadlines in his diary; and mine, only two weeks earlier. That way I remind the boss that the deadline is getting close. My boss is the best organized, most relaxed manager in the company. None of his colleagues can understand how he does it."

"What are some of the things about which you and your supervisor disagreed?"

It is safest to state that you did not disagree.

"In what areas do you feel your supervisor could have done a better job?"

The same goes for this one. No one admires a Monday-morning quarterback.

You could reply, though: "I have always had the highest respect for my supervisor. I have always been so busy learning from Mr. Jones that I don't think he could have done a better job. He has really brought me to the point where I am ready for greater challenges. That's why I'm here."

"What are some of the things your supervisor did that you disliked?"

If you and the interviewer are both nonsmokers, for example, and your boss isn't, use it. Apart from that: "You know, I've never thought of our relationship in terms of like or dislike. I've always thought our role was to get along together and get the job done."

"How well do you feel your boss rated your job performance?"

This is one very sound reason to ask for written evaluations of your work before leaving a company. Some performance-review procedures include a written evaluation of your performance—perhaps your company employs it. If you work for a company that asks you to sign your formal review, you are quite entitled to request a copy of it. You should also ask for a letter of recommendation whenever you leave a job: You have nothing to lose. While I don't recommend thrusting recommendations under unwilling interviewers' noses (they smell a rat when written endorsements of any kind are offered unrequested), the time will come when you are asked and can produce them with a flourish. If you don't have written references, perhaps: "My supervisor always rated my job performance well. In fact, I was always rated as being capable of accepting further responsibilities. The problem was there was nothing available in the company—that's why I'm here."

If your research has been done properly you can also quote verbal appraisals of your performance from prior jobs. "In fact, my boss said only a month ago that I was the most valuable [e.g.] engineer in the work group, because . . ."

"How did your boss get the best out of you?"

This is a manageability question, geared to probing whether you are going to be a pain in the neck or not. Whatever you say, it is important for your ongoing happiness that you make it clear you don't appreciate being treated like a dishrag. You can give a short, general answer: "My last boss got superior effort and performance by treating me like a human being and giving me the same personal respect with which she liked to be treated herself." This book is full of answers that get you out of tight corners and make you shine, but this is one instance in which you really should tell it like it is. You don't want to work for someone who is going to make life miserable for you.

"How interested are you in sports?"

A recently completed survey of middle- and upper-management personnel found that the executives who listed group sports/activities among their extracurricular activities made an average of $3,000 per year more than their sedentary colleagues. Don't you just love baseball suddenly? The interviewer is looking for your involvement in groups, as a signal that you know how to get along with others and pull together as a team.

"I really enjoy most team sports. Don't get a lot of time to indulge myself, but I am a regular member of my company's softball team." Apart from team sports, endurance sports are seen as a sign of determination: swimming, running, and cycling are all okay. Games of skill (bridge, chess, and the like) demonstrate analytical skills. Being a Grand Master of Dungeons and Dragons doesn't demonstrate a damned thing.

"What personal characteristics are necessary for success in your field?"

You know the answer to this one: It's a brief recital of key personality profiles.

You might say: "To be successful in my field? Drive, motivation, energy, confidence, determination, good communication, and analytical skills. Combined, of course, with the ability to work with others."

"Do you prefer working with others or alone?"

This question is usually used to determine whether you are a team player. Before answering, however, be sure you know whether the job requires you to work alone. Then answer appropriately. Perhaps: "I'm quite happy working alone when necessary. I don't need much constant reassurance. But I prefer to work in a group—so much more gets achieved when people pull together."

"Explain your role as a group/team member."

You are being asked to describe yourself as either a team player or a loner. Most departments depend on harmonious teamwork for their success, so describe yourself as a team player, by all means: "I perform my job in a way that helps others to do theirs in an efficient fashion. Beyond the mechanics, we all have a responsibility to make the workplace a friendly and pleasant place to be. That means everyone working for the common good and making the necessary personal sacrifices toward that good."

"How would you define a conducive work atmosphere?"

This is a tricky question, especially because you probably have no idea what kind of work atmosphere exists in that particular office. So, the longer your answer, the greater your chances of saying the wrong thing. Keep it short and sweet. "One where the team has a genuine interest in its work and desire to turn out a good product/deliver a good service."

"Do you make your opinions known when you disagree with the views of your supervisor?"

If you can, state that you come from an environment where input is encouraged when it helps the team's ability to get the job done efficiently. "If opinions are sought in a meeting, I will give mine, although I am careful to be aware of others' feelings. I will never criticize a coworker or a superior in open forum; besides, it is quite possible to disagree without being disagreeable. However, my past manager made it clear that she valued my opinion by asking for it. So, after a while, if there was something I felt strongly about, I would make an appointment to sit down and discuss it one-on-one." You might choose to end by turning the tables with a question of your own: "Is this a position where we work as a team to solve problems and get the job done, or one where we are meant to be seen and not heard and speak when spoken to?"

"What would you say about a supervisor who was unfair or difficult to work with?"

For this job, you'll definitely want to meet your potential supervisor—just in case you have been earmarked for the company Genghis Khan without warning. The response, "Do you have anyone in particular in mind?" will probably get you off the hook. If you need to elaborate, try: "I would make an appointment to see the supervisor and diplomatically explain that I felt uncomfortable in our relationship, that I felt he or she was not treating me as a professional colleague, and therefore that I might not be performing up to standard in some way—that I wanted to right matters and ask for his or her input as to what I must do to create a professional relationship. I would enter into the discussion in the frame of mind that we were equally responsible for whatever communication problems existed, and that this wasn't just the manager's problem."

"Do you consider yourself a natural leader or a born follower?"

Ow! How you answer depends a lot on the job offer you are chasing. If you are a recent graduate, you are expected to have high aspirations, so go for it. If you are already on the corporate ladder with some practical experience in the school of hard knocks, you might want to be a little more cagey. Assuming you are up for (and want) a leadership position, you might try something like this: "I would be reluctant to regard anyone as a natural leader. Hiring, motivating, and disciplining other adults and at the same time molding them into a cohesive team involves a number of delicately tuned skills that no honest people can say they were born with. Leadership requires first of all the desire; then it is a lifetime learning process. Anyone who reckons they have it all under control and have nothing more to learn isn't doing the employer any favors."

Of course, a little humility is also in order, because just about every leader in every company reports to someone, and there is a good chance that you are talking to such a someone right now. So you might consider including something like, "No matter how well developed any individual's leadership qualities, an integral part of the skills of a leader is to take direction from his or her immediate boss, and also to seek the input of the people being supervised. The wise leader will always follow good advice and sound business judgment wherever it comes from. I would say that given the desire to be a leader, the true leader in the modern business world must embrace both." How can anyone disagree with that kind of wisdom?

"Why do you feel you are a better [e.g.] secretary than some of your coworkers?"

If you speak disparagingly of your coworkers, you will not put yourself in the best light. That is what the question asks you to do, so it poses some difficulties. The trick is to answer the question but not to accept the invitation to show yourself from anything other than a flattering perspective. "I think that question is best answered by a manager. It is so difficult to be objective, and I really don't like to slight my coworkers. I don't spend my time thinking about how superior I am, because that would be detrimental to our working together as a team. I believe, however, some of the qualities that make me an outstanding secretary are . . ." and you go on to illustrate job-related personal qualities that make you a beacon of productivity and a joy to work with.

"You have a doctor's appointment arranged for noon. You've waited two weeks to get in. An urgent meeting is scheduled at the last moment, though. What do you do?"

What a crazy question, you mutter. It's not. It is even more than a question—it is what I call a question shell. The question within the shell—in this instance, "Will you sacrifice the appointment or sacrifice your job?—can be changed at will. This is a situational-interviewing technique, which poses an on-the-job problem to see how the prospective employee will respond. A Chicago company asks this question as part of its initial screening, and if you give the wrong answer, you never even get a face-to-face interview. So what is the right answer to this or any similar shell question?

Fortunately, once you understand the interviewing technique, it is quite easy to handle—all you have to do is turn the question around. "If I were the manager who had to schedule a really important meeting at the last moment, and someone on my staff chose to go to the doctor's instead, how would I feel?"

It is unlikely that you would be an understanding manager unless the visit were for a triple bypass. To answer, you start with an evaluation of the importance of the problem and the responsibility of everyone to make some sacrifices for the organization, and finish with: "The first thing I would do is reschedule the appointment and save the doctor's office inconvenience. Then I would immediately make sure I was properly prepared for the emergency meeting."

"How do you manage to interview while still employed?"

As long as you don't explain that you faked a dentist appointment to make the interview you should be all right. Beware of revealing anything that might make you appear at all underhanded. Best to make the answer short and sweet and let the interviewer move on to richer areas of inquiry. Just explain that you had some vacation time due, or took a day off in lieu of overtime payments. "I had some vacation time, so I went to my boss and explained I needed a couple of days off for some personal business, and asked her what days would be most suitable. Although I plan to change jobs, I don't in any way want to hurt my current employer in the process by being absent during a crunch."

"When do you expect a promotion?"

Tread warily, show you believe in yourself, and have both feet firmly planted on the ground. "That depends on a few criteria. Of course, I cannot expect promotions without the performance that marks me as deserving of promotion. I also need to join a company that has the growth necessary to provide the opportunity. I hope that my manager believes in promoting from within and will help me grow so that I will have the skills necessary to be considered for promotion when the opportunity comes along."

If you are the only one doing a particular job in the company, or you are in management, you need to build another factor into your answer. For example: "As a manager, I realize that part of my job is to have done my succession planning, and that I must have someone trained and ready to step into my shoes before I can expect to step up. That way I play my part in preserving the chain of command." To avoid being caught off-guard with queries about your having achieved that in your present job, you can finish with: "Just as I have done in my present job, where I have a couple of people capable of taking over the reins when I leave."

"Tell me a story."

Wow. What on earth does the interviewer mean by that question? You don't know until you get him or her to elaborate. Ask, "What would you like me to tell you a story about?" To make any other response is to risk making a fool of yourself. Very often the question is asked to see how analytical you are: People who answer the question without qualifying show that they do not think things through carefully. The subsequent question will be about either your personal or professional life. If it is about your personal life, tell a story that shows you like people and are determined. Do not discuss your love life. If the subsequent question is about your professional life, tell a story that demonstrates your willingness and manageability.

"What have your other jobs taught you?"

Talk about the professional skills you have learned and the personality traits you have polished. Many interviewees have had success finishing their answer with: "There are two general things I have learned from past jobs. First, if you are confused, ask—it's better to ask a dumb question than make a stupid mistake. Second, it's better to promise less and produce more than to make unrealistic forecasts."

"Define cooperation."

The question asks you to explain how to function as a team player in the workplace. Your answer could be: "Cooperation is a person's ability to sacrifice personal wishes and beliefs whenever necessary to assure the department reaches its goals. It is also a person's desire to be part of a team, and by hard work and goodwill make the department greater than the sum of its parts."

"What difficulties do you have tolerating people with different backgrounds and interests from yours?"

Another "team player" question with the awkward implication that you do have problems. Give the following answer: "I don't have any."

"In hindsight, what have you done that was a little harebrained?"

You are never harebrained in your business dealings, and you haven't been harebrained in your personal life since graduation, right? The only safe examples to use are ones from your deep past that ultimately turned out well. One of the best to use, if it applies to you, is this one: "Well, I guess the time I bought my house. I had no idea what I was letting myself in for, and at the time, I really couldn't afford it. Still, I managed to make the payments, though I had to work like someone possessed. Yes, my first house—that was a real learning experience." Not only can most people relate to this example, but it also gives you the opportunity to sell one or two of your very positive and endearing traits.

□　□　□

If you think the interview is only tough for the interviewee, it's time to take a look at the other side of the desk. Knowing what's going on behind those Foster Grants can really help you shine.

16 | The Other Side of the Desk

Two types of interviewers can spell disaster for the unprepared: the Highly Skilled and the Unconscious Incompetent. Find out how to recognize and respond to each one.

There are two terrible places to be during an interview—sitting in front of the desk wondering what on earth is going to happen next and sitting behind the desk asking the questions. The average interviewer dreads the meeting almost as much as the interviewee, yet for opposite reasons.

American business frequently yields to the mistaken belief that any person, on being promoted to the ranks of management, becomes mystically endowed with all necessary managerial skills. That is a fallacy. Comparatively few management people have been taught to interview; most just bumble along and pick up a certain proficiency over a period of time.

There are two distinct types of interviewers who can spell disaster for you if you are unprepared. One is the highly skilled interviewer, who has been trained in systematic techniques for probing your past for all the facts and evaluating your potential. The other is the totally incompetent interviewer, who may even lack the ability to phrase a question adequately. Both are equally dangerous when it comes to winning the job offer.

The Skillful Interviewer

Skillful interviewers know exactly what they want to discover. They have taken exhaustive steps to learn the strategies that will help them hire only the best for their company. They follow a set format for the interview process to ensure objectivity in selection and a set sequence of questions to ensure the facts are gathered. They will definitely test your mettle.

There are many ways for a manager to build and conduct a structured interview, but all have the same goals:

- To ensure a systematic coverage of your work history and applicable job-related skills
- To provide a technique for gathering all the relevant facts
- To provide a uniform strategy that objectively evaluates all job candidates
- To determine ability, willingness, and manageability

Someone using structured interview techniques will usually follow a standard format. The interview will begin with small talk and a brief introduction to relax you. Following close on the heels of that chit-chat comes a statement geared to assure you that baring your faults is the best way to get the job. Your interviewer will then outline the steps in the interview. That will include you giving a chronological description of your work history, and then the interviewer asking specific questions about your experience. Then, prior to the close of the interview, you will be given an opportunity to ask your own questions.

Sounds pretty simple, huh? Well, watch out! The skilled interviewer knows exactly what questions to ask, why they will be asked, in what order they will be asked, and what the desired responses are. He or she will interview and evaluate every applicant for the job in exactly the same fashion. You are up against a pro.

Like the hunter who learns to think like his or her prey, you will find that the best way to win over the interviewer is to think like the interviewer. In fact, take that idea a little further: You must win, but you don't want the other guys to realize you beat them at their own game. To do that, you must learn how the interviewer has prepared for you; and by going through the same process you will beat out your competitors for the job offer.

The dangerous part of this type of structured interview is called "skills evaluation." The interviewer has analyzed all the different skills it takes to do the job, and all the personality traits that complement those skills. Armed with that data, he or she has developed a series of carefully sequenced questions to draw out your relative merits and weaknesses.

Graphically, it looks like this:

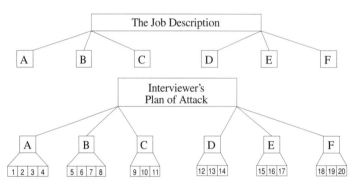

Letters A–F are the separate skills necessary to do the job; numbers 1–20 are questions asked to identify and verify each particular skill. This is where many of the tough questions will arise, and the only way to prepare effectively is to take the interviewer's viewpoint and complete this exercise in its entirety. That effort requires a degree of objectivity, but will generate multiple job offers.

☐ Look at the position you seek. What role does it play in helping the company achieve its corporate mission and make a profit?

☐ What are the five most important duties of that job?

☐ From a management viewpoint, what are the skills and attributes necessary to perform each of these tasks?

Write it all down. Now, put yourself in the interviewer's shoes. What topics would you examine to find out whether a person can really do the job? If for some reason you get stuck in the process, just use your past experience. You have worked with good and bad people, and their work habits and skills will lead you to develop both the potential questions and the correct answers.

Each job skill you identify is fertile ground for the interviewer's questions. Don't forget the intangible skills that are so important to many jobs, like self-confidence and creativity, because the interviewer won't. Develop a number of questions for each job skill you identify.

Again, looking back at coworkers (and still wearing the manager's mask), what are the personal characteristics that would make life more comfortable for you as a manager? Those are also dimensions that are likely to be probed by the interviewer. Once you have identified the questions you would ask in the interviewer's position, the answers should come easily.

That's the way managers are trained to develop structured interview questions— I just gave you the inside track. Complete the exercise by developing the answers you would like to hear as a manager. Take time to complete the exercise conscientiously, writing out both the questions and the appropriate answers.

☐   ☐   ☐

These sharks have some juicy questions to probe your skills, attitude, and personality. Would you like to hear some of them? Notice that these questions tend to lay out a problem for you to solve, but in no way lead you toward the answer. They are often two- and three-part questions as well. The additional question that can be tagged onto them all is, "What did you learn from this experience?" Assume it is included whenever you get one of these questions—you'll be able to sell different aspects of your success profile.

"You have been given a project that requires you to interact with different levels within the company. How do you do this? What levels are you most comfortable with?"

This is a two-part question that probes communication and self-confidence skills. The first part asks how you interact with superiors and motivate those working with and for you on the project. The second part of the question is saying, "Tell me whom you regard as your peer group—help me categorize you." To cover those bases, you will want to include the essence of this: "There are basically two types of people I would interact with on a project of this nature. First, there are those I report to, who bear the ultimate responsibility for its success. With them, I determine deadlines and how they will evaluate the success of the project. I outline my approach, breaking the project down into component parts, getting approval on both the approach and the costs. I would keep my supervisors up-to-date on a regular basis, and seek input whenever needed. My supervisors would expect three things from me: the facts, an analysis of potential problems, and that I not be intimidated, as that would jeopardize the project's success. I would comfortably satisfy those expectations.

"The other people to interact with on a project like this are those who work with and for me. With those people, I would outline the project and explain how a successful outcome will benefit the company. I would assign the component parts to those best suited to each, and arrange follow-up times to assure completion by deadline. My role here would be to facilitate, motivate, and bring the different personalities together to form a team.

"As for comfort level, I find this type of approach enables me to interact comfortably with all levels and types of people."

"Tell me about an event that really challenged you. How did you meet the challenge? In what way was your approach different from others'?"

This is a straightforward two-part question. The first probes your problem-solving abilities. The second asks you to set yourself apart from the herd. First of all, outline the problem. The blacker you make the situation, the better. Having done that, go ahead and explain your solution, its value to your employer, and how it was different from other approaches.

"My company has offices all around the country; I am responsible for seventy of them. My job is to visit each office on a regular basis and build market-penetration strategies with management, and to train and motivate the sales and customer-service force. When the recession hit, the need to service those offices was more important than ever, yet the traveling costs were getting prohibitive.

"Morale was an especially important factor; you can't let outlying offices feel defeated. I reapportioned my budget and did the following: I dramatically increased telephone contact with the offices. I instituted a monthly sales-technique letter—how to prospect for new clients, how to negotiate difficult sales, and so forth. I bought and rented sales training and motivational tapes and sent them to my managers with instructions on how to use them in a sales meeting. I stopped visiting all the offices. Instead, I scheduled weekend training meetings in central locations throughout my area: one day of sales training and one day of management training, concentrating on how to run sales meetings, early termination of low producers, and so forth.

"While my colleagues complained about the drop in sales, mine increased, albeit by a modest 6 percent. After two quarters, my approach was officially adopted by the company."

"Give me an example of a method of working you have used. How did you feel about it?"

You have a choice of giving an example of either good or bad work habits. Give a good example, one that demonstrates your understanding of corporate goals, your organizational skills, analytical ability, or time management skills.

You could say: "I believe in giving an honest day's work for a day's pay. That requires organization and time management. I do my paperwork at the end of each day, when I review the day's achievements; with this done, I plan for tomorrow. When I come to work in the morning, I'm ready to get going without wasting time. I try to schedule meetings right before lunch; people get to the point more quickly if it's on their time. I feel that is an efficient and organized method of working."

"When you joined your last company and met the group for the first time, how did you feel? How did you get on with them?"

Your answer should include: "I naturally felt a little nervous, but I was excited about the new job. I shared that excitement with my new friends, and told them that I was enthusiastic about learning new skills from them. I was open and friendly, and when given the opportunity to help someone myself, I jumped at it."

"In your last job, how did you plan to interview?"

That's an easy one. Just give a description of how the skilled interviewer prepares.

"How have you benefited from your disappointments?"

Disappointments are different from failures. It is an intelligent—probably trained—interviewer who asks this one; it is also an opportunity for the astute interviewee to shine. The question itself is very positive—it asks you to show how you benefited. Note also that it doesn't ask you to give specific details of specific disappointments, so you don't have to open your mouth and insert your foot. Instead, be general. Edison once explained his success as an inventor by claiming that he knew more ways not to do something than anyone else living; you can do worse than quote him. In any event, sum up your answer with, "I treat disappointments as a learning experience; I look at what happened, why it happened, and how I would do things differently in each stage should the same set of circumstances appear again. That way, I put disappointment behind me and am ready with renewed vigor and understanding to face the new day's problems."

A side note. A person with strong religious beliefs may be tempted to answer a question like this in terms of religious values. If you benefit from disappointments in a spiritual way, remember that not everyone feels the same as you do. More important, the interviewer is, by law, prohibited from talking about religion with you, so you can unwittingly put the interviewer in an awkward position of not knowing how to respond. And making an interviewer feel awkward in any way is not the way to win the job offer.

"What would you do when you have a decision to make and no procedure exists?"

This question probes your analytical skills, integrity, and dedication. Most of all, the interviewer is testing your manageability and adherence to procedures—the "company way of doing things." You need to cover that with: "I would act without my manager's direction only if the situation were urgent and my manager were not available. Then, I would take command of the situation, make a decision based on the facts, and implement it. I would update my boss at the earliest opportunity." If possible, tell a story to illustrate.

"That is an excellent answer. Now to give me a balanced view, can you give me an example that didn't work out so well?"

There are two techniques that every skilled interviewer will use, especially if you are giving good answers. In this question, the interviewer looks for negative balance; in the follow-up, the person will look for negative confirmation. Here, you are required to give an example of an inadequacy. The trick is to pull something from the past, not the present, and to finish with what you learned from the experience. For example: "That's easy. When I first joined the work force, I didn't really understand the importance of systems and procedures. There was one time when I was too anxious to contribute and didn't have the full picture. There was a sales visit report everyone had to fill out after visiting a customer. I always put a lot of effort into it until I realized it was never read; it just went in the files. So I stopped doing it for a few days to see if it made any difference. I thought I was gaining time to make more sales for the company. I was so proud of my extra sales calls I told the boss at the end of the week. My boss explained that the records were for the long term, so that should my job change, the next salesperson would have the benefit of a full client history. It was a long time ago, but I have never forgotten the lesson: There's always a reason for systems and procedures. I've had the best-kept records in the company ever since."

To look for negative confirmation, the interviewer then may say something like, "Thank you. Now can you give me another example?" He or she is trying to confirm a weakness. If you help, you could well do yourself out of a job. Here's your reaction: You sit deep in thought for a good ten seconds, then look up and say firmly, "No, that's the only occasion when anything like that happened." Shut up and refuse to be enticed further.

The Unconscious Incompetent

Now you should be ready for almost anything a professional interviewer could throw at you. Your foresight and strategic planning will generate multiple offers of employment for you in all circumstances except one, and that's when you face the unconsciously incompetent interviewer. He or she is probably more dangerous to your job-offer status than everything else combined.

The problem is embodied in the experienced manager who is a poor interviewer, but who does not know it. He or she, consciously or otherwise, bases hiring decisions on "experience" and "knowledge of mankind" and "gut feeling." In any event, he or she is an unconscious incompetent. You have probably been interviewed by one in your time. Remember leaving an interview and, upon reflection, feeling the interviewer knew absolutely nothing about you or your skills? If so, you know how frustrating that can be. Here, you'll see how to turn that difficult situation to your advantage. In the future, good managers who are poor interviewers will be offering jobs with far greater frequency than ever before. Understand that a poor interviewer can be a wonderful manager; interviewing skills are learned, not inherited or created as a result of a mystical corporate blessing.

The unconscious incompetents abound. Their heinous crime can only be exceeded by your inability to recognize and take advantage of the proffered opportunity.

As in handling the skilled interviewer, it is necessary to imagine how the unconscious incompetent thinks and feels. There are many manifestations of the poor interviewer. Each of the next examples is followed by instructions for appropriate handling of the unique problems posed for you.

☐ **Example One:** The interviewer's desk is cluttered, and the resume or application that was handed to him or her a few minutes before cannot be found.

Response: Sit quietly through the bumbling and searching. Check out the surroundings. Breathe deeply and slowly to calm any natural interview nerves. As you bring your adrenaline under control, you bring a certain calming effect to the interviewer and the interview. (This example, by the way, is usually the most common sign of the unconscious incompetent.)

☐ **Example Two:** The interviewer experiences constant interruptions from the telephone or people walking into the office.

Response: This provides good opportunities for selling yourself. Make note on your pad of where you were in the conversation and refresh the interviewer on the point when you start talking again. He or she will be impressed with your level head and good memory. The interruptions also give time, perhaps, to find something of common interest in the office, something you can compliment. You will also have time to compose the suitable value key follow-up to the point made in the conversation prior to the interruption.

☐ **Example Three:** The interviewer starts with an explanation of why you are both sitting there, and then allows the conversation to degenerate into a lengthy diatribe about the company.

Response: Show interest in the company and the conversation. Sit straight, look attentive (the other applicants probably fall asleep), make appreciative murmurs, and nod at the appropriate times until there is a pause. When that occurs, comment that you appreciate the background on the company, because you can now see more clearly how the job fits into the general scheme of things and that you see, for example, how valuable communication skills would be for the job. Could the interviewer please tell you some of the other job requirements? Then, as the job's functions are described, you can interject appropriate information about your background with: "Would it be of value, Mr. Smith, if I described my experience with . . . ?"

☐ **Example Four:** The interviewer begins with, or quickly breaks into, the drawbacks of the job. The job may even be described in totally negative terms. That is often done without giving a balanced view of the duties and expectations of the position.

Response: An initial negative description often means that the interviewer has had bad experiences hiring for the position. Your course is to empathize (not sympathize) with his or her bad experiences, and make it known that you recognize the importance of (for example) reliability, especially in this particular type of job. (You will invariably find in these instances that what your interviewer has lacked in the past is someone with a serious understanding of value keys.) Illustrate your proficiency in that particular aspect of your profession with a short example from your work history. Finish your statements by asking the interviewer what some of the biggest problems to be handled in the job are. The questions demonstrate your understanding, and the interviewer's answers outline the areas from your background and skills to which you should draw attention.

☐ **Example Five:** The interviewer spends considerable time early in the interview describing "the type of people we are here at XYZ Corporation."

Response: Very simple. You have always wanted to work for a company with that atmosphere. It creates the type of work environment that is conducive to a person really giving his or her best efforts.

☐ **Example Six:** The interviewer asks closed-ended questions, ones that demand no more than a yes/no answer (e.g., "Do you pay attention to detail?"). Such questions are hardly adequate to establish your skills, yet you must handle them effectively to secure the job offer.

Response: A yes/no answer to a closed-ended question will not get you that offer. The trick is to treat each closed-ended question as if the interviewer has added, "Please give me a brief yet thorough answer." Closed-ended questions also are often mingled with statements followed by pauses. In those instances, agree with the statement in a way that demonstrates both a grasp of your job and the interviewer's statement. For example: "That's an excellent point, Mr. Smith. I couldn't agree more that the attention to detail you describe naturally affects cost containment. My track record in this area is . . . ."

☐ **Example Seven:** The interviewer asks a continuing stream of negative questions (as described in chapter 17, "The Stress Interview").

Response: Use the techniques and answers described earlier. Give your answers with a smile and do not take the questions as personal insults; they are not intended that way. The more stressful the situations the job is likely to place you in, the greater the likelihood of your having to field negative questions. The interviewer wants to know if you can take the heat.

☐ **Example Eight:** The interviewer has difficulty looking at you while speaking.
Response: The interviewer is someone who finds it uncomfortable being in the spotlight. Try to help him or her to be a good audience. Ask specific questions about the job responsibilities and offer your skills in turn.

☐   ☐   ☐

Often a hiring manager will arrange for you to meet with two or three other people. Frequently, the other interviewers have been neither trained in appropriate interviewing skills nor told the details of the job for which you are interviewing. So you will take additional copies of your Executive Briefing with you to the interview to aid them in focusing on the appropriate job functions.

When you understand how to recognize and respond to these different types of interviewers, you will leave your interview having made a favorable first impression. No one forgets first impressions.

17 | The Stress Interview

Your worst nightmare can come true at a stress interview, but once you learn that these questions are just amplified versions of much simpler ones, you'll remain cool and calm. Also: a vital discussion on handling illegal interview questions.

For all intents and purposes, every interview is a stress interview; the interviewer's negative and trick questions can act as the catalyst for your own fear. And the only way to combat that fear is to be prepared, to know what the interviewer is trying to do, and to anticipate the various directions he or she will take. Whenever you are ill-prepared for an interview, no one will be able to put more pressure on you than you do on yourself. Remember: A stress interview is just a regular interview with the volume turned all the way up—the music is the same, just louder. Only preparedness will keep you cool and collected.

You've heard the horror stories. An interviewer demands of a hapless applicant, "Sell me this pen," or asks, "How would you improve the design of a teddy bear?" Or the candidate is faced with a battery of interviewers, all demanding rapid-fire answers to questions like, "You're giving a dinner party. Which ten famous people would you invite and why?" When the interviewee offers evidence of foot-in-mouth disease by asking, "Living or dead?" he receives his just desserts in reply: "Ten of each."

Such awful-sounding questions are thrown in to test your poise, to see how you react under pressure, and to plumb the depths of your confidence. Many people ruin their chances by reacting to them as personal insults rather than the challenges and opportunities to shine that they really are.

Previously restricted to the executive suite for the selection of high-powered executives, stress interviews are now widespread throughout the professional world. And they can come complete with all the intimidating and treacherous tricks your worst nightmare can devise. Yet a good performance at a stress interview can mean the difference between a job in the fast lane and a stalled career. The interviewers in a stress interview are invariably experienced and well organized, and have developed tightly structured procedures and advanced interviewing techniques. The questions and tension they generate have the cumulative effect of throwing you off balance and revealing the "real" you—rather than someone who can respond with last night's rehearsed answers to six or seven stock questions.

Stress questions can be turned to your advantage or merely avoided with nifty footwork. Whichever approach you choose, you will be among a select few who understand this line of questioning. As always, when addressing the questions in this chapter, remember to develop personalized answers that reflect your experience and profession. Practice your responses aloud—by doing that, your responses to these interview gambits will become more natural, and will help you feel more confident during an interview. You might even consider making a tape of tough questions, spacing them at intervals of thirty seconds to two minutes. You can then play the tape back and answer the questions in real time.

As we will see in this chapter, reflexive questions can prove especially useful when the heat is on. Stress questions are designed to sort out the clutch players from those who freeze under pressure. Used with discretion, the reflexives (" . . . don't you think?") will demonstrate to the interviewer that you are able to function well under pressure. At the same time, of course, you put the ball back in the interviewer's court.

One common stress interview technique is to set you up for a fall: a pleasant conversation, one or a series of seemingly innocuous questions to relax your guard, then a dazzling series of jabs and body blows that leave you gibbering. For instance, an interviewer might lull you into a false sense of security by asking some relatively stress-free questions: "What was your initial starting salary at your last job?" then, "What is your salary now?" then, "Do you receive bonuses?" etc. To put you on the ropes, he or she might then completely surprise you with, "Tell me what sort of troubles you have living within your means," or "Why aren't you earning more at your age?" Such interviewers are using stress in an intelligent fashion, to simulate the unexpected and sometimes tense events of everyday business life. Seeing how you handle simulated pressure gives a fair indication of how you will react to the real thing.

The sophisticated interviewer talks very little, perhaps only 20 percent of the time, and that time is spent asking questions. Few comments, and no editorializing on your answers, means that you get no hint, verbal or otherwise, about your performance.

The questions are planned, targeted, sequenced, and layered. The interviewer covers one subject thoroughly before moving on. Let's take the simple example of "Can you work under pressure?" As a reader of *Knock 'em Dead,* you will know to answer that question with an example, and thereby deflect the main thrust of the stress technique. The interviewer will be prepared for a simple yes/no answer; what follows will keep the unprepared applicant reeling.

☐ *"Can you work under pressure?"* A simple, closed-ended question that requires just a yes/no answer, but you won't get off so easy.

☐ *"Good, I'd be interested to hear about a time when you experienced pressure on your job."* An open-ended request to tell a story about a pressure situation. After this, you will be subjected to the layering technique—six layers in the following instance. Imagine how tangled you could get without preparation.

☐ *"Why do you think this situation arose?"* It's best if the situation you describe is not a peer's or manager's fault.

☐ *"When exactly did it happen?"* Watch out! Your story of saving thousands from the burning skyscraper may well be checked with your references.

☐ *"What in hindsight were you most dissatisfied with about your performance?"* Here we go. You're trying to show how well you perform under pressure, then suddenly you're telling tales against yourself.

☐ *"How do you feel others involved could have acted more responsibly?"* An open invitation to criticize peers and superiors, which you should diplomatically decline.

☐ *"Who holds the responsibility for the situation?"* Another invitation to point the finger of blame.

☐ *"Where in the chain of command could steps be taken to avoid that sort of thing happening again?"* This question probes your analytical skills and whether you are the type of person who always goes back to the scene of the crime to learn for the next time.

You have just been through an old reporter's technique of asking why, when, who, what, how, and where. The technique can be applied to any question you are asked and is frequently used to probe those success stories that sound just too good to be true. You'll find them suddenly tagged on to the simple closed-ended questions, as well as to the open-ended ones. Typically, they'll start with something like: "Share with me," "Tell me about a time when," or, "I'm interested in finding out about," and then request specific examples from your work history.

After you've survived that barrage, a friendly tone may conceal another zinger: "What did you learn from the experience?" This question is geared to probing your judgment and emotional maturity. Your answer should emphasize whichever of the key personality traits your story was illustrating.

When an interviewer feels you were on the edge of revealing something unusual in an answer, you may well encounter "mirror statements." Here, the last key phrase of your answer will be repeated or paraphrased, and followed by a steady gaze and silence. For example, "So, you learned that organization is the key to management." The idea is that the quiet and an expectant look will work together to keep you talking. It can be disconcerting to find yourself rambling on without quite knowing why. The trick is knowing when to stop. When the interviewer gives you an expectant look in this context, expand your answer (you have to), but by no more than a couple of sentences. Otherwise, you will get that creepy feeling that you're digging yourself into a hole.

There will be times when you face more than one interviewer at a time. When that happens, remember the story of a female attorney who had five law partners all asking questions at the same time. As the poor interviewee got halfway through one answer, another question would be shot at her. Pausing for breath, she smiled and said, "Hold your horses, ladies and gentlemen. These are all excellent questions, and given time, I'll answer them all. Now who's next?" In so doing, she showed the interviewers exactly what they wanted to see and what, incidentally, is behind every stress interview and every negatively phrased question—finding the presence of poise and calm under fire, combined with a refusal to be intimidated.

You never know when a stress interview will raise its ugly head. Often it can be that rubber-stamp meeting with the senior vice president at the end of a series of grueling meetings. That is not surprising. While other interviewers are concerned with determining whether you are able, willing, and a good fit for the job in question, the senior executive who eventually throws you for a loop may be probing you for potential promotability.

The most intimidating stress interviews are recognizable before the interviewer speaks: no eye contact, no greeting, either silence or a noncommittal grunt, and no small talk. You may also recognize such an interviewer by his general air of boredom, lack of interest, or thinly veiled aggression. The first words you hear could well be, "O.K., so go ahead. I don't have all day." In these situations, forewarned is forearmed, so here are some of the questions you can expect to follow such openings.

"What is your greatest weakness?"

This is a direct invitation to put your head in a noose. Decline the invitation.

If there is a minor part of the job at hand where you lack knowledge—but knowledge you will obviously pick up quickly—use that. For instance: "I haven't worked with this type of spreadsheet program before, but given my experience with six other types, I don't think it should take me more than a couple of days to pick it up." Here you remove the emphasis from weakness and put it onto a developmental problem that is easily overcome. Be careful, however; this very effective ploy must be used with discretion.

Another good option is to give a generalized answer that takes advantage of value keys. Design the answer so that your weakness is ultimately a positive characteristic. For example: "I enjoy my work and always give each project my best shot. So when sometimes I don't feel others are pulling their weight, I find it a little frustrating. I am aware of that weakness, and in those situations I try to overcome it with a positive attitude that I hope will catch on."

Also consider the technique of putting a problem in the past. Here you take a weakness from way back when, and show how you overcame it. It answers the question but ends on a positive note. An illustration: "When I first got into this field, I always had problems with my paperwork—you know, leaving an adequate paper trail. And to be honest, I let it slip once or twice. My manager sat me down and explained the potential troubles such behavior could cause. I really took it to heart, and I think you will find my paper trails some of the best around today. You only have to tell me something once." With that kind of answer, you also get the added bonus of showing that you accept and act on criticism.

Congratulations! You have just turned a bear of a question into an opportunity to sell yourself. In deciding on the particular answer you will give, remember that the interviewer isn't really concerned about your general weaknesses—no one is a saint outside of the interview room. He or she is simply concerned about any red flags that might signal your inability to perform the job or work well under supervision.

"With hindsight, how could you have improved your progress?"
Here's a question that demands, "Tell me your mistakes and weaknesses." If you can mention ways of improving your performance without damaging your candidacy, do so. The end of your answer should contain something like: "Other than that, I don't know what to add. I have always given it my best shot." Then shut up.

"What kinds of decisions are most difficult for you?"
You are human, admit it, but be careful what you admit. If you have ever had to fire someone, you are in luck, because no one likes to do that. Emphasize that, having reached a logical conclusion, you act. If you are not in management, tie your answer to key profiles: "It's not that I have difficulty making decisions—some just require more consideration than others. A small example might be vacation time. Now, everyone is entitled to it, but I don't believe you should leave your boss in a bind at short notice. I think very carefully at the beginning of the year when I'd like to take my vacation, and then think of alternate dates. I go to my supervisor, tell him what I hope to do, and see whether there is any conflict. I wouldn't want to be out of the office for the two weeks prior to a project deadline, for instance. So by carefully considering things far enough in advance, I don't

procrastinate, and I make sure my plans jibe with my boss and the department for the year."

Here you take a trick question and use it to demonstrate your consideration, analytical abilities, and concern for the department—and for the company's bottom line.

"Tell me about the problems you have living within your means."

This is a twister to catch you off-guard. Your best defense is first of all to know that it exists, and second to give it short shrift. "I know few people who are satisfied with their current earnings. As a professional, I am continually striving to improve my skills and to improve my living standard. But my problems are no different from that of this company or any other—making sure all the bills get paid on time and recognizing that every month and year there are some things that are prudent to do and other expenses that are best deferred."

"What area of your skills/professional development do you want to improve at this time?"

Another tell-me-all-your-weaknesses question. You should try to avoid damaging your candidacy by tossing around careless admissions. One effective answer to this is to say, "Well, from what you told me about the job, I seem to have all the necessary skills and background. What I would really find exciting is the opportunity to work on a job where . . ." At this point, you replay the interviewer's hot buttons about the job. You emphasize that you really have all the job-related skills and also tell the interviewer what you find exciting about the job. It works admirably.

Another safe response is to reiterate one or two areas that combine personal strengths and the job's most crucial responsibilities, and finish with saying, "These areas are so important that I don't think anyone can be too good or should ever stop trying to polish their skills."

"Your application shows you have been with one company a long time without any appreciable increase in rank or salary. Tell me about this."

Ugh. A toughie. To start with, you should analyze why this state of affairs does exist (assuming the interviewer's assessment is accurate). Then, when you have determined the cause, practice saying it out loud to yourself as you would say it during an actual interview. It may take a few tries. Chances are that no matter how valid your explanation really is, it will come off sounding a little tinny or vindictive without some polishing. Avoid the sour-grapes syndrome at all costs.

Here are some tactics you can use. First of all, try to avoid putting your salary history on application forms. No one is going to deny you an interview for lack of a salary history if your skills match those the job requires. Of course, you should never put such trivia on your resume.

If the interviewer is intent, and asks you outright for this information, you'll find a great response in the section on salary histories in chapter 23.

Now then. Next, we'll address the delicate matter of "hey-wait-a-minute-why-no-promotions?" This is one case where saying the wrong thing can get you in just as much trouble as failing to say the right thing. The interviewer has posed a truly negative inquiry; the more time either of you spend on it, the more time the interviewer gets to devote to concentrating on negative aspects of your candidacy. Make your answer short and sweet, then shut up. For instance, "My current employer is a stable company with a good working environment, but there's minimal growth there in my area—in fact, there hasn't been any promotion in my area since _____. Your question is the reason I am meeting here with you; I have the skills and ability to take on more responsibility and I'm looking for a place to do that."

"Are you willing to take calculated risks when necessary?"

First, qualify the question: "How do you define calculated risks? What sort of risks? Give me an example of a risk you have in mind; what are the stakes involved?" That will show you exactly the right analytical approach to evaluating a calculated risk, and while the interviewer is rattling on, you have bought time to come up with an answer. Whatever your answer, you will include, "Naturally, I would never take any risk that would in any way jeopardize the safety or reputation of my company or colleagues. In fact, I don't think any employer would appreciate an employee at any level taking risks of any nature without first having a thorough briefing and chance to give input."

"See this pen I'm holding? Sell it to me."

Not a request, as you might think, that would be asked only of a salesperson. In today's business world, everyone is required to sell—sometimes products, but more often ideas, approaches, and concepts. As such, you are being tested to see whether you understand the basic concepts of features-and-benefits selling, how quickly you think on your feet, and how effective your verbal communication is. For example, the interviewer holds up a broad-tip yellow highlighter. You say calmly, "Let me tell you about the special features of this product. First of all, it's a highlighter that will emphasize important points in reports or articles, and that will save you time in recalling the important features. The casing is wide enough to enable you to use it comfortably at your desk or on a flip chart. It has a flat base you can stand it up on. At one dollar, it is disposable—and affordable enough for you to have a handful for your desk, briefcase, car, and at home. And the bright yellow color means you'll never lose it."

Then close with a smile and a question of your own that will bring a smile to your interviewer's face: "How many gross shall we deliver?"

"How will you be able to cope with a change in environment after [e.g.] five years with your current company?"

Another chance to take an implied negative and turn it into a positive. "That's one of the reasons I want to make a change. After five years with my current employer, I felt I was about to get stale. Everyone needs a change of scene once in a while. It's just time for me to make some new friends, face some new challenges, and experience some new approaches; hopefully, I'll have the chance to contribute from my experience."

"Why aren't you earning more at your age?"

Accept this as a compliment to your skills and accomplishments. "I have always felt that solid experience would stand me in good stead in the long run and that earnings would come in due course. Also, I am not the type of person to change jobs just for the money. At this point, I have a solid background that is worth something to a company." Now, to avoid the interviewer putting you on the spot again, finish with a question: "How much should I be earning now?" The figure could be your offer.

"What is the worst thing you have heard about our company?"

This question can come as something of a shock. As with all stress questions, your poise under stress is vital: If you can carry off a halfway decent answer as well, you are a winner. The best response to this question is simple. Just say with a smile: "You're a tough company to get into because your interviews and interviewers are so rigorous." It's true, it's flattering, and it shows that you are not intimidated.

"How would you define your profession?"

With questions that solicit your understanding of a topic, no matter how good your answer, you can expect to be interrupted in mid-reply with "That has nothing to do with it," or "Whoever put that idea into your head?" While your response is a judgment call, 999 times out of a thousand these comments are not meant to be taken as serious criticisms. Rather, they are tests to see how well you would be able to defend your position in a no-holds-barred conversation with the chairman of the board, who says exactly what he or she thinks at all times. So go ahead and defend yourself, without taking or showing offense.

Your first response will be to gain time and get the interviewer talking. "Why do you say that?" you ask, answering a question with a question. And turning the tables on your aggressor displays your poise, calm, and analytical skills better than any other response.

"Why should I hire an outsider when I could fill the job with someone inside the company?"

The question isn't as stupid as it sounds. Obviously, the interviewer has examined existing employees with an eye toward their promotion or reassignment. Just as obviously, the job cannot be filled from within the company. If it could be, it would be, and for two very good reasons: It is cheaper for the company to promote from within, and it is good for employee morale.

Hiding behind this intimidating question is actually a pleasant invitation: "Tell me why I should hire you." Your answer should include two steps. The first is a simple recitation of your skills and personality profile strengths, tailored to the specific requirements of the job.

For the second step, realize first that whenever a manager is filling a position, he or she is looking not only for someone who can do the job but also for someone who can benefit the department in a larger sense. No department is as good as it could be—each has weaknesses that need strengthening. So in the second part of your answer, include a question of your own: "Those are my general attributes. However, if no one is promotable from inside the company, that means you are looking to add strength to your team in a special way. In what ways do you hope the final candidate will be able to benefit your department?" The answer to this is your cue to sell your applicable qualities.

"Have you ever had any financial difficulties?"

The potential employer wants to know whether you can control not only your own finances but also finances in general. If you are in the insurance field, for example—in claims, accounting, supervision, or management—you can expect to hear this one. The question, though, is not restricted to insurance: Anyone, especially a person who handles money in day-to-day business, is fair game.

Remember that for someone to check your credit history, he or she must have your written consent. That is required under the 1972 Fair Credit and Reporting Act. Invariably, when you fill out a job application form, sign it, and date it, you've also signed a release permitting the employer to check your credit history. If you have already filled out the form, you might not hear this specific question during your interview, but your creditors might. I should note here that the reader who asked me about this question also described how she'd handled it during the interview: by describing her past problems with bankruptcy in every detail. However, in trying to be open and honest, she had actually done herself a disservice.

The interviewer does not want to hear sob stories. If your credit history is spotty, concentrate on the information that will damage your candidacy least and enhance it most. You might find it appropriate to bring the matter up yourself if you work in an area where your credit history is likely to be checked. If you choose to wait until the interviewer brings it up, you might say (if you had to file for bankruptcy, for instance), "I should tell you that some years ago, for reasons beyond my control, I was forced into personal bankruptcy. That has been behind me for some time. Today, I have a sound credit rating and no debts. Bankruptcy is not something I'm proud of, but I did learn from the experience, and I feel it has made me a more proficient account supervisor." The answer concentrates on today, not past history.

"How do you handle rejection?"

This question is common if you are applying for a job in sales, including face-to-face sales, telemarketing, public relations, and customer service. If you are after a job in one of these areas and you really don't like the heavy doses of rejection that are any salesperson's lot, consider a new field. The anguish you will experience will not lead to a successful career or a happy life.

With that in mind, let's look behind the question. The interviewer simply wants to know whether you take rejection as rejection of yourself or whether you simply accept it as a temporary rejection of a service or product. Here is a sample answer that you can tailor to your particular needs and background: "I accept rejection as an integral part of the sales process. If everyone said 'yes' to a product, there would be no need for the sales function. As it is, I see every rejection as bringing me closer to the customer who will say 'yes.' " Then, if you are encouraged to go on: "I regard rejection as simply a fact of life, that the customer has no need for the product today. I can go on to my next call with the conviction that I am a little closer to my next sale."

"Why were you out of work for so long?"

You must have a sound explanation for any and all gaps in your employment history. If not, you are unlikely to receive a job offer. Emphasize that you were not just looking for another paycheck—you were looking for a company with which to settle and to which to make a long-term contribution.

"I made a decision that I enjoy my work too much just to accept another paycheck. So I determined that the next job I took would be one where I could settle down and do my best to make a solid contribution. From everything I have heard about this company, you are a group that expects people to pull their weight, because you've got a real job to do. I like that, and I would like to be part of the team. What do I have to do to get the job?"

You answer the question, compliment the interviewer, and shift the emphasis from your being unemployed to how you can get the job offer.

"Why have you changed jobs so frequently?"

If you have jumped around, blame it on youth (even the interviewer was young once). Now you realize what a mistake your job-hopping was, and with your added domestic responsibilities, you are now much more settled. Or you may wish to impress on the interviewer that your job-hopping was never as a result of poor performance, and that you grew professionally as a result of each job change.

You could reply: "My first job had a long commute. I soon realized that, but I knew it would give me good experience in a very competitive field. Subsequently, I found a job much closer to home where the commute was only a half hour each way. I was very happy at my second job. However, I got an opportunity to really broaden my experience base with a new company that was just starting up. With the wisdom of hindsight, I realize that move was a mistake; it took me six months to realize I couldn't make a contribution there. I've been with my current company a reasonable length of time. So I have broad experience in different environments. I didn't just job-hop; I have been following a path to gain broad experience. So you see, I have more experience than the average person of my years, and a desire to settle down and make it pay off for me and my employer."

Or you can say: "Now I want to settle down and make my diverse background pay off in my contributions to my new employer. I have a strong desire to contribute and am looking for an employer that will keep me challenged; I think this might be the company to do that. Am I right?"

"Tell me about a time when you put your foot in your mouth."

Answer this question with caution. The interviewer is examining your ability and willingness to interact pleasantly with others. The question is tricky because it asks you to show yourself in a poor light. Your answer should downplay the negative impact of your action and end with positive information about your candidacy. The best thing to do is to start with an example outside of the workplace and show how the experience improved your performance at work.

"About five years ago, I let the cat out of the bag about a surprise birthday party for a friend, a terrific *faux pas*. It was a mortifying experience, and I promised myself not to let anything like that happen again." Then, after this fairly innocuous statement, you can talk about communications in the workplace. "As far as work is concerned, I always regard employer/employee communications on any matter as confidential unless expressly stated otherwise. So, putting my foot in my mouth doesn't happen to me at work."

"Why do you want to leave your current job?" or *"Why did you leave your last job?"*

This is a common trick question. You should have an acceptable reason for leaving every job you have held, but if you don't, pick one of the six acceptable reasons from the employment industry formula, the acronym for which is CLAMPS:

- Challenge: You weren't able to grow professionally in that position.
- Location: The commute was unreasonably long.
- Advancement: There was nowhere for you to go. You had the talent, but there were too many people ahead of you.
- Money: You were underpaid for your skills and contribution.
- Pride or prestige: You wanted to be with a better company.
- Security: The company was not stable.

For example: "My last company was a family-owned affair. I had gone as far as I was able. It just seemed time for me to join a more prestigious company and accept greater challenges."

"What interests you least about this job?"

This question is potentially explosive, but easily defused. Regardless of your occupation, there is at least one repetitive, mindless duty that everyone groans about and that goes with the territory. Use that as your example in a statement of this nature: "Filing is probably the least demanding part of the job. However, it is important to the overall success of my department, so I try to do it with a smile." This shows that you understand that it is necessary to take the rough with the smooth in any job.

"What was there about your last company that you didn't particularly like or agree with?"

You are being checked out as a potential fly in the ointment. If you have to answer, it might be about the way the company policies and/or directives were sometimes consciously misunderstood by some employees who disregarded the bottom line—the profitability of the corporation.

Or: "You know how it is sometimes with a big company. People lose awareness of the cost of things. There never seemed to be much concern about economy or efficiency. Everyone wanted his or her year-end bonus, but only worried about it in

December. The rest of the year, nobody gave a hoot. I think that's the kind of thing we could be aware of almost every day, don't you agree?"

Or: "I didn't like the way some people gave lip service to 'the customer comes first,' but really didn't go out of their way to keep the customer satisfied. I don't think it was a fault of management, just a general malaise that seemed to affect a lot of people."

"What do you feel is a satisfactory attendance record?"

There are two answers to this question—one if you are in management, one if you are not. As a manager: "I believe attendance is a matter of management, motivation, and psychology. Letting the employees know you expect their best efforts and won't accept half-baked excuses is one thing. The other is to keep your employees motivated by a congenial work environment and the challenge to stretch themselves. Giving people pride in their work and letting them know you respect them as individuals have a lot to do with it, too."

If you are not in management, the answer is even easier: "I've never really considered it. I work for a living, I enjoy my job, and I'm rarely sick."

"What is your general impression of your last company?"

Always answer positively. Keep your real feelings to yourself, whatever they might be. There is a strong belief among the management fraternity that people who complain about past employers will cause problems for their new ones. Your answer is, "Very good" or "Excellent." Then smile and wait for the next question.

"What are some of the problems you encounter in doing your job, and what do you do about them?"

Note well the old saying, "A poor workman blames his tools." Your awareness that careless mistakes cost the company good money means you are always on the lookout for potential problems. Give an example of a problem you recognized and solved.

For example: "My job is fairly repetitive, so it's easy to overlook problems. Lots of people do. However, I always look for them; it helps keep me alert and motivated, so I do a better job. To give you an example, we make computer-memory disks. Each one has to be machined by hand, and once completed, the slightest abrasion will turn one into a reject. I have a steady staff and little turnover, and everyone wears cotton gloves to handle the disks. Yet about six months ago, the reject rate suddenly went through the roof. Is that the kind of problem you mean? Well, the cause was one that could have gone unnoticed for ages. Jill, the section head who inspects all the disks, had lost a lot of weight, her diamond engagement ring was slipping around her finger, and it was scratching the disks as she passed them and stacked them to be shipped. Our main client was giving us a big problem over it, so my looking for problems and paying attention to detail really paid off."

The interviewer was trying to get you to reveal weak points; you avoided the trap.

"What are some of the things you find difficult to do? Why do you feel that way?"

This is a variation on a couple of earlier questions. Remember, anything that goes against the best interests of your employer is difficult to do. If you are pressed for a job function you find difficult, answer in the past tense; that way, you show that you recognize the difficulty, but that you obviously handle it well.

"That's a tough question. There are so many things that are difficult to learn in our business if you want to do the job right. I used to have forty clients to sell to every month, and I was so busy touching bases with all of them, I never got a chance to sell to any of them. So I graded them into three groups. I called on the top 20 percent with whom I did business every three weeks. The next group were those I sold to occasionally. I called on them once a month, but with a difference—each month, I marked ten of them to spend time with and really get to know. I still have difficulty reaching all forty of my clients in a month, but my sales have tripled and are still climbing."

"Jobs have pluses and minuses. What were some of the minuses on your last job?"

A variation on the question, "What interests you least about this job?" which was handled earlier. Use the same type of answer. For example, "Like any salesperson, I enjoy selling, not doing the paperwork. But as I cannot expect the customer to get the goods, and me my commission, without following through on this task, I grin and bear it. Besides, if I don't do the paperwork, that holds up other people in the company."

If you are not in sales, use the sales force as a scapegoat. "In accounts receivable, it's my job to get the money in to make payroll and good things like that. Half the time, the goods get shipped before I get the paperwork because sales says, 'It's a rush order.' That's a real minus to me. It was so bad at my last company, we tried a new approach. We met with sales and explained our problem. The result was that incremental commissions were based on cash in, not on bill date. They saw the connection, and things are much better now."

"What kinds of people do you like to work with?"

This is the easy part of a tricky three-part question. Obviously, you like to work with people who have pride, honesty, integrity, and dedication to their work. Now—

"What kinds of people do you find it difficult to work with?"

The second part of the same question. You could say: "People who don't follow procedures, or slackers—the occasional rotten apples who don't really care about the quality of their work. They're long on complaints, but short on solutions." Which brings us to the third part of the question:

"How have you successfully worked with this difficult type of person?"

This is the most difficult part to answer. You might reply: "I stick to my guns, keep enthusiastic, and hope some of it will rub off. I had a big problem with one guy—all he did was complain and always in my area. Eventually, I told him how I felt. I said if I were a millionaire, I'd have all the answers and wouldn't have to work, but as it was, I wasn't, and had to work for a living. I told him that I really enjoyed his company, but I didn't want to hear it any more. Every time I saw him after that, I presented him with a work problem and asked his advice. In other words I challenged him to come up with positives, not negatives."

You can go on that sometimes you've noticed that such people simply lack enthusiasm and confidence, and that energetic and cheerful coworkers can often change that. If the interviewer follows up with an inquiry about what you would do if no amount of good effort on your part solved the problem, respond, "I would maintain cordial relations, but not go out of my way to seek more than a business-like acquaintance. Life is too short to be demotivated by people who always think their cup is half empty."

"How did you get your last job?"

The interviewer is looking for initiative. If you can, show it. At the least, show determination.

"I was actually turned down for my last job for having too little experience. I asked the manager to give me a trial before she offered it to anyone else. I went in and asked for a list of companies they'd never sold to, picked up the phone, and in that hour I arranged two appointments. How did I get the job? In a word, determination!"

"How would you evaluate me as an interviewer?"

The question is dangerous, maybe more so than the one asking you to criticize your boss. Whatever you do, of course, don't tell the truth if you think the interviewer is an incompetent. It may be true, but it won't get you a job offer. This is an instance where honesty is not the best policy. It is best to say, "This is one of the toughest interviews I have ever been through, and I don't relish the prospect of going through another. Yet I do realize what you are trying to achieve." Then go on to explain that you understand the interviewer wants to know whether you can think on your feet, that there is pressure on the job, and that he or she is trying to simulate some of that real-life pressure in the interview. You may choose to finish the answer with a question of your own: "How do you think I fit the profile of the person you need?"

"I'm not sure you're suitable for the job."

Don't worry about the tone of the question—the interviewer's "I'm not sure" really means, "I'd like to hire you, so here's a wide-open opportunity to sell me on yourself." He or she is probing three areas from your personal profile: your confidence, determination, and listening profiles. Remain calm and put the ball straight back into the interviewer's court: "Why do you say that?" You need both the information and time to think up an appropriate reply, but it is important to show that you are not intimidated. Work out a program of action for this question; even if the interviewer's point regarding your skills is valid, come back with value keys and alternate compatible skills. Counter with other skills that show your competence and learning ability, and use them to show you can pick up the new skills quickly. Tie the two together and demonstrate that with your other attributes you can bring many pluses to the job. Finish your answer with a reflexive question that encourages a "yes" answer.

"I admit my programming skills in that language are a little light. However, all languages have similarities, and my experience demonstrates that with a competence in four other languages, getting up to speed with this one will take only a short while. Plus, I can bring a depth of other experience to the job." Then, after you itemize your experience: "Wouldn't you agree?"

If the reason for the question is not a lack of technical skills, it must be a question about one of your key profile areas. Perhaps the interviewer will say, "You haven't convinced me of your determination." This is an invitation to sell yourself, so tell a story that demonstrates determination.

For example: "It's interesting you should say that. My present boss is convinced of my determination. About a year ago we were having some problems with a union organization in the plant. Management's problem was our 50 percent Spanish monolingual production work force. Despite the fact that our people had the best working conditions and benefits in the area, they were strongly prounion. If they were successful, we would be the first unionized division in the company. No one in management spoke Spanish, so I took a crash Berlitz course—two hours at home every night for five weeks. I got one of the maintenance crew to help me with my grammar and diction. Then a number of other production workers started saying simple things to me in Spanish and helping me with the answers. I opened the first meeting with the work force to discuss the problems. My 'Buenos dias. Me llamo

Brandon' got a few cheers. We had demonstrated that we cared enough to try to communicate. Our division never did unionize, and my determination to take the extra step paid off and allowed my superiors to negotiate from a position of caring and strength. That led to English lessons for the Spanish-speaking, and Spanish classes for the English-speaking. We are now a bilingual company, and I think that shows we care. Wouldn't you agree my work in that instance shows determination?"

"Wouldn't you feel better off in another firm?"

Relax, things aren't as bad as you might assume. This question is usually asked if you are really doing quite well, or if the job involves a certain amount of stress. A lawyer, for example, might well be expected to face this one. The trick is not to be intimidated. Your first step is to qualify the question. Relax, take a breath, sit back, smile, and say, "You surprise me. Why do you say that?" The interviewer must then talk, giving you precious time to collect your wits and come back with a rebuttal.

Then answer "no," and explain why. All the interviewer wants to see is how much you know about the company and how determined you are to join its ranks. Your earlier research and knowledge of personal profile keys (determination) will pay off again. Overcome the objection with an example, and show how that will help you contribute to the company; end with a question of your own. In this instance, the question has a twofold purpose: one, to identify a critical area to sell yourself; and two, to encourage the interviewer to consider an image of you working at the company.

You could reply: "Not at all. My whole experience has been with small companies. I am good at my job and in time could become a big fish in a little pond. But that is not what I want. This corporation is a leader in its business. You have a strong reputation for encouraging skills development in your employees. This is the type of environment I want to work in. Now, coming from a small company, I have done a little bit of everything. That means that no matter what you throw at me, I will learn it quickly. For example, what would be the first project I would be involved with?"

And you end with a question of your own that gets the interviewer focusing on those immediate problems. You can then explain how your background and experience can help.

"What would you say if I told you your presentation this afternoon was lousy?"

"If" is the key word here, with the accusation there only for the terminally neurotic. The question is designed to see how you react to criticism, and so tests your "manageability." No company can afford to employ the thin-skinned applicant today. You will come back and answer the question with a question of your own. An appropriate response would be: "First of all, I would ask which aspects of my presentation were lousy. My next step would be to find out where you felt the problem was. If there was miscommunication, I'd clear it up. If the problem was elsewhere, I would seek your advice and be sure that the problem was not recurrent." This would show that when it is a manager's duty to criticize performance, you are an employee who will respond in a businesslike and emotionally mature manner.

The Illegal Question

Of course, one of the most stressful—and negative—questions is the illegal one, a question that delves into your private life or personal background. Such a question will make you uncomfortable if it is blatant, and could also make you angry.

Your aim, however, is to overcome your discomfort and to avoid getting angry: You want to get the job offer, and any self-righteousness or defensive reaction on your part will ensure that you *don't* get it. You may feel angry enough to get up and walk out, or say things like, "These are unfair practices; you'll hear from my lawyer in the morning." But the result will be that you won't get the offer, and therefore won't have the leverage you need. Remember, no one is saying you can't refuse the job once it's offered to you.

So what is an illegal question? Title VII is a federal law that forbids employers from discriminating against any person on the basis of sex, age, race, national origin, or religion. More recently, the Americans with Disabilities Act was passed to protect this important minority.

☐ An interviewer may not ask about your religion, church, synagogue, or parish, the religious holidays you observe, or your political beliefs or affiliations. He or she may not ask, for instance, "Does your religion allow you to work on Saturdays?" *But* the interviewer may ask something like, "This job requires work on Saturdays. Is that a problem?"

☐ An interviewer may not ask about your ancestry, national origin, or parentage; in addition, you cannot be asked about the naturalization status of your parents, spouse, or children. The interviewer cannot ask about your birthplace. *But* the interviewer may ask (and probably will, considering the current immigration laws) whether you are a U.S. citizen or a resident alien with the right to work in the United States.

☐ An interviewer may not ask about your native language, the language you speak at home, or how you acquired the ability to read, write, or speak a foreign language.

But he or she may ask about the languages in which you are fluent, if knowledge of those languages is pertinent to the job.

☐ An interviewer may not ask about your age, your date of birth, or the ages of your children. *But* he or she may ask you whether you are over eighteen years old.

☐ An interviewer may not ask about maiden names or whether you have changed your name; your marital status, number of children or dependents, or your spouse's occupation; or whether (if you are a woman) you wish to be addressed as Miss, Mrs., or Ms. *But* the interviewer may ask about how you like to be addressed (a common courtesy) and whether you have ever worked for the company before under a different name. (If you have worked for this company or other companies under a different name, you may want to mention that, in light of the fact that this prospective manager may check your references and additional background information.)

As you consider a question that seems to verge on illegality, you should take into account that the interviewer may be asking it innocently, and may be unaware of the laws on the matter. Your best bet is to be polite and straightforward, as you would in any other social situation. You also want to move the conversation to an examination of your skills and abilities, not your status. Here are some sample illegal questions—and some possible responses. Remember, your objective is to get job offers; if you later decide that this company is not for you, you are under no obligation to accept the position.

"What religion do you practice?"

If you do practice, you can say "I attend my church/synagogue/mosque regularly, but I make it my practice not to involve my personal beliefs in my work. My work for the company and my career are too important for that."

If you do not practice a religion, you may want to say something like, "I have a set of personal beliefs that are important to me, but I do not attend any organized services. And I do not mix those beliefs with my work, if that's what you mean."

"How old are you?"

Age discrimination is still prevalent, but with older people joining the work force every day and the increasing need for experienced workers, you will hear this question less and less. Answer the question in terms of your experience. For example: "I'm in my fifties and have more than twenty-five years of experience in this field." Then list your skills as they apply to the job.

"Are you married?"

If you are, the company is concerned with the impact your family duties and future plans will have on your tenure there. Your answer could be, "Yes, I am. Of course, I make a separation between my work life and my family life that allows me to give my all to a job. I have no problem with travel or late hours; those things are part of this line of work. I'm sure my references will confirm this for you."

"Do you plan to have children?"

This isn't any of the interviewer's business, but he or she wants to know whether you will leave the company early to raise a family. You can answer "no," of course. If you answer "yes," you might add, "But those plans are for the future, and they depend on the success of my career. Certainly, I want to do the best, most complete job for this company I can. I consider that my skills are right for the job and that I can make a long-range contribution. I certainly have no plans to leave the company just as I begin to make meaningful contributions."

If the questions become too pointed, you may want to ask—innocently—"Could you explain the relevance of that issue to the position? I'm trying to get a handle on it." That response, however, can seem confrontational; you should only use it if you are *extremely* uncomfortable, or are quite certain you can get away with it. Sometimes, the interviewer will drop the line of questioning.

Illegal questions tend to arise not out of brazen insensitivity, but rather out of an interest in you. The employer is familiar with your skills and background, feels you can do the job, and wants to get to know you as a person. Outright discrimination these days is really quite rare. With illegal questions, your response must be positive—that's the only way you're going to get the job offer, and getting a job offer allows you to leverage other jobs. You don't have to work for a discriminatory company, but you can certainly use the firm to get to something better.

Mock Meetings, Role Plays, and In-Basket Tests

Some employers use even more elaborate versions of the stress interview when selecting personnel. Groups of candidates may be put in a room together and asked to stage a mock meeting, or be asked to give an impromptu presentation. You may even be asked to demonstrate your organization and time management skills by sorting out and acting on an in-basket full of an overwhelming amount of supposedly urgent data, all while being interrupted by telephone calls.

Collectively, these approaches are referred to as assessment center techniques. They are frequently run—on an employer's behalf—by a third-party operation that specializes in this corporate manifestation of the Spanish Inquisition. Some companies use this approach when hiring executives, some for choosing sales and customer service professionals, and others for identifying the best candidates for administrative positions. Unfortunately, assessment center techniques are so common today that anyone in the job market risks facing their myriad tortures. The good news is that I have one or two techniques that can help you face these latter-day Torquemadas with equanimity.

One of the reasons that assessment center techniques are growing in popularity is the corporate world's increasing focus on teamwork. Many employers figure they can hire the best workers for a team environment by using group interviews. (Forget the fact that assessment centers haven't proven themselves better or worse than other selection methods!) Since you may encounter this old-new approach during your job search, I want you to be ready for it.

Racks, Beds of Nails, and Iron Maidens

Assessment centers use a broad variety of techniques, including:

* mock meetings
* in-basket tests
* role playing

Let me give you some background on each of these techniques, and show you how you can prepare yourself to make a great impression in any situation. With these selection techniques, forewarned is forearmed. With a little bit of time to prepare, and an understanding of how these situations work, you can survive anything they might throw at you. Besides, it's only pretend—so there's no need to break out in a cold sweat.

Mock Meetings: Taking Control, Taking Charge, and Being a Team Player

Some employers will want to see you take charge of, perhaps take over, the leadership of the group; others want to see your skills at interacting with people; some will want to see both. Your first step in preparing for a mock meeting is to outline the challenges you would face in the average daily routine of the job you've applied for. These challenges are likely to form the basis of the situations you'll be asked to respond to. For example, if your job will involve making sales presentations on big-ticket items to groups of people, you can expect the mock meeting to include all of the difficult questions, problems, and people you would be likely to meet in such a context. There are only two differences: First, the whole range of problems is going to appear in one meeting; and second, it's just pretend. If you are a competent professional, and react to the situations you face in a professional manner, you will do just fine.

Your assessors may set up a leaderless group discussion and watch what happens. These groups may include an assortment of applicants, existing employees, and selection center staff, some of them "planted" there to cause disruption or otherwise throw you off balance. Just knowing who is who and why they're there can be a big help. Now that overwhelmingly belligerent SOB can be treated as what he really is: a test of your assertiveness skills.

Anything you face in one of these situations will mirror the challenges you face in the real work world. If your appraisal of the job is that "Taking Control" and "Demonstrating Leadership" are likely to be the goals of the mock meeting, *how* you take control and demonstrate leadership will be crucial to your success. You need to set a standard of democratic leadership; you have to become the parent who sets firm limits, but gives support. Be sure to give everyone "air time," while keeping the group on-target and on-schedule.

Sometimes taking charge can be dangerous, however. If you come across as too tough, bossy, or autocratic, forget it! You can't just say, "Okay, this is a test of my decision-making and leadership skills, so move over, rover, and let *me* take over." You should encourage a more team-oriented approach: "Let's take a moment to gather our thoughts, and then each, in turn, address the issues from our unique perspective." You must keep the meeting moving if someone tries to dominate the discussion or move it away from the agenda. You can then demonstrate your leadership by thanking everyone for their contributions.

If someone else beats you to the punch and assumes the leadership role, don't try to show everyone how tough you are by fighting to regain control. Instead, act like the archetypal active team member. Use the time you have while the leader is busy managing the meeting to plan your strategy and develop your contributions to the idea or plan the group is working on. Position yourself as a team player and consensus builder, but show you can take the initiative, too.

From this position, you can be ready to scoop the opposition at the end of the meeting. While the "leader" is busy making sure that every voice gets heard, you can prepare to help the group summarize its common ground, and establish possible next steps.

For more information on what the testers will be looking for in terms of team work and leadership, see the related questions on pages 155 and 156.

In-basket: A Test of Organized Action

You're staring at a huge stack of reports, memos, and phone messages on your desk. The red light on the phone is flashing to let you know you've got voice mail messages. The computer screen glares at you, with a dozen as-yet-unread e-mail messages. Confronting applicants with a virtual day at the office is yet another way companies try to screen out the wheat from the chaff. In this example, you're facing an in-basket test, and it is being used primarily to examine your time management and organization skills.

The in-basket test confronts the job candidate with overwhelming amounts of information, and often conflicting priorities. Then the observers sit back, put their feet up, and watch you wither or shine before their eyes. There are many ways to tackle this kind of test, but the main thing is to make sure that you come prepared with a system to prioritize and organize the work.

Alan Lakein, the godfather of time management, introduced me to a wildly effective and widely accepted approach to time management. Take everything out of the in-basket and place it in one of three piles:

- The A pile is *urgent*, and you will act on it "today"—in other words, during the test.
- The B pile is *important* and needs attention. You'll start on it when and if you get through your A pile. If not, much of it will move into your A pile, as you plan for "tomorrow" at the end of "today."
- The C pile is to file or just put in a drawer. It is still important work, but not as urgent as your A and B work. If someone makes it urgent for you—via a telephone call or an urgent e-mail message—you'll know where to find it.

Working out these priorities is the first step in acing an in-basket test. Once established, you'll be able to prioritize those pesky interruptions that are always programmed into this particular type of test. When the calls come in, as they will, you must have a system in place that can help you decide how to respond. For example, you need to find out:

- Who's calling, and who that person is. You want to establish their name, department, and reporting relationship. If your "cyber boss" of the day calls, he or she has the power to move something from your C pile directly to your A pile.
- What they're calling about. You can put the person on hold while you find the appropriate paperwork, consider the relative importance of the call, and decide how to handle it with efficiency and professionalism.

It is important, at the end of the test, to make sure that the assessor understands that you have been using an effective and logical system. *How to Get Control of Your Time and Your Life,* by Alan Lakein, can teach you world-class time management and organization skills.

For more information on what assessors are looking for in this kind of test, see the question about scheduling on page 158, and the question on working methods on page 159.

Role Playing

You may be asked to handle a sticky personnel problem, an employee calling in sick from the golf course, a malfunctioning team, an inventory problem, a broken machine, or cold calls to a series of prospective "clients." The goal of role playing is invariably to see how you handle the people and situations that are likely to crop up in the day-to-day execution of your duties.

Are you a hard-nosed SOB, or do you cave in at the slightest pressure? Do you want the world to love and admire you, or are you out to settle a score? How do you handle a belligerent customer or salvage a tough sale when it turns sour at the last moment?

What's the best way to handle these situations? Consider the role you are playing: Is it to land a job as a customer service representative, sales training specialist, vice president of finance, or union lawyer? In handling role-playing tests, you need to be clear about the job you're facing—and the challenges it typically generates. You will then understand exactly what the testers are looking for, and the role you should choose to play in their scenarios.

In each of these stressful interviewing situations the key is to determine which professional hat you should be wearing, and to demonstrate the behaviors the testers will expect from someone wearing that hat. For more on getting in touch with the professional you, see "How to Ace the Psychological Tests," chapter 26.

☐   ☐   ☐

Interviewers may pull all kinds of tricks on you, but you will come through with flying colors once you realize that they're trying to discover something extremely simple—whether or not you can take the heat. After all, those interviewers are only trying to sort out the good corporate warriors from the walking wounded. If you are asked and successfully handle these trick and negatively phrased questions, the interviewer will end up looking at you favorably. Stay calm, give as good as you get, and take it all in stride. Remember that no one can intimidate you without your permission.

18 | Strange Venues

Learn the tips that will help you master interviews in noisy, distracting hotel lobbies, restaurants, poolsides, and other unusual settings.

Why are some interviews conducted in strange places? Are meetings in noisy, distracting hotel lobbies designed as a form of torture? What are the real reasons that an interviewer invites you to eat at a fancy restaurant?

For the most part, these tough-on-the-nerves situations happen because the interviewer is a busy person, fitting you into a busy schedule. Take the case of a woman I know. She had heard stories about tough interview situations but never expected to face one herself. It happened at a retail convention in Arizona, and she had been asked to meet for a final interview by the pool. The interviewer was there, taking a short break between meetings, in his bathing suit. And the first thing the interviewer did was suggest that my friend slip into something comfortable.

That scenario may not lurk in your future, but the chances are that you will face many tough interview situations in your career. They call for a clear head and a little gamesmanship to put you ahead of the competition. The interviewee at the pool used both. She removed her jacket, folded it over the arm of the chair and seated herself, saying pleasantly, "That's much better. Where shall we begin?"

It isn't easy to remain calm at such times. On top of interview nerves, you're worried about being overheard in a public place, or (worse) surprised by the appearance of your current boss. That last item isn't too far-fetched. It actually happened to a reader from San Francisco. He was being interviewed in the departure lounge at the airport when his boss walked through the arrivals door. Oops—he had asked for the day off "to go to the doctor."

Could he have avoided the situation? Certainly, if he had asked about privacy when the meeting was arranged. That would have reminded the interviewer of the need for discretion. The point is to do all you can in advance to make such a meeting as private as possible. Once that's done, you can ignore the rest of the world and concentrate on the interviewer's questions.

Hotel Lobbies and Other Strange Places

Strange interview situations provide other wonderful opportunities to embarrass yourself. You come to a hotel lobby in full corporate battle dress: coat, briefcase, perhaps an umbrella. You sit down to wait for the interviewer. "Aha," you think to yourself, opening your briefcase, "I'll show him my excellent work habits by delving into this computer printout."

That's not such a great idea. Have you ever tried rising with your lap covered with business papers, then juggling the briefcase from right hand to left to accommodate the ritual handshake? It's quite difficult. Besides, while you are sitting in nervous anticipation, preinterview tension has no way of dissipating. Your mouth will become dry, and your "Good morning, I'm pleased to meet you" will come out sounding like the cat being strangled.

To avoid such catastrophes in places like hotel lobbies, first remove your coat on arrival. Then, instead of sitting, walk around a little while you wait. Even in a small lobby, a few steps back and forth will help you reduce tension to a manageable level. Keep your briefcase in your left hand at all times—it makes you look purposeful, and you won't trip over it when you meet the interviewer.

If, for any reason, you must sit down, make a conscious effort to breathe deeply and slowly. This will help control the adrenaline that makes you feel jumpy.

A strange setting can actually put you on equal footing with the interviewer. Neither of you is on home turf, so in many cases, the interviewer will feel just as awkward as you do. A little gamesmanship can turn the occasion to your advantage.

To gain the upper hand, get to the meeting site early to scout the territory. By knowing your surroundings, you will feel more relaxed. Early arrival also allows you to control the outcome of the meeting in other subtle ways. You will have time to stake out the most private spot in an otherwise public place. Corners are best. They tend to be quieter, and you can choose the seat that puts your back to the wall (in a practical sense, that is). In this position, you have a clear view of your surroundings and will feel more secure. The fear of being overheard will evaporate.

The situation is now somewhat in your favor. You know the locale, and the meeting place is as much yours as the interviewer's. You will have a clear view of your surroundings, and odds are that you will be more relaxed than the interviewer. When he or she arrives, say, "I arrived a little early to make sure we had some privacy. I think over here is the best spot." With that positive demonstration of your organizational abilities, you give yourself a head start over the competition.

The Meal Meeting

Breakfast, lunch, or dinner are the prime choices for interviewers who want to catch the seasoned professional off-guard. In fact, the meal is arguably the toughest of all tough interview situations. The setting offers the interviewer the chance to see you in a nonoffice (and therefore more natural) setting, to observe your social graces, and to consider you as a whole person. Here, topics that would be impossible to address in the traditional office setting will naturally surface, often with virtually no effort on the part of the interviewer. The slightest slip in front of that wily old sea pirate opposite—thinly disguised in a Brooks Brothers suit—could get your candidacy deep-sixed *tout de suite*.

Usually you will not be invited to an "eating meeting" until you have already demonstrated that you are capable of doing the job. It's a good sign, actually: An invitation to a meal means that you are under strong consideration, and, by extension, intense scrutiny.

The meeting is often the final hurdle and could lead directly to the job offer— assuming, of course, that you properly handle the occasional surprises that arise. The interviewer's concern is not whether you can do the job, but whether you have the growth potential that will allow you to fill more senior slots as they become available.

But be careful. Many have fallen at the final hurdle in a close-run race. Being interviewed in front of others is bad enough; eating and drinking in front of them at the same time only makes it worse. If you knock over a glass or dribble spaghetti sauce down your chin, the interviewer will be so busy smirking that he or she won't hear what you have to say.

To be sure that the interviewer remains as attentive to the positive points of your candidacy as possible, let's discuss table manners.

Your social graces and general demeanor at the table can tell as much about you as your answer to a question. For instance, overordering food or drink can signal poor self-discipline. At the very least, it will call into question your judgment and maturity. High-handed behavior toward waiters and buspeople could reflect negatively on your ability to get along with subordinates and on your leadership skills. Those concerns are amplified when you return food or complain about the service, actions which, at the very least, find fault with the interviewer's choice of restaurant.

By the same token, you will want to observe how your potential employer behaves. After all, you are likely to become an employee, and the interviewer's behavior to servers in a restaurant can tell you a lot about what it will be like on the job.

☐ **Alcohol:** Soon after being seated, you will be offered a drink—if not by your host, then by the waiter. There are many reasons to avoid alcohol at interview meals. The most important reason is that alcohol fuzzes your mind, and research proves that stress increases the intoxicating effect of alcohol. So, if you order something to drink, try to stick with something nonalcoholic, such as a club soda or simply a glass of water. If pressed, order a white-wine spritzer, a sherry, or a light beer—it depends on the environment and what your host is drinking.

If you do have a drink, never have more than one. If there is a bottle of wine on the table, and the waiter offers you another glass, simply place your hand over the top of your glass. It is a polite way of signifying no.

You may be offered alcohol at the end of the meal. The rule still holds true—turn it down. You need your wits about you even if the interview seems to be drawing to a close. Some interviewers will try to use those moments, when your defenses are at their lowest, to throw in a couple of zingers.

☐ **Smoking:** Smoking is another big problem that is best handled by taking a simple approach. Don't do it unless encouraged. If both of you are smokers, and you are encouraged to smoke, follow a simple rule: Never smoke between courses, only at the end of a meal. Even most confirmed nicotine addicts, like the rest of the population, hate smoke while they are eating.

☐ **Utensils:** Keep all your cups and glasses at the top of your place setting and well away from you. Most glasses are knocked over at a cluttered table when one stretches for the condiments or gesticulates to make a point. Of course, your manners will prevent you from reaching rudely for the pepper shaker.

When you are faced with an array of knives, forks, and spoons, it is always safe to start at the outside and work your way in as the courses come. Keep your elbows at your sides and don't slouch in the chair. When pausing between mouthfuls (which, if you are promoting yourself properly, should be frequently), rest your knife and fork on the plate this way.

The time to start eating, of course, is when the interviewer does; the time to stop is when he or she does. At the end of a course or the meal, rest your knife and fork together on the plate, at five o'clock.

Here are some other helpful hints:

- Never speak with your mouth full.
- To be on the safe side, eat the same thing, or close to it, as the interviewer. Of course, while this rule makes sense in theory, the fact is that you probably will be asked to order first, so ordering the same thing can become problematic. Solve the problem before you order by complimenting the restaurant during your small talk and then, when the menus arrive, asking, "What do you think you will have today?"
- Do not change your order once it is made, and never send the food back.
- Be polite to your waiters, even when they spill soup in your lap.
- Don't order expensive food. Naturally, in our heart of hearts, we all like to eat well, especially on someone else's tab. But don't be tempted. When you come right down to it, you are there to talk and be seen at your best, not to eat.
- Eat what you know. Stay away from awkward, messy, or exotic foods (e.g., artichokes, long pasta, and escargot, respectively). Ignore finger foods, such as lobster or spare ribs. In fact, you should avoid eating with your fingers altogether, unless you are in a sandwich joint, in which case you should make a point of avoiding the leaky, overstuffed menu items.
- Don't order salad. The dressing can often get messy. If a salad comes with the meal, request that the dressing be on the side. Then, before pouring it on, cut up the lettuce.
- Don't order anything with bones. Stick with filets; there are few simple, gracious ways to deal with any type of bone.

☐ **Checks and Goodbyes:** I know an interviewer whose favorite test of composure is to have the waiter, by arrangement, put the bill on the interviewee's side of the table. She then chats on, waiting for something interesting to happen. If you ever find yourself in a similar situation, never pick up the check, however long it is left by your plate. When ready, your host will pick it up, because that's the simple protocol of the occasion. By the same token, you should never offer to share payment.

When parting company, always thank the host for his or her hospitality and the wonderful meal. Of course, you should be sure to leave on a positive note by asking good naturedly what you have to do to get the job.

☐   ☐   ☐

Strange interview situations can arise at any time during the interview cycle, and in any public place. Wherever you are asked to go, keep your guard up. Your table manners, listening skills, and overall social graces are being judged. The question on the interviewer's mind is: Can you be trusted to represent the company graciously?

19 | Welcome to the Real World

For the most recent graduate, here are some tough questions specifically tailored to discover your business potential.

Of all the steps a recent graduate will take up the ladder of success over the years, none is more important or more difficult than getting a foot on the first rung. And the interviewing process designed for recent graduates is particularly rigorous, because management regards the hiring of entry-level professionals as one of its toughest jobs.

When a company hires experienced people, there is a track record to evaluate. With recent graduates, there is little or nothing. Often, the only solid things an interviewer has to go on are high-school, SAT, and/or college grades. That's not much on which to base a hiring decision—grades don't tell the interviewer whether you will fit in or make a reliable employee. Many recruiters liken the gamble of hiring recent graduates to laying down wines for the future: They know that some will develop into full-bodied, reliable vintages, but that others will be disappointments. So, recruiters have to find different ways to predict your potential accurately.

After relying, as best they can, on school performance to evaluate your ability, interviewers concentrate on questions that reveal how willing you are to learn and get the job done, and how manageable you are likely to be, both on average days and when the going gets rough.

Your goal is to stand out from all the other entry-level candidates as someone altogether different and better. For example, don't be like thousands of others who, in answer to questions about their greatest strength, reply lamely, "I'm good with people," or, "I like working with others." As you know by now, such answers do not separate you from the herd. In fact, they brand you as average. To stand out, a recent graduate must recount a past situation that illustrates how good he or she is with people, or one that demonstrates an ability to be a team player.

Fortunately, the key personality traits discussed throughout the book are just as helpful for getting your foot on the ladder as they are for aiding your climb to the top.

They will guide you in choosing what aspects of your personality and background you should promote at the interview.

It isn't necessary to have snap answers ready for every question, because you never will. In fact, it is more important for you to pause after a question and collect your thoughts before answering: You must show that you think before you speak. That way, you will demonstrate your analytical abilities, which age feels youth has in short supply.

By the same token, occasionally asking for a question to be repeated is useful to gain time and is quite acceptable, as long as you don't do it with every question. And if a question stumps you, as sometimes happens, do not stutter incoherently. It is sometimes best to say simply, "I don't know." Or, you might say, "I'd like to come back to that later"—the odds are even that the interviewer will forget to ask again; if he or she doesn't, at least you've had some time to come up with an answer.

Knowing everything about a certain entry-level position is not necessary, because business feels it can teach you most things. But, as a vice president of Merrill Lynch once said, "You must bring to the table the ability to speak clearly." So, knowing what is behind those questions designed especially for recent graduates will give you the time to build informative and understandable answers.

"How did you get your summer jobs?"

All employers look favorably on recent graduates who have any work experience, no matter what it is. "It is far easier to get a fix on someone who has worked while at school," says Dan O'Brien, head of employment at Grumman. "They manage their time better, are more realistic, and more mature. Any work experience gives us much more in common." So, as you make your answer, add that you learned that business is about making a profit, doing things more efficiently, adhering to procedures, and putting out whatever effort it takes to get the job done. In short, treat your summer jobs, no matter how humble, as any other business experience.

In this particular question, the interviewer is looking ideally for something that shows initiative, creativity, and flexibility. Here's an example: "In my town, summer jobs were hard to come by, but I applied to each local restaurant for a position waiting tables, called the manager at each one to arrange an interview, and finally landed a job at one of the most prestigious. I was assigned to the afternoon shift, but with my quick work, accurate billing, and ability to keep customers happy, they soon moved me to the evening shift. I worked there for three summers, and by the time I left, I was responsible for the training and management of the night-shift waiters, the allotment of tips, and the evening's final closing and accounting. All in all, my experience showed me the mechanics of a small business and of business in general."

"Which of the jobs you have held have you liked least?"

The interviewer is trying to trip you up. It is likely that your work experience contained a certain amount of repetition and drudgery, as all early jobs in the business world do. So beware of saying that you hated a particular job "because it was boring." Avoid the negative and say something along these lines: "All of my jobs had their good and bad points, but I've always found that if you want to learn, there's plenty to be picked up every day. Each experience was valuable." Then describe a seemingly boring job, but show how it taught you valuable lessons or helped you hone different aspects of your personality profile.

"What are your future vocational plans?"

This is a fancy way of asking, "Where do you want to be five years from now?" The trap all entry-level professionals make is to say, "In management," because they think that shows drive and ambition. It has become such a trite answer, though, that it immediately generates a string of questions that most recent graduates can't answer: What is the definition of management? What is a manager's prime responsibility? A manager in what area? Your safest answer identifies you with the profession you are trying to break into, and shows you have your feet on the ground. "My vocational plans are that I want to get ahead. To do that I must be able to channel my energies and expertise into those areas my industry and employer need. So in a couple of years I hope to have become a thorough professional with a clear understanding of the company, the industry, and where the biggest challenges, and therefore opportunities, lie. By that time, my goals for the future should be sharply defined." An answer like that will set you far apart from your contemporaries.

"What college did you attend, and why did you choose it?"

The college you attended isn't as important as your reasons for choosing it— the question is trying to examine your reasoning processes. Emphasize that it was your choice, and that you didn't go there as a result of your parents' desires or because generations of your family have always attended the Acme School of Welding. Focus on the practical. "I went to Greenbriar State—it was a choice based on practicality. I wanted a school that would give me a good education and prepare me for the real world. State has a good record for turning out students fully prepared to take on responsibilities in the real world. It is [or isn't] a big school, but/and it has certainly taught me some big lessons about the value of [whatever personality values apply] in the real world of business."

If the interviewer has a follow-up question about the role your parents played in selection of your school, be wary—he or she is plumbing your maturity. It is best to reply that the choice of the school was yours, though you did seek the advice of your parents once you had made your selection, and that they supported your decision.

"Are you looking for a permanent or temporary job?"

The interviewer wants reassurance that you are genuinely interested in the position and won't disappear in a few months to pursue postdoctoral studies in St. Tropez. Try to go beyond saying simply "yes." Explain why you want the job. You might say, "Of course, I am looking for a permanent job. I intend to make my career in this field, and I want the opportunity to learn the business, face new challenges, and learn from experienced professionals." You will also want to qualify the question with one of your own at the end of your answer: "Is this a permanent or a temporary position you are trying to fill?" And don't be scared to ask. The occasional unscrupulous employer will hire someone fresh out of school for a short period of time—say, for one particular project—and then lay him or her off.

"How did you pay for college?"

Avoid saying "Oh, Daddy handled all of that," as it probably won't create quite the impression you'd like. Your parents may well have helped you out, but you should explain, if it's appropriate, that you worked part-time and took out loans (as most of us must during college).

"We have tried to hire people from your school/your major before, and they never seem to work out. What makes you different?"

Here's a stress question to test your poise and analytical skills. You can shout that, yes, of course you are different and can prove it. So far, though, all you know is that there was a problem, not what caused the problem. Respond this way: "First, may I ask you exactly what problems you've had with people from this background?" Once you know what the problem is (if one really exists at all—it may just be a curve ball to test your poise) then you can illustrate how you are different. But only then. Otherwise, you run the risk of your answer being interrupted with, "Well, that's what everyone else said before I hired them. You haven't shown me that you are different."

"I'd be interested to hear about some things you learned in school that could be used on the job."

While specific job-related courses could form part of your answer, they cannot be all of it. The interviewer wants to hear about "real-world" skills, so oblige by explaining what the experience of college taught you rather than a specific course. In other words, explain how the experience honed your relevant personality profiles.

"Within my major and minor I tried to pursue those courses that had most practical relevance, such as . . . However, the greatest lessons I learned were the importance of . . ." and then list your personality profile strengths.

"Do you like routine tasks/regular hours?"

A trick question. The interviewer knows from bitter experience that most recent graduates hate routine and are hopeless as employees until they come to an acceptance of such facts of life. Explain that, yes, you appreciate the need for routine, that you expect a fair amount of routine assignments before you are entrusted with the more responsible ones, and that that is why you are prepared to accept it as necessary. As far as regular hours go you could say, "No, there's no problem there. A company expects to make a profit, so the doors have to be open for business on a regular basis."

"What have you done that shows initiative and willingness to work?"

Again, tell a story about how you landed or created a job for yourself, or even got involved in some volunteer work. Your answer should show initiative in that you both handled unexpected problems calmly and anticipated others. Your willingness is demonstrated by the ways you overcame obstacles. For example: "I worked for a summer in a small warehouse. I found out that a large shipment was due in a couple of weeks, and I knew that room had to be made. The inventory system was outdated, and the rear of the warehouse was disorganized, so I came in on a Saturday, figured out how much room I needed, cleaned up the mess in the rear, and catalogued it all on the new inventory forms. When the shipment arrived, the truck just backed in. There was even room to spare."

Often after an effort above and beyond the call of duty, a manager might congratulate you, and if it had happened to you in this instance, you might conclude your answer with the verbal endorsement: "The divisional manager happened along just when I was finishing the job, and said he wished he had more people who took such pride in their work."

"Can you take instructions without feeling upset or hurt?"

This is a manageability question. If you take offense easily or bristle when your mistakes are pointed out, you won't last long with any company. Competition is fierce at the entry level, so take this as another chance to set yourself apart. "Yes, I can take instruction—and more important, I can take constructive criticism without feeling hurt. Even with the best intent, I will still make mistakes, and at times someone will have to put me back on the right track. I know that if I ever expect to rise in the company, I must first prove myself to be manageable."

"Have you ever had difficulties getting along with others?"

This is a combination question, probing willingness and manageability. Are you a team player or are you going to disrupt the department and make the interviewer's life miserable? This is a closed-ended question that requires only a yes/no answer, so give one and shut up.

"What type of position are you interested in?"

This again is one of those questions that tempts you to mention management. Don't. Say you are interested in what you will be offered anyway, which is an entry-level job. "I am interested in an entry-level position that will enable me to learn this business inside and out, and will give me the opportunity to grow when I prove myself, either on a professional or a managerial ladder."

"What qualifications do you have that will make you successful in this field?"

There is more to answering this question than reeling off your academic qualifications. In addition you will want to stress relevant work experience and illustrate your strong points as they match the key personality traits as they apply to the position you seek. It's a simple, wide-open question that says, "Hey, we're looking for an excuse to hire you. Give us some help."

"Why do you think you would like this type of work?"

This is a deceptively simple question because there is no pat answer. It is usually asked to see whether you really understand what the specific job and profession entails on a day-to-day basis. So, to answer it requires you to have researched the company and job functions as carefully as possible. Preparation for this should include a call to another company in the field and a request to speak to someone doing the job you hope to get. Ask what the job is like and what that person does day to day. How does the job fit into the department? What contribution does it make to the overall efforts of the company? Why does he or she like that type of work? Armed with that information, you will show that you understand what you are getting into; most recent graduates do not.

"What's your idea of how industry works?"

The interviewer does not want a long dissertation, just the reassurance that you don't think it works along the same lines as a registered charity. Your understanding should be something like this: "The role of any company is to make as much money as possible, as quickly and efficiently as possible, and in a manner that will encourage repeat business from the existing client base and new business from word of mouth and reputation." Finish with the observation that it is every employee's role to play as a team member in order to achieve those goals.

"What do you know about our company?"

You can't answer this question unless you have enough interest to research the company thoroughly. If you don't have that interest, you should expect someone who has made the effort to get the job.

"What do you think determines progress in a good company?"

Your answer will include all the positive personality traits you have been illustrating throughout the interview. Include allusions to the listening profile, determination, ability to take the rough with the smooth, adherence to systems and procedures, and the good fortune to have a manager who wants you to grow.

"Do you think grades should be considered by first employers?"

If your grades were good, the answer is obviously "yes." If they weren't, your answer needs a little more thought. "Of course, an employer should take everything into consideration, and along with grades will be an evaluation of willingness and manageability, an understanding of how business works, and actual work experience. Combined, such experience and professional skills can be more valuable than grades alone."

□   □   □

Many virtuous candidates are called for entry-level interviews, but only those who prepare themselves to answer the tough questions will be chosen. Interviews for recent graduates are partly sales presentations. And the more you interview, the better you get, so don't leave preparing for them until the last minute. Start now and hone your skills to get a head start on your peers. Finally, here's what a professor from a top-notch business school once told me: "You are taking a new product to market. Accordingly, you've got to analyze what it can do, who is likely to be interested, and how you are going to sell it to them." Take some time to get to know yourself and your particular values as they will be perceived in the world of business.

20 | The Graceful Exit

Is parting such sweet sorrow? The end of an interview will more likely mean relief, but here are some dos and don'ts to bear in mind as your meeting comes to a close.

To paraphrase Shakespeare, all the employment world's a stage, and all the people on it merely players making their entrances and exits. Curtains rise and fall, and your powerful performance must be capped with a professional and memorable exit. To ensure you leave the right impression, this chapter will review the dos and don'ts of leaving an interview.

A signal that the interview is drawing to a close comes when you are asked whether you have any questions. Ask questions, and by doing so, highlight your strengths and show your enthusiasm. Your goal at the interview is to generate a job offer, so you should find it easy to avoid the crimes that damage your case.

Dos:

1. **Ask appropriate job-related questions.** When the opportunity comes to ask any final questions, review your notes. Bring up any relevant strengths that haven't been addressed.
2. **Show decisiveness.** If you are offered the job, react with enthusiasm. Then sleep on it. If it's possible to do so without making a formal acceptance, lock the job up now and put yourself in control; you can always change your mind later. But before you make any commitment with regard to compensation, see chapter 23, "Negotiating the Offer."
3. **When you are interviewed by more than one person, be sure you have the correct spelling of their names.** "I enjoyed meeting your colleagues, Ms. Smith. Could you give me the correct spelling of their names, please?" This question will give you the names you forgot in the heat of battle and will demonstrate your consideration.
4. **Review the job's requirements with the interviewer.** Match them point by point with your skills and attributes.
5. **Find out whether this is the only interview.** If so, you must ask for the job in a positive and enthusiastic manner. Find out the time frame for a decision

and finish with: "I am very enthusiastic about the job and the contributions I can make. If your decision will be made by the fifteenth, what must I do in the meantime to assure I get the job?"

6. **Ask for the next interview.** When there are subsequent interviews in the hiring procedure, ask for the next interview in the same honest and forthright manner. "Is now a good time to schedule our next meeting?" If you do not ask, you do not get.

7. **Keep yourself in contention.** A good leading question to ask is, "Until I hear from you again, what particular aspects of the job and this interview should I be considering?"

8. **Always depart in the same polite and assured manner you entered.** Look the interviewer in the eye, put on a smile (there's no need to grin), give a firm handshake, and say, "This has been an exciting meeting for me. This is a job I can do, and I feel I can contribute to your goals, because the atmosphere here seems conducive to doing my very best work. When will we speak again?"

Don'ts:

1. **Don't discuss salary, vacation, or benefits**. It is not that the questions are invalid, just that the timing is wrong. Bringing such topics up before you have an offer is asking what the company can do for you—instead, you should be saying what you can do for the company. Those topics are part of the negotiation (handled in chapter 23, "Negotiating the Offer"); remember, without an offer you have nothing to negotiate.

2. **Don't press for an early decision.** Of course you should ask, "When will I know your decision?" But don't press it. And don't try to use the "other-opportunities-I-have-to-consider" gambit as leverage when no such offers exist—that annoys the interviewer, makes you look foolish, and may even force you to negotiate from a position of weakness. Timing is everything; the issue of how to handle other opportunities as leverage is explored in detail later.

3. **Don't show discouragement.** Sometimes a job offer can occur on the spot. Usually it does not. So don't show discouragement if you are not offered the job at the interview, because discouragement shows a lack of self-esteem and determination. Avoiding a bad impression is merely the foundation of leaving a good one, and the right image to leave is one of enthusiasm, guts, and openness—just the traits you have been projecting throughout the interview.

4. **Don't ask for an evaluation of your interview performance.** That forces the issue and puts the interviewer in an awkward position. You *can* say that you want the job, and ask what you have to do to get it.

Part IV | Finishing Touches

Statistics show that the last person to interview usually gets the job. Here are some steps you can take that will keep your impression strong.

The successful completion of every interview is a big stride toward getting job offers, yet it is not the end of your job hunt. A company rarely hires the first competent person it sees. A hiring manager will sometimes interview as many as fifteen people for a particular job, but the strain and pace of conducting interviews naturally dim the memory of each applicant. Unless you are the last person to be interviewed, the impression you make will fade with each subsequent interview the interviewer undertakes. And if you are not remembered, you will not be offered the job. You must develop a strategy to keep your name and skills constantly in the forefront of the interviewer's mind. These finishing touches often make all the difference.

Some of the suggestions here may not seem earth-shattering, just simple, sensible demonstrations of your manners, enthusiasm, and determination. But remember that today all employers are looking for people with that extra little something. You can avoid the negative or merely indifferent impression and be certain of creating a positive one by following these guidelines.

21 | Out of Sight, Out of Mind

Don't let the interviewer forget you! The follow-up is simple, and here are seven steps that guarantee the continuation of your candidacy.

The first thing you do on leaving the interview is breathe a sigh of relief. The second is to make sure that "out of sight, out of mind" will not apply to you. You do this by starting a follow-up procedure immediately after the interview.

Sitting in your car, on the bus, train, or plane, do a written recap of the interview while it's still fresh in your mind. Answer these questions:

- Whom did you meet? (names and titles)
- What does the job entail?
- What are the first projects, the biggest challenges?
- Why can you do the job?
- What aspects of the interview went poorly? Why?
- What is the agreed-upon next step?
- What was said during the last few minutes of the interview?

Probably the most difficult—and most important—thing to do is to analyze what aspects of the interview went poorly. A person does not get offered a job based solely on strength. On the contrary, many people get new jobs based on their relative lack of negatives as compared with the other applicants. So it is mandatory that you look for and recognize any negatives from your performance. That is the only way you will have an opportunity to package and overcome those negatives in your follow-up procedure and during subsequent interviews.

The next step is to write the follow-up letter to the interviewer to acknowledge the meeting and to keep you fresh in his or her mind. Writing a follow-up letter also shows that you are both appreciative and organized, and it refreshes the urgency of your candidacy at the expense of other candidates. But remember that a canned follow-up form letter could hurt your candidacy.

☐ **1. Type the letter.** It exhibits greater professionalism. If you don't own a typewriter, the local library will frequently allow the use of theirs. If not, a typing service will do it for a nominal fee. If, for any reason, the letter cannot be typed, make sure it is legibly and neatly written. The letter should make four points clear to the company representative:

- You paid attention to what was being said.
- You understood the importance of the interviewer's comments.
- You are excited about the job, can do it, and want it.
- You can contribute to those first major projects.

☐ **2. Use the right words and phrases in your letter.** Here are some you might want to use:

- "Upon reflection," or "Having thought about our meeting . . ."
- Recognize—"I recognize the importance of . . ."
- Listen—"Listening to the points you made . . ."
- Enthusiasm—Let the interviewer catch your enthusiasm. It is very effective, especially as your letter will arrive while other applicants are nervously sweating their way through the interview.
- Impressed—Let the interviewer know you were impressed with the people/product/service/facility/market/position, but do not overdo it.
- Challenge—Show that you feel you would be challenged to do your best work in this environment.
- Confidence—There is a job to be done and a challenge to be met. Let the interviewer know you are confident of doing both well.
- Interest—If you want the job (or next interview), say so. At this stage, the company is buying and you are selling. Ask for the job in a positive and enthusiastic manner.
- Appreciation—As a courtesy and mark of professional manners, you must express appreciation for the time the interviewer took out of his or her busy schedule.

☐ **3. Whenever possible and appropriate, mention the names of the people you met at the interview.** Draw attention to one of the topics that was of general interest to the interviewers.

☐ **4. Address the follow-up letter to the main interviewer.** Send a copy to personnel with a note of thanks as a courtesy.

☐ **5. Don't gild the lily.** Keep it short—less than one page—and don't make any wild claims that might not withstand close scrutiny.

☐ **6. Mail the letter within twenty-four hours of the interview.** If the decision is going to be made in the next couple of days, hand-deliver the letter or make a strong point by sending a mailgram. The follow-up letter will help to set you apart from other applicants and will refresh your image in the mind of the interviewer just when it would normally be starting to dim.

☐ **7. If you do not hear anything after five days (which is quite normal), put in a telephone call to the company representative.** Reiterate the points made in the letter, saying that you want the job (or next interview), and finish your statements with a question: "Mr. Smith, I feel confident about my ability to contribute to your department's efforts, and I really want the job. Could you tell me what I have to do to get it?" Then be quiet and wait for the answer.

☐ ☐ ☐

Of course, you may be told you are no longer in the running. The next chapter will show you that that is a great opportunity to snatch victory from the jaws of defeat.

22 | Snatching Victory from the Jaws of Defeat

Rejection? Impossible! Then again, you won't be right for every job. Here are some techniques that help you to create opportunity in the face of rejection.

During the interviewing process, there are bound to be interviewers who erroneously come to the conclusion that you are not the right person for the job they need to fill. When that happens, you will be turned down. Such an absurd travesty of justice can occur in different ways:

- At the interview
- In a letter of rejection
- During your follow-up telephone call

Whenever the turn-down comes, you must be emotionally and intellectually prepared to take advantage of the opportunity being offered to you.

When you get turned down for the only opportunity you have going, the rejection can be devastating to your ego. That is why I have stressed the wisdom of having at least a few interviews in process at the same time.

You will get turned down. No one can be right for every job. The right person for a job doesn't always get it, however—the best prepared and most determined often does. While you may be responsible in part for the initial rejection, you still have the power to correct the situation and win the job offer. What you do with the claimed victory is a different matter—you will then be in a seller's market with choice and control of your situation.

To turn around a turn-down often requires only willpower and determination. Almost every job you desire is obtainable once you understand the hiring process from the interviewer's side of the desk. Your initial—and temporary—rejection is attributable to one of these reasons:

- The interviewer does not feel you can do the job.
- The interviewer feels you lack a successful profile.

- The interviewer did not feel your personality would contribute to the smooth functioning of the department—perhaps you didn't portray yourself as either a team player, or as someone willing to take the extra step.

With belief in yourself, you can still succeed. Repeat to yourself constantly through the interview cycle: "I will get this job, because no one else can give as much to this company as I can!" Do that and implement the following plan immediately when you hear of rejection, whether in person, via mail, or over the telephone.

☐ **Step One:** Thank the interviewer for the time and consideration. Then ask politely: "To help my future job search, why wasn't I chosen for the position?" Assure the interviewer that you would truly appreciate an honest, objective analysis. Listen to the reply and do not interrupt regardless of the comments. Use your time constructively and take notes furiously. When the company representative finishes speaking, show you understood the comments. (Remember, understanding and agreeing are different animals.)

"Thank you, Mr. Smith, now I can understand the way you feel. Because I am not a professional interviewer, I'm afraid my interview nerves got in the way. I'm very interested in working for your company [use an enthusiastic tone] and am determined to get the job. Let me meet with you once again. This time, when I'm not so nervous, I am confident you will see I really do have the skills you require" [then provide an example of a skill you have in the questionable area]. "You name the time and the place, and I will be there. What's best for you, Mr. Smith?"

End with a question, of course. An enthusiastic request like that is very difficult to refuse and will usually get you another interview. An interview, of course, at which you must shine.

☐ **Step Two:** Check your notes and accept the company representative's concerns. Their validity is irrelevant; the important point is that the negative points represent the problem areas in the interviewer's perception of you. List the negative perceptions, and using the techniques, exercises, and value keys discussed throughout the book, develop different ways to overcome or compensate for every negative perception.

☐ **Step Three:** Reread Part III of this book.

☐ **Step Four:** Practice aloud the statements and responses you will use at the interview. If you can practice with someone who plays the part of the interviewer, so much the better. That will create a real interview atmosphere and be helpful to your success. Lacking a role-play partner, you can create that live answer by putting the anticipated objections and questions on a tape and responding to them.

☐ **Step Five:** Study all available information on the company.

☐ **Step Six:** Congratulate yourself continually for getting another interview after initial rejection. This is proof of your self-worth, ability, and tenacity. You have nothing to lose and everything to gain, having already risen phoenix-like from the ashes of temporary defeat.

☐ **Step Seven:** During the interview, ask for the job in a positive and enthusiastic manner. Your drive and staying power will impress the interviewer. All you must do to win the job is overcome the perceived negatives, and you have been given the time to prepare. Go for it.

☐ **Step Eight:** Even when all has failed at the subsequent interview, do not leave without a final request for the job. Play your trump card: "Mr. Smith, I respect the fact that you allowed me the opportunity to prove myself here today. I am convinced I am the best person for the job. I want you to give me a trial, and I will prove on the job that I am the best hiring decision you have made this year. Will you give us both the opportunity?"

A reader once wrote to me as I was revising *Knock 'em Dead*. The letter read in part, "I read the chapter entitled 'Snatching Victory from the Jaws of Defeat' and did everything you said to salvage what appeared to be a losing interview. My efforts did make a very good impression on the interviewer, but as it was finally explained to me, I really did not have equal qualifications for the job, and finally came in a close second. I really want to work for this growing company, and they say they have another position coming up in six months. What should I do?"

I know of someone in the airline business who wanted a job working on that most prestigious of aircraft, the Concorde. He had been recently laid off and had high hopes for a successful interview. As it happened, he came in second for the Concorde position. He was told that the firm would speak to him again in the near future. So he waited—for eight months. Finally, he realized that waiting for the job could only leave him unemployed. The moral of the story is that you must be brutally objective when you come out second-best, and whatever the interviewer says, you must sometimes assume that you are getting the polite brush-off.

With that in mind, let's see what can be done on the positive side. First of all, send a thank-you note to the interviewer, acknowledging your understanding of the state of affairs and reaffirming your desire to work for the company. Conclude with a polite request to bear you in mind for the future.

Then, keep an eye out for any news item about the company in the press. Whenever you see something, cut it out and mail it to the interviewer with a very brief note that says something like: "I came across this in *Forbes* and thought you might find it interesting. I am still determined to be your next account manager, so please keep me in mind when the next opening occurs."

You can also call the interviewer once every couple of months, just to check in. Remember, of course, to keep the phone call brief and polite—you simply want to keep your name at the top of the interviewer's mind.

And maybe something will come of it. Ultimately, however, your only choice is to move on. There is no gain waiting on an interviewer's word. Go out and keep looking, because chances are that you will come up with an even better job. Then, if you still want to work for that company that gave you the brush-off, you will have some leverage.

Most people fail in their endeavors by quitting just before the dawn of success. Follow these directions and you can win the job. You have proved yourself to be a fighter, and that is universally admired. The company representative will want you to succeed because you are made of stuff that is rarely seen today. You are a person of guts, drive, and endurance—the hallmarks of a winner. Job turn-downs are an opportunity to exercise and build your strengths, and by persisting, you may well add to your growing number of job offers, now and in the future.

23 | Negotiating the Offer

They want you! Before you sign on the dotted line, however, you should be well schooled in the essentials of good salary and benefits negotiations. After all, you're never going to have this much leverage again unless you start over from square one, right?

The crucial period after you have received a formal offer and before you accept is probably the one point in your relationship with an employer at which you can say with any accuracy that you have the whip hand. The advantage, for now, is yours. They want you but don't have you; and their wanting something they don't have gives you a negotiating edge. An employer is also more inclined to respect and honor a person who has a clear understanding of his or her worth in the marketplace—they want a savvy and businesslike person.

You don't have to accept or reject the first offer, whatever it is. In most instances you can improve the initial offer in a number of ways, but you have to know something about the existing market conditions for those employed in your area of endeavor. If you are female, bear in mind that simply settling for a few points above your current rate of pay is bad advice for anyone and downright crazy for you. A word or two on the sober topic of pay discrimination is in order here.

The Women's Bureau of the U.S. Department of Labor tells us that men outearn women in nearly every field. (For what it's worth, my research could not turn up a single industry in which this was not the case.) Even if a woman's responsibilities, background, and accomplishments are exactly the same as those of her male colleague, she is statistically unlikely to take home a paycheck equal to his.

According to the Women's Bureau, male engineers make 14.3 percent more than their female counterparts. Male mathematicians make 16.3 percent more. Male advertising and public relations professionals make 28 percent more. Male lawyers and judges make 28 percent more. And male editors and reporters make a whopping 43 percent more than women performing the same or comparable work.

Those are big discrepancies, and they're just the tip of the iceberg. On average, a woman earns seventy cents for every dollar a man performing the same work earns.

ONLINE RESOURCE

Bureau of Labor Statistics
http://www.bls.gov
This website contains a wealth of job-related and economic information from around the nation. The only downside is that some of the information tends to be a little outdated. Regardless, you'll find information on state unemployment rates; salary information; anticipated job growth rates for particular industries; growing fields; and publications and research papers on prices, living conditions, and technology.

That's up from fifty-nine cents, which was the figure back in 1981, but it's still a depressing figure for women in the workplace today. At this rate, American industry will not be able to reach gender-based pay equity until the year 2020.

Is this a conscious male conspiracy against women? I think not. My personal belief is that much of the gap can be attributed to a simple lack of knowledge of professional negotiating skills, and that women in the workplace are picking these skills up fast. A recent *Industry Week* survey showed that 75 percent of men believe their firms pay men and women equally, even though only a little over half of all American corporations have standardized pay scales. This indicates that qualified female hires are now in a position, at least at the majority of firms, to receive fair consideration of their requests for equitable pay rates. But they have to ask.

Man or woman, there is no guarantee that you are being paid what you are worth. The simple facts are these: If you don't get it while they want you and don't have you, you sure as shootin' can't count on getting it once they do have you. When a thirty-year-old undernegotiates his or her salary by just $2,000 on a new job, it will cost that person a minimum of $70,000 over the course of a career. And remember, every subsequent raise will come from a proportionately lower base; real dollars lost over an entire career span could actually be double this figure.

To get what you have coming at the negotiating table, you must take the time to understand what you have achieved, what you have to offer, and what you are worth to the employer. You should be able to get a better handle on that final item by doing good research, but remember that regional influences can affect pay levels, as can current business conditions.

Everything in this book has been written toward maximizing your professional worth, and salary negotiation is certainly no exception. Please bear in mind that there are no shortcuts. The ideas presented in this chapter will be helpful to you if they represent the culmination of your successful campaign to set yourself apart from the competition, but you cannot negotiate a terrific salary package if an employer is not convinced that you are in the top tier of applicants.

Follow this three-step procedure in planning your salary discussions with employers.

☐ **Step One:** Before getting into negotiation with any employer, work out your minimum cash requirements for any job; you must know what it is going to take to keep a roof over your head and bread on the table. It's necessary to know this figure, but you need never discuss it with anyone—knowing it is the foundation of getting both what you need and what you are worth.

☐ **Step Two:** Get a grip on what your skills are worth in the current market. There are a number of ways to do that. Consider the resources and methods outlined below:

- You may be able to find out the salary range for the level above you and the level beneath you at the company in question.
- You can get information from the Bureau of Labor Statistics in Washington, DC, which keeps stats on hundreds of job titles. Be warned, however, that those titles are often a little out-of-date.
- Your state labor office may have salary ranges available for you to review.
- Ask headhunters—they know better than anyone what the market will bear. You should, as a matter of career prudence, establish an ongoing relationship with a reputable headhunter, because you never know when his or her services will come in handy.
- Many professional journals publish annual salary surveys you can consult.
- The *National Business Employment Weekly*, a magazine published by The *Wall Street Journal*, runs ongoing salary surveys by profession; back issues are available.

☐ **Step Three:** This is the fun part. Come up with the figure that would make you smile, drop dead, and go to heaven on the spot. (But try to keep it somewhere within the bounds of reality—multimillion-dollar offers with stock options being in relatively short supply for most of us.)

☐   ☐   ☐

You now have three figures: a minimum, a realistic midpoint desired salary, and a dream salary.

Your minimum is, as I have said, for personal consumption—never discuss it with anyone. Put it aside, and what do you have left? A salary range, just like the one every employer has for every interview you attend. Yours extends from your midpoint to your dream salary. Yes, that range represents the "top half" of what you want or, more accurately, could conceivably accept—but there's a reason for that. In the event, you will find that it is far easier to negotiate down than it is to negotiate up, and you must find a starting point that gives you every possible advantage.

Negotiate When You Can

I have said throughout *Knock 'em Dead* that your sole aim at the interview is to get the job offer, because without it you have nothing to negotiate. Once the offer is extended, the time to negotiate has arrived, and there will never be a more opportune time. Your relationship with the potential employer has gone through a number of distinct changes—from "Perhaps we should speak to this one" to "Yes, he might be able to do the job" through "This is the top candidate, we really like him and want to have him on board." But now is the only point in the relationship when you will have the upper hand. Enjoy it while you can.

Although questions of salary are usually brought up after you are under serious consideration, you must be careful to avoid painting yourself into a corner when you fill out the initial company application form that contains a request for required salary. Usually you can get away with "open" as a response; sometimes the form will instruct you not to write "open," in which case you can write "negotiable" or "competitive."

□   □   □

So much for basic considerations. Let's move on to the money questions that are likely to be flying around the room.

The salary/job negotiation begins in earnest in two ways. The interviewer can bring up the topic with statements like:

- "How do you think you would like working here?"
- "People with your background always fit in well with us."
- "You could make a real contribution here."
- "Well, you certainly seem to have what it takes."

Or, if it is clearly appropriate to do so, you can bring on the negotiating stage. In that case, you can make mirror images of the above, which make the interviewer face the fact that you certainly are able to do the job, and that the time has therefore come to talk turkey:

- "How do you think I would fit in with the group?"
- "I feel my background and experience would definitely complement the work group, don't you?"
- "I think I could make a real contribution here. What do you think?"
- "I know I have what it takes to do this job. What questions are lingering in your mind?"

Now then. What do you do when the question of money is brought up before you have enough details about the job to negotiate from a position of knowledge and strength? Postpone money talk until you have the facts in hand. Do that by asking something like: "I still have one or two questions about my responsibilities, and it will be easier for me to talk about money when I have cleared them up. Could I first ask you a few questions about . . . ?"

Then proceed to clarify duties and responsibilities, being careful to weigh the relative importance of the position and the individual duties to the success of the department you may join.

The employer is duty-bound to get your services as reasonably as possible, while you have an equal responsibility to do the best you can for yourself. Your goal is not to settle for less than will enable you to be happy on the job—unhappiness at work can taint the rest of your life. It is far easier to negotiate down than it is to negotiate up. The value of the offer you accept depends on your performance throughout the interview and hiring cycle, and especially the finesse you display in the final negotiations. The rest of the chapter is going to address the many questions that might be asked, or that you might ask, to bring matters to a successful conclusion.

"What is an adequate reward for your efforts?"

A glaring manageability question and money probe all in one. The interviewer probably already has a typist on staff who expects a Nobel Prize each time he or she gets out a faultless letter. Your answer should be honest and cover all bases. "My primary satisfaction and reward comes from a job well done and completed on time. The occasional good word from my boss is always welcome. Last but not least, I think everyone looks forward to a salary review."

"What is your salary history?" or ***"What was your salary progress on your last job?"***

The interviewer is looking for a couple of things here. First, he or she is looking for the frequency, percentage, and dollar value of your raises, which in turn tell him or her about your performance and the relative value of the offer that is about to be made. What you want to avoid is tying the potential offer to your salary history—the offer you negotiate should be based solely on the value of the job in hand. Again, this is even more important if you are a woman.

Your answer needs to be specifically vague. Perhaps: "My salary history has followed a steady upward path, and I have never failed to receive merit increases. I would be glad to give you the specific numbers if needed, but I shall have to sit down and give it some thought with a pencil and paper." The odds are that the interviewer will not ask you to do that; if he or she does, nod in agreement and say that you'll get right to it when you get home. Don't begin the task until you are requested a second time, which is unlikely.

If for any reason you do get your back against the wall with this one, be sure to include in the specifics of your answer that "one of the reasons I am leaving my current job is that raises were standard for all levels of employees, so that despite my superior contributions, I got the same percentage raise as the tardy employee. I want to work in an environment where I will be recognized and rewarded for my contributions." Then end with a question: "Is this the sort of company where I can expect that?"

"What were you making on your last job?"

A similar but different question. It could also be phrased, "What are you making now?" or "What is your current salary?"

While I have said that your current earnings should bear no relation to your starting salary on the new job, it can be difficult to make that statement clear to the interviewer without appearing objectionable. Although the question asks you to be specific, you needn't get too specific. Instead, you should try to draw attention to the fact that the two jobs are different. A short answer might include: "I am earning $X, although I'm not sure how that will help you in your evaluation of my worth for this job, because the two jobs are somewhat different."

It is important to understand the "areas of allowable fudge." For instance, if you are considerably underpaid, you may want to weigh the dollar-value of such perks as medical and dental plans, pay in lieu of vacation, profit-sharing and pension plans, bonuses, stock options, and other incentives. For many people, those can add between 20 to 35 percent to their base salary—you might honestly be able to mention a higher figure than you at first thought possible. Also, if you are due for a raise imminently, you are justified in adding it in.

It isn't common for current or previous salaries to be verified by employers, although certain industries, because of legal requirements, check more than others do (for instance, the stock market or the liquor business). Before your "current salary" disappears through the roof, however, you should know that the interviewer can ask to see a payroll stub or W2 form at the time you start work, or could make the offer dependent on verification of salary. After you are hired, the new employer may request verbal or written confirmation from previous employers, or might use an outside verification agency. In any instance where the employer contacts someone verbally or in writing, the employer must by law have your written permission to do so. That small print on the bottom of the job application form followed by a request for your signature usually authorizes the employer to do just that.

"Have you ever been refused a salary increase?"

This implies that you asked. An example of your justifiable request might parallel the following true story. An accountant in a tire distributorship made changes to an accounting system that saved $65,000 a year, plus thirty staff hours a week. Six months after the methods were obviously working smoothly, he requested a salary review, was refused, but was told he would receive a year-end bonus. He did: $75. If you can tell a story like that, by all means tell how you were turned down for a raise. If not, it is best to play it safe and explain that your work and salary history showed a steady and marked continual improvement over the years.

"How much do you need to support your family?"

As we have seen, your best advice is to find some way to sidestep this by discussing your midpoint desired salary.

This question is sometimes asked of people who will be working in a sales job, where remuneration is based upon a draw against forthcoming commissions. If this scenario describes your income patterns, be sure you have a firm handle on your basic needs before you accept the position.

For salaried positions, this question is of questionable relevance. It implies the employer will try to get you at a subsistence salary, which is not why you are there. In this instance, give a range from your desired high-end salary down to your desired midpoint salary.

"How much will it take to get you?" "How much are you looking for?" "What are your salary expectations?" "What are your salary requirements?"

You are being asked to name a figure here. Give the wrong answer and you can get eliminated. It is always a temptation to ask for the moon, knowing you can come down later, but there are better approaches. It is wise to confirm your understanding of the job and its importance before you start throwing numbers around, because you will have to live with the consequences. You need the best possible offer without pricing yourself out of the market, so it's time to dance with one of the following responses.

"Well, let's see if I understand the responsibilities fully . . ." You then proceed to itemize exactly what you will be doing on a daily basis and the parameters of your responsibilities and authority. Once that is done you will seek agreement: "Is this the job as you see it or have I missed anything?" Remember to describe the job in its most flattering and challenging light, paying special attention to the way you see it fitting into the overall picture and contributing to the success of department, work group, and company. You can then finish your response with a question of your own: "What figure did you have in mind for someone with my track record?" or "What range has been authorized for this position?" Your answer will include, in part, something along the lines of, "I believe my skills and experience will warrant a starting salary between _____ and _____."

You also could ask, "What would be the salary range for someone with my experience and skills?" or "I naturally want to make as much as my background and skills will allow. If I am right for the job, and I think my credentials demonstrate that I am, I am sure you will make me a fair offer. What figure do you have in mind?"

Another good response is: "I would expect a salary appropriate to my experience and ability to do the job successfully. What range do you have in mind?"

Such questions will get the interviewer to reveal the salary range, and concentrate his or her attention on the challenges of the job and your ability to accept and work with those challenges.

When you are given a range, you can adjust your money requirements appropriately, latching on to the upper part of the range. For example, if the range is $30,000–$35,000 a year, you can come back with a range of $34,000–$37,000.

```
30 ┌
   │
   │        ┐ 34
   │        │
35 └        │
            │
            └ 37
```

Consequently, your response will include: "That certainly means we have something to talk about. While your range is $30,000–$35,000, I am looking for a minimum of $34,000 with an ideal of $37,000. Tell me, what flexibility is there at the top of your salary range?" You need to know this to put yourself in the strongest negotiating position, and this is the perfect time and opportunity to gain the information and the advantage.

All this fencing is aimed at getting the interviewer to show his or her hand first. Ask for too much, and it's "Oh dear, I'm afraid you're overqualified"—to which you can reply, "So overpay me." (Actually, that works when you can carry it off with an ingratiating smile.) If your request is too low, you are likely to be ruled out as lacking the appropriate experience.

When you have tried to get the interviewer to name a range and failed, you must come up with specific dollars and cents. At this point, the key is to understand that all jobs have salary ranges attached to them. Consequently, the last thing you will ever do is come back with a specific dollar figure—that traps you. Instead, you will mention your own range, which will not be from your minimum to your maximum but rather from your midpoint to your maximum. Remember, you can always negotiate down, but can rarely negotiate up.

"What kind of salary are you worth?"

This is a how-much-do-you-want question with a slight twist. It is asking you to name a desired figure, but the twist is that it also asks you to justify that figure. It requires that you demonstrate careful analysis of your worth, industry norms, and job requirements. You are recommended to try for a higher figure rather than a lower one. "Having compared my background and experience with industry norms and salary surveys, I feel my general worth is in the region of $X to $Y. My general background and credentials fit your needs, and my first-hand knowledge of the specific challenges and projects I would face in this job are an exact match, so I feel worthy of justifying an offer toward the top of this range. Don't you agree?"

After your response to a salary question, you can expect to hear, "That's too much," or "Oh, that is more than we were hoping to pay," or "That would be stretching the budget to the breaking point." When that happens, accept it as no more than a negotiating gambit and come back with your own calm rebuttal: "What did you have in mind?"

"What do you hope to be earning two to five years from now?"

A difficult question. The interviewer is probing your desired career and earning path and is trying to see whether you have your sights set high enough—or too high.

Perhaps a jocular tone doesn't hurt here: "I'd like to be earning just about as much as my boss and I can work out!" Then, throw the ball back with your own question: "How much is it possible to make here?"

If you give a specific figure, the interviewer is going to want justification. If you come up with a salary range, you are advised also to have a justified career path to go along with it.

You could also say, "In two years, I will have finished my C.P.A. requirements, so with that plus my additional experience, industry norms say I should be earning between $X and $Y. I would hope to be earning at least within that range, but hopefully with a proven track record of contributions, I would be making above the norm." The trick is to use industry statistics as the backbone of your argument, express confidence in doing better than the norm, and whenever possible stay away from specific job titles unless pressed.

"Do you think people in your occupation should be paid more?"

This one can be used prior to serious salary negotiation to probe your awareness of how your job really contributes to the bottom line. Or it can occur in the middle of salary negotiations to throw you off balance. The safe and correct answer is to straddle the fence. "Most jobs have salary ranges that reflect the job's relative importance and contribution to a company. And those salary ranges reflect the norm for the great majority of people within that profession. That does not mean, however, that the extraordinary people in such a group are not recognized for the extra performance and skills. There are always exceptions to the rule."

Good Offers, Poor Offers

After a period of bantering back and forth like this, the interviewer names a figure, hopefully meant as a legitimate offer. If you aren't sure, qualify it: "Let me see if I understand you correctly: Are you formally offering me the position at $X a year?"

The formal offer can fall into one of two categories.

☐ **It sounds fair and equitable:** In that case, you still want to negotiate for a little more—employers almost expect it of you, so don't disappoint them. Mention a salary range again, the low end of which comes at about the level of their offer and the high end somewhat above it. You can say, "Well it certainly seems that we are close. I was hoping for something more in the range of $X to $Y. How much room do we have for negotiation here?"

No one will withdraw an offer because you say you feel you are worth more. After all, the interviewer thinks you are the best person for the job, and has extended a formal offer, and the last thing he or she needs now is to start from square one again. The employer has a vested interest in bringing the negotiation to a satisfactory conclusion. In a worst-case scenario, the interviewer can stick to the original offer.

☐ **It isn't quite what you expected:** Even if the offer isn't what you thought it would be, you still have options other than accepting or rejecting the offer as it stands. But your strategy for now is to run the money topic as far as you can in a calm and businesslike way; then once you have gone that far, you can back off and examine the other potential benefits of the job. That way you will leave yourself with an opening, if you need it, to hit the money topic once more at the close of negotiations.

If you feel the salary could do with a boost, say so. "I like the job, and I know I have what it takes to be successful in it. I would also be prepared to give you a start date of [e.g.] March 1 to show my sincerity. But quite honestly, I couldn't justify it with your initial salary offer. I just hope that we have some room for negotiation here."

Or you can say, "I could start on March 1, and I do feel I could make a contribution here and become an integral part of the team. The only thing standing in the way is my inability to make ends meet based on your initial offer. I am sincerely interested in the opportunity and flattered by your interest in me. If we could just solve this money problem, I'm sure we could come to terms. What do you think can be done about it?"

The interviewer will probably come back with a question asking how much you want. "What is the minimum you would be prepared to work for?" he or she might ask. Respond with your range again—with your minimum really your midpoint—and the interviewer may well then come back with a higher offer and ask for your concurrence. This is the time to be noncommittal but encouraged, and to move on to the benefits included with the position: "Well, yes, that is a little better. Perhaps we should talk about the benefits."

Alternatively, the interviewer may come back with another question: "That's beyond our salary range for this job title. How far can you reduce your salary needs to fit our range?"

That question shows good faith and a desire to close the deal, but don't give in too easily—the interviewer is never going to want you as much as he or she does now. Your first response might be: "I appreciate that, but if it is the job title and its accompanying range that is causing the problem, couldn't we upgrade the title, thereby putting me near the bottom of the next range?" Try it—it often works. If is doesn't, it is probably time to move to other negotiable aspects of the job offer.

But not before one last try. You can take that final stab by asking, "Is that the best you can do?" With this question, you must look the interviewer directly in the eye, ask the question, and maintain eye contact. It works surprisingly well. You should also remember to try it as a closing gambit *at the very end of negotiations* when you have received everything you can hope for. You may get a surprise.

Negotiating Your Future Salary

At this point, you have probably ridden present salary as hard as you reasonably can (for a while, anyway)—so the time has come to shift the conversation to future remuneration.

"Even though the offer isn't quite what I'd hoped for to start the job, I am still interested. Can we talk about the future for a while?" Then you move the conversation to an on-the-job focus. Here are a few arrangements corporate headhunters frequently negotiate for their recruits.

☐ **A single, lump-sum signing bonus**—nice to have, though it is money here today and gone tomorrow. Don't make the mistake of adding it onto the base. If you get a $2,500 signing bonus, that money won't be figured in for your year-end review— your raise will be based on your actual salary, so the bonus is a little less meaningful than it appears.

☐ **A 60-, 90-, or 120-day performance review with raise attached.** You can frequently negotiate a minimum percentage increase here, if you have confidence in your abilities.

☐ **A title promotion and raise after two, three, or four months.**

☐ **A year-end bonus.** When you hear talk about a year-end bonus, don't rely on "what it's going to be this year" or "what it was last year," because the actual bonus will never bear any resemblance to either figure. Base the realism of any bonus expectations on a five-year performance history.

☐ **Things other than cash.** Also in the realm of real disposable income are things like a company car, gas, maintenance, and insurance. They represent hard dollars you would not have to spend. It's not unusual to hear of employers paying car or insurance allowances, picking up servicing bills for your personal automobile, or paying gas up to a certain amount each month. But if you don't ask, you can never expect an employer to offer. What have you got to lose? Remember, though, to get any of those unusual goodies in writing—even respectable managers in respected companies can suffer amnesia.

Questions to Leverage and Evaluate the Offer

No two negotiations are going to be alike, so there is no absolute model you can follow. Nevertheless, when you have addressed present and future remuneration, this might be the time to get some more information on the company and the job itself.

Even if you haven't agreed on money, you are probably beginning to get a feeling as to whether or not you can put the deal together; you know the employer wants to. Many of the following questions will be appropriate here; some might even be appropriate at other times during the interview cycle.

Full knowledge of all the relevant facts is critical to your successful final negotiation of money and benefits. Your prudent selection of questions from this list will help you negotiate the best offers and choose the right job for you. (At this point, asking some pertinent questions from the following list also serves as a decompression device of sorts for both parties.)

☐   ☐   ☐

The questions come in these categories:

- Nuts-and-bolts job clarification
- Job and department growth
- Corporate culture
- Company growth and direction

The following section is also worth reading between first and second interviews.

Nuts and Bolts

First, if you have career aspirations, you want to land in an outfit that believes in promoting from within. To find out, ask a few of these questions: How long has the job been open? Why is it open? Who held the job last? What is he doing now?

Promoted, fired, quit? How long was he in that job? How many people have held this job in the last three years? Where are they now? How often and how many people have been promoted from this position—and to where?

Other questions that might follow would include:

"What is the timetable for filling the position?"

The longer the job has been open and the tighter the time frame for filling it, the better your leverage. That can also be determined by asking, "When do you need me to start? Why on that date particularly?"

"What are the first projects to be addressed?" or ***"What are the major problems to be tackled and conquered?"***

"What do you consider the five most important day-to-day responsibilities of this job? Why?"

"What personality traits do you consider critical to success in this job?"

"How do you see me complementing the existing group?"

"Will I be working with a team, or on my own? What will be my responsibilities as a team member? What will be my leadership responsibilities?"

"How much overtime is involved?"

"How much travel is involved?" and ***"How much overnight travel?"***

With overnight travel you need to find out the number of days per week and month; and more important, whether you will be paid for weekend days or given comp time. I have known companies who regularly expect you to get home from a long weekend trip at one o'clock in the morning and be at work at 8:30 A.M. on Monday—all without extra pay or comp time.

"How frequent are performance and salary reviews? And what are they based on—standard raises for all, or are they weighted toward merit and performance?

How does the performance appraisal and reward system work? Exactly how are outstanding employees recognized, judged, and rewarded?"

"What is the complete financial package for someone at my level?"

Job and Department Growth

Not everyone wants a career path—in fact, careers and career paths are fairly new to business and are a phenomenon of the latter part of the twentieth century. The fast track may or may not be for you. Gauging the potential for professional growth in a job is very important for some; for others, it comes slightly lower down the list. Even if you aren't striving to head the corporation in the next few years, you will still want to know what the promotional and growth expectations are so that you don't end up with a company expecting you to scale the heights.

"To what extent are the functions of the department recognized as important and worthy of review by upper management?"
If upper management takes an interest in the doings of your work group, rest assured you are in a visible position for recognition and reward.

"Where and how does my department fit into the company pecking order?"

"What does the department hope to achieve in the next two to three years? How will that help the company? How will it be recognized by the company?"

"What do you see as the strengths of the department? What do you see as weaknesses that you are looking to turn into strengths?"

"What role would you hope I would play in these goals?"

"What informal/formal benchmarks will you use to measure my effectiveness and contributions?"

"Based on my effectiveness, how long would you anticipate me holding this position? When my position and responsibilities change, what are the possible titles and responsibilities I might grow into?"

"What is the official corporate policy on internal promotion? How many people in this department have been promoted from their original positions since joining the company?"

"How do you determine when a person is ready for promotion?"

"What training and professional development programs are available to help me grow professionally?"

"Does the company encourage outside professional development training? Does the company sponsor all or part of any costs?"

"What are my potential career paths within the company?"

"To what jobs have people with my title risen in the company?"

"Who in the company was in this position the shortest length of time? Why? Who has remained in this position the longest? Why?"

Corporate Culture

All companies have their own way of doing things—that's corporate culture. Not every corporate culture is for you.

"What is the company's mission? What are the company's goals?"

"What approach does this company take to its marketplace?"

"What is unique about the way this company operates?"

"What is the best thing you know about this company? What is the worst thing you know about this company?"

"How does the reporting structure work? What are the accepted channels of communication and how do they work?"

"What kinds of checks and balances, reports, or other work-measurement tools are used in the department and company?"

"What do you and the company consider important in my fitting into the corporate culture—the way of doing things around here?"

"Will I be encouraged or discouraged from learning about the company beyond my own department?"

Company Growth and Direction

For those concerned about career growth, a healthy company is mandatory; for those concerned about stability of employment, the same applies.

"What expansion is planned for this department, division, or facility?"

"What markets does the company anticipate developing?"

"Does the company have plans for mergers or acquisitions?"

"Currently, what new endeavors is the company actively pursuing?"

"How do market trends affect company growth and progress? What is being done about them?"

"What production and employee layoffs and cutbacks have you experienced in the last three years?"

"What production and employee layoffs and cutbacks do you anticipate? How are they likely to affect this department, division, or facility?"

"When was the last corporate reorganization? How did it affect this department? When will the next corporate reorganization occur? How will it affect this department?"

"Is this department a profit center? How does that affect remuneration?"

The Package

Take-home pay is the most important part of your package. (You'll probably feel that the only thing wrong with your pay is that it gets taxed before you get to take it home!) That means you must carefully negotiate any possible benefits accruing to the job that have a monetary value but are nontaxable, and/or add to your physical and mental happiness. The list is almost endless, but here is a comprehensive listing of commonly available benefits. Although many of these benefits are available to all employees at some companies, you should know that, as a rule of thumb, the higher up the ladder you climb, the more benefits you can expect. Because the corporate world and its concepts of creating a motivated and committed work force are constantly in flux, you should never assume that a particular benefit will not be available to you.

The basic rule is to ask—if you don't ask, there is no way you will get. A few years ago, it would have been unthinkable that anyone but an executive could expect something as glamorous as an athletic club membership in a benefits package. In the 1990s, however, more companies have a membership as a standard benefit; an increasing number are even building their own health club facilities. In New York you can easily pay between $250 and $700 for membership in a good club. What's this benefit worth in your area? Call a club and find out.

Benefits Your Package May Include:

- 401K and other investment matching programs
- "Cafeteria" insurance plans—you pick the insurance benefits you want
- Car allowance
- Car insurance or an allowance
- Car maintenance and gas or an allowance
- Car
- Compensation days—for unpaid overtime/business travel time
- Country club or health club membership
- Accidental death insurance
- Deferred compensation
- Dental insurance—note deductibles and the percentage that is employer-paid
- Employment contract and/or termination contract
- Expense account
- Financial planning help and tax assistance
- Life insurance
- Medical insurance—note deductibles and percentage that is employer-paid
- Optical insurance—note deductibles and percentage that is employer-paid
- Paid sick leave
- Pension plans
- Personal days off
- Profit sharing
- Short- or long-term disability compensation plans
- Stock options
- Vacation

Evaluating the Offer

Once the offer has been negotiated to the best of your ability, you need to evaluate it—and that doesn't have to be done on the spot. Some of your requests and questions will take time to get answered, and very often the final parts of negotiation—"Yes, Mr. Jones, we can give you the extra $20,000 and six months of vacation you requested"—will take place over the telephone. Regardless of where the final negotiations are completed, never accept or reject the offer on the spot.

Be positive, say how excited you are about the prospect and that you would like a little time (overnight, a day, two days) to think it over, discuss it with your spouse,

ONLINE RESOURCE

Wall Street Journal
http://www.careers.wsj.com
This site contains excellent information for the jobseeker including average salaries for specific jobs and industries. This information is extremely useful when contemplating job offers to determine how they stack up to industry averages.

consult your tarot cards, whatever. Not only is this delay standard practice, but it will also give you the opportunity to leverage other offers, as discussed in the next chapter.

Use the time you gain to speak to your mentors or advisors. But a word of caution: In asking advice from those close to you, be sure you know exactly where that advice is coming from—you need clear-headed objectivity at this time.

Once the advice is in, and not before, weigh it along with your own observations—no one knows your needs and aspirations better than you do. While there are many ways of doing that, a simple line down the middle of a sheet of paper, with the reasons to take the job written on one side and the reasons to turn it down on the other, is about as straightforward and objective as you can get.

You will weigh salary, future earnings and career prospects, benefits, commute, lifestyle, and stability of the company, along with all those intangibles that are summed up in the term *gut feelings*. Make sure you answer these questions for yourself:

- Do you like the work?
- Can you be trained in a reasonable period of time, thus having a realistic chance of success on the job?
- Are the title and responsibilities likely to provide you with challenge?
- Is the opportunity for growth in the job compatible with your needs and desires?
- Are the company's location, stability, and reputation in line with your needs?
- Is the atmosphere/culture of the company conducive to your enjoying working at the company?
- Can you get along with your new manager and immediate work group?
- Is the money offer and total compensation package the best you can get?

Notice that money is but one aspect of the evaluation process. There are many other factors to take into account as well. Even a high-paying job can be less advantageous than you think. For instance, you should be careful not to be foxed by the gross figure. It really is important that you get a firm handle on those actual, spendable, after-tax dollars—the ones with which you pay the rent. Always look at an offer in the light of how many more spendable dollars a week it will put in your pocket.

Evaluating the New Boss

When all that is done, you must make a final but immensely important determination—whether or not you will be happy with your future manager. Remember, you are going to spend the majority of your waking hours at work, and the new job can only be as good as your relationship with your new boss. If you felt uncomfortable with the person after an interview or two, you need to evaluate carefully the kind of discomfort and unhappiness it could generate over the coming months and years.

You'll want to know about the manager's personal style: Is he or she confrontational, authoritarian, democratic, hands-off? How would reprimands or differing viewpoints be handled? Does he or she share information on a need-to-know basis, the old military-management style of keep-'em-in-the-dark? When a group member makes a significant contribution, who gets the credit as far as senior management is concerned—the person, the manager, or the group? You can find out some of that information from the manager; other aspects you'll need to review when you meet team members, or the people from personnel.

Accepting New Jobs, Resigning from Others

Once your decision is made, you should accept the job verbally. Spell out exactly what you are accepting: "Mr. Smith, I'd like to accept the position of engineer at a starting salary of $42,000. I will be able to start work on March 1. And I understand my package will include life, health, and dental insurance, a 401K plan, and a company car." Then you finish with: "I will be glad to start on the above date pending a written offer received in time to give my present employer adequate notice of my departure. I'm sure that's acceptable to you."

Until you have the offer in writing, you have nothing. A verbal offer can be withdrawn—it happens all the time. That's not because the employer suddenly doesn't like you, but because of reasons that affect, but bear no real relationship to, your candidacy. I have known of countless careers that have stalled through reneged verbal offers—they lead to unemployment, bitterness, and even lawsuits. So avoid the headaches and play it by the numbers.

Once you have the offer in writing, notify your current employer in the same fashion. Quitting is difficult for almost everyone, so you can write a pleasant resignation letter, walk into your boss's office, hand it to him or her, then discuss things calmly and pleasantly once he or she has read it.

You will also want to notify any other companies who have been in negotiation with you that you are no longer on the market, but that you were most impressed with meeting them and would like to keep communications open for the future. (Again, see the next chapter for details on how to handle—and encourage—multiple job offers.)

24 | Multiple Interviews, Multiple Offers

Relying on one interview at a time can only lead to anxiety, so you must create and foster an ever-growing network of interviews and, consequently, job offers.

False optimism and laziness lead many job hunters to be content with only one interview in process at any given time. That severely reduces the odds of landing the best job in town within your chosen time frame. Complacency guarantees that you will continue to operate in a buyer's market.

The recommended approach is to generate as many interviews as possible in a two- to three-week period. Interviewing skills are learned and consequently improve with practice. With the improved skills comes a greater confidence, and those natural interview nerves disperse. Your confidence shows through to potential employers, and you are perceived in a positive light. And because other companies are interested in you, everyone will move more quickly to secure your services. That is especially important if you are unfortunate enough to be unemployed. Being out of work is when you need money the most and is the time when the salary you can command on the open market is substantially reduced. The interview activity you generate will help offset this.

By generating multiple interviews, you bring the time of the first job offer closer and closer. That one job offer can be quickly parlayed into a number of others. And with a single job offer, your unemployed status has, to all intents and purposes, passed.

Immediately, you can call every company with whom you've met, and explain the situation. "Mr. Johnson, I'm calling because while still under consideration with your company I have received a job offer from one of your competitors. I would hate to make a decision without the chance of speaking with you again. I was very impressed by my meeting with you. Can we get together in the next couple of days?" End, of course, with a question that carries the conversation forward.

If you were in the running at all, your call will usually generate another interview; Mr. Johnson does not want to miss out on a suddenly prized commodity. Remember: It is human nature to want the very things one is about to lose. So you see, your simple offer can be multiplied almost by the number of interviews you have in process at the time.

A single job offer can also be used to generate interviews with new firms. It is as simple as making your usual telephone networking presentation, but you end it differently. You would be very interested in meeting with them because of your knowledge of the company/product/service, but also because you have just received a job offer—would it be possible to get together in the next couple of days?

Relying on one interview at a time can only lead to prolonged anxiety, disappointment, and, possibly, unemployment. That reliance is due to the combination of false optimism, laziness, and fear of rejection. Those are traits that cannot be tolerated except by confirmed defeatists, for defeat is the inevitable result of those traits. As Heraclitus said, "Character is destiny." Headhunters say, "The job offer that cannot fail will."

Self-esteem, on the other hand, is vital to your success, and happiness is found with it. And with it you will begin to awake each day with a vitality previously unknown. Vigor will increase, your enthusiasm will rise, and desire to achieve will burn within. The more you do today, the better you will feel tomorrow.

Even when you follow this plan to the letter, not every interview will result in an offer. But with many irons in the fire, an occasional firm "no" should not affect your morale. It won't be the first or last time you face rejection. Be persistent, and above all, close your mind to all negative and discouraging influences. The success you experience from implementing this plan will increase your store of willpower and determination, affect the successful outcome of your job hunt, and enrich your whole life. Start today.

The key to your success is preparation. Remember, it is necessary to plan and organize in order to succeed. Failing is easy—it requires no effort. It is the achievement of success that requires effort; and that means effort today, not tomorrow, for tomorrow never comes. So start building that well-stocked briefcase today.

25 | What If I Am Asked to Take a Drug Test?

A "false positive" can derail your career. Protect yourself.

"Would you be willing to take a drug test as a condition of employment?"

More and more often, you're likely to see the statement, "Employment is contingent upon a negative drug test" on your initial application form. You will probably hear no more on the topic until after an offer has been extended. You are only likely to be tested if you are the choice for the job. At this point, you can expect to be called in for a couple of hours of pre-employment paperwork; this is when you are most likely to be asked to produce a urine specimen for drug testing.

Rightly or wrongly, drug testing as a condition of employment is much more common than in years past, and it is likely to remain part of the job search landscape for the foreseeable future. I wrote in 1979 that "we can reasonably expect that by the mid-nineties, up to one out of every three jobs will require some form of drug testing as part of the selection process." From the vantage point of 1998 we can see that this projection was too conservative. Today almost seven out of every ten jobs require a negative drug test as a condition of employment.

The Supreme Court has upheld drug testing programs for federal employees holding law enforcement positions and for customs personnel involved in drug interdiction activities. While there is no direct link between these governmental policies and private industry hiring, the rulings have been interpreted as reflecting our society's general acceptance of drug testing.

The vast majority of testing is done to screen potential employees; the Employment Management Association has concluded that once hired, you are less likely to be subjected to drug testing than you were as an applicant (unless, of course, you exhibit signs of drug abuse on the job). However, expect a steady increase in random on-the-job testing too, as companies and unions make it a matter of policy.

Perhaps you are reading this section out of curiosity, because drugs and drug testing are in the news these days. You may even think to yourself, "Well, this is all very interesting, but I don't take drugs; none of this applies to me." Unfortunately, you couldn't be more wrong.

Drug testing is everyone's business, because even those who have no problem with abusing controlled substances can be hurt if a "false positive" reading shows up on their drug test. Although there have been significant improvements in testing technologies, inaccurate readings are still all too common.

Over the last decade drug testing has grown from a fad to a largely well-run industry. The acceptance of drug testing procedures as a standard part of employee selection in much of corporate America has reduced the cost of testing, which in turn has added to its popularity.

In the last couple of years employers (on the whole) have been taking a far more responsible role in demanding accurate testing and in protecting the job applicant's right to privacy. For example, at one time a repulsive practice called "observed collection" looked like it was going to become the norm. This meant you produced your specimen under surveillance. Fortunately, this practice has become much less fashionable. (More on what has replaced it later.)

However, despite the growing sophistication of the industry, some drug tests still come back with false positives. These mistakes provide seemingly authoritative "evidence" that you have used illicit drugs when you have not. To say the least, this finding would not add to your professional reputation.

What Causes False Positives?

There are a number of things that can cause false positives. First, many everyday foods, beverages, and over-the-counter drugs can set off alarms meant to identify serious drug abuse. By taking a pain reliever that contains ibuprofen, for instance—as millions do for the relief of any number of aches and pains—you run the risk that you will test positive for marijuana use. If you suffer from a cold and want to be sure to get the sleep necessary to put in a good day at work tomorrow, you may decide to take a nighttime cold medication; but if there is a surprise drug test the next day, you may learn to your amazement that you are an abuser of opiates.

False positives can also occur as the result of taking prescription asthma medications, or because of cross-reacting chemicals from that doctor-prescribed and -controlled diet plan you're on. Has your physician instructed you to take the sedative Valium? If so, a drug test could earn you a reputation as an angel dust fan. You are likely to show up as a morphine addict if you've suffered a bad cold or cough and have been prescribed codeine or certain other medications. This may also happen if you indulge in that most wicked of all addictions: lust for poppy seed bagels. That's what two bagel-munching Navy doctors discovered: Their careers nearly ran aground when two consecutive tests branded them as users of morphine. A few weeks later, however, the Navy discovered the error and traced it to the ship's commissary. The consumption levels of the bagels in question, the Navy eventually admitted, were well within the range of "normal dietary use."

The pharmaceutical companies that sell the tests identify the *known* substances that are *proven to* cross-react, but that doesn't mean that those administering the tests can always be depended upon to possess this information or use it wisely. It should be noted, too, that the test manufacturers admit the tests are sometimes just plain wrong, poppy seeds or no poppy seeds. Their line is that urinalysis (the most common form of drug testing) carries no more than a 5 percent inaccuracy rate. (This is misleading, however, as we shall see.)

Five percent doesn't seem like much, does it? Many businesses and organizations seem to have decided that a 5 percent error rate is an acceptable level of risk. Stop for a moment, though, and ask yourself this: What happens if you are the unlucky one out of twenty who is wrongly identified as a drug abuser?

A little background is probably in order here. Drug testing recognizes (or, at any rate, is meant to recognize) whether minuscule traces of a certain substance are present in the urine. Marijuana, which accounts for over 90 percent of all positive findings, stays in an average-sized body for up to three weeks. Of course, the length of time any substance stays in your system is affected by your actual body weight and your general health.

Now then. Since the question is not whether you *decided* to put a substance in your body, but whether it is *present,* an interesting set of issues arises. We are all well aware of the ongoing conflict over secondhand cigarette smoke; current evidence indicates that even those who don't smoke tobacco can, if they breathe air polluted by cigarette smoke, *suffer* adverse health effects as a result. The smoke still enters the body, even if you don't have a cigarette between your lips.

Marijuana makes smoke, too. And you don't have to smoke it for it to show up in your system. Just go to a party where someone else is smoking it, or sit next to a puffing Wall Streeter at a Grateful Dead concert, and you could have your professional reputation destroyed by an "accurate" drug test the next day! I should note that a number of tests have established minimum levels, below which the results will be considered negative. This has been done to accommodate the passive smoke concerns, so maybe you can go to Lollapalooza after all.

What's more, the 5 percent inaccuracy rate claimed by the manufacturers of urinalysis tests is, while true in the strict sense, not meaningful in practical terms. In clinical testing conditions, these tests have indeed been shown to perform at or under a 5 percent error ratio. But your drug test will not be conducted in clinical testing conditions. It will be conducted "in the field"—out in the real world, where things aren't monitored quite so closely. When the lab's emphasis is on weeding out drug users (rather than on research), the error rate can be expected to balloon to 14 percent, according to estimates made in the *Journal of Analytic Toxicology*.

Let's examine the history of drug testing accuracy. The Center for Disease Control (CDC) and the National Institute on Drug Abuse (NIDA) ran a nine-year study on the accuracy of private-sector laboratories. Private-sector labs, where your specimen is most likely to be handled, hardly inspire confidence: They don't have to be licensed, they usually operate without legislated training requirements, and they are often staffed by workers receiving only minimum wage. The results of the study? Brace yourself.

When the labs knew the specimens in question came from the CDC and the NIDA, the results were extremely impressive and could serve as a model for any testing program. But when the labs did not know where the specimens were coming from—when the specimen, in other words, could have been yours—a very different picture emerged. Up to sixty-six out of a hundred samples showed false positives. That translates to two-thirds of a given group of people having their reputations destroyed for no particular reason. At the same time, the inaccuracy rate for screening known abusers under these "blind" conditions was shown to rise to as high as 100 percent! Translation: The labs gave a clean bill of health to up to 100 percent of the sample specimens *known* to contain traces of illegal drugs.

In response to horror stories like these, the government's department of Health and Human Services has taken on the responsibility of accrediting testing labs. Fortunately, this accreditation and policing is catching on with employers and labs alike—employers because it reduces the chances of lawsuits, and the labs because losing accreditation could cost them business. But it's quite clear, the claims of the pharmaceutical industry and the good efforts of everyone at remedying the problems notwithstanding, there is still considerable cause for concern.

What causes testing inaccuracy? First of all, juggling urine specimens all day long is not everyone's idea of ultimate career fulfillment, and as the pay isn't a king's ransom either, it is not surprising that the quality of lab work is less than exemplary. Second, urine testing is easy to do incorrectly. The specimens go stale quickly and react poorly to extremes of heat and cold. In addition, urine that is too acidic or too alkaline can skew the test results; this can be caused simply by the subject's eating spicy foods before the test.

Now for the Relatively Good News

Believe it or not, the steadily increasing volume in the urine testing business has its benefits for the job hunter. While EIA (urinalysis) is still the test of choice, it is becoming standard practice that when a urinalysis test comes back positive, it is automatically followed up with the far more accurate GCMS test. This automatic application of GCMS should help counteract the problems caused by false positives.

The Fairest Drug Test of All

You can feel most relaxed about a drug test if your potential employer uses a third-party testing company referred to as an MRO. MRO is an acronym for Medical Review Officer, the medical practitioner who usually heads the testing firm. MRO companies treat accuracy and confidentiality very seriously, because a breach of either can result in loss of accounts. MROs are becoming more popular because employers are concerned about their legal exposure with less than exemplary drug testing programs.

Pre-employment screening tests, both urinalysis and others, typically test for abuse in five areas:

- Cannabis (marijuana)
- Opiates (codeine/morphine)
- Phencyclidines (PCP/angel dust)
- Amphetamines (speed)
- Cocaine (crack)

If you test positive on a urinalysis test, a GCMS will automatically be performed. If the GCMS comes back with a "verified positive" (see box), the MRO will contact you directly, say that you have tested positive in one of the five areas, and ask if you have an explanation.

If you can confirm, through your doctor, that you have a prescription that contains the offending substance, or a similar or cross-reactive drug, you will be in the clear. Alternatively, if you have been overseas in a place where this drug is legal, or where it was administered under medical supervision, you are again in the clear—so long as the appropriate travel dates appear on your passport.

Both MROs and employers I have spoken with tell me that the biggest danger for most job applicants is taking a spouse's prescription medication. It is something many of us do from time to time. Popping your loved one's pills, *for whatever reason*, is unacceptable. A verified positive test, *for whatever reason* (except as described above), will invariably result in the withdrawal of a job offer.

> A verified positive test is one that is positive on an initial EIA (immunoassay test) and confirmed by a GCMS (gas chromatography/mass spectrometry assay test).

Facing the Test

While the dangers of drug testing to your job hunt and career are gradually diminishing with the advent of HMO and HHS-certified testing laboratories, these are still new on the scene and have yet to dominate the market. In the meantime you still have a job to get, a career to nurture, and a reputation to protect.

When a drug test looms in your future, there are three questions that should help to put your mind at ease. They are questions that no responsible employer will object to:

1. Is the drug testing program administered by a Medical Review Officer?
2. Does the program use HHS (Health and Human Services)-certified labs exclusively?
3. Is there a right to retesting?

In reference to this third question, if the test should show a positive result, reputable pharmaceutical companies and laboratories will recommend an additional test; you are well within your rights to ask whether you will be given this basic consideration. If the company's program is using an MRO or HHS lab, a positive urinalysis test will automatically be followed up by the very accurate GCMS tests. Consequently, you are likely to be told that you do have a right to another test; however, the employer will want you to pay for it; and will only reimburse you if the results contradict the previous GCMS test. This happens about as often as a blue moon.

Being asked in advance to list drugs you are taking is becoming far less common with the move towards MROs and HHS-certified labs. However, not all companies are using these labs.

In these other instances you will likely be given a form to read, fill in, and sign. This formalizes your permission to conduct the test, and affirms your willingness to comply with company policies on the matter. The form should also list all the over-the-counter and prescription drugs and other ingestible substances known to cross-react with the test that will be used. Be sure to indicate on the form any of these substances and all drugs and medications you have taken recently. The form often asks you to note what has been taken "within the week," but you should also list any medications you have taken in the past few weeks. Depending on your body weight, one week may not be enough to flush the residues from your system.

Do not fail to note *every* applicable item! Five minutes ago you had no idea that a bagel or a cold medication could earn you a reputation as a drug abuser; no substance is "innocent" when it comes to cross-reaction in drug tests.

As I noted above, observed collection, which is corporate gobbledygook for urinating in front of witnesses, is thankfully on the decline. However, don't settle down with the *New York Times* crossword while producing your specimen. These days the tester will slap an adhesive thermometer on that warm little tube once you emerge to check that the temperature falls between the 94–99 degree range. The thermometer approach is seen as a more dignified approach to the problem with switched specimens.

Protecting your privacy and maintaining the security of your specimen has led to the development of a carefully controlled "chain of possession" process that all the better labs adhere to. Unfortunately, you can destroy this chain of possession and your chances of getting the job within five minutes of leaving the sanctum sanctorum. You'll be asked to write your phone number on an adhesive strip attached to the now-sealed vial. If you don't write down a phone number the MRO (Medical Review Officer) will not bother to track you down through other channels; and may report that the test was not completed and that the candidate in question is "medically unqualified." That sound you're hearing? Your job offer flushing down the toilet.

Suppose that, somewhere during the interview process, someone at the firm comments suspiciously that you seem remarkably well briefed on the topic of drug testing. You might reply along these lines:

"Being a person who is attentive to detail and proud of it, I took the time to research this issue thoroughly. It is my understanding that some programs are more carefully run than others. I think we are both just trying to protect our reputations. I don't know your company as well as you do, as you do not know me as well as I do."

While the drug testing industry is making a concerted effort to improve its security and accuracy, and all employers are equally concerned with fairness, you should still give yourself every advantage before taking the test. Here are some suggestions to put the odds in your favor:

You should note that drug tests are often scheduled to coincide with other pre-employment paperwork. When you schedule your appointment, keep in mind that some companies will not allow you to reschedule, and others, although not all, will rescind a job offer if you don't make the appointment, or if you fail to take the test within 48 hours. This is because some substances, like marijuana, begin to wash out of the system very quickly.

If you can, schedule the test for the afternoon, or even after work hours. The most concentrated urine specimens are those generated first thing in the morning; those given later in the afternoon are less potent.

The moment you learn that you may have to take a test, your objective should be to flush any possibly objectionable substances out of your body. Drink lots and lots of water; seize every opportunity to void yourself the day of the test.

Diuretic beverages such as coffee, tea, and juices will also flush out your system; although beer is also a diuretic, you should not drink alcohol prior to an interview, for obvious reasons.

Jogging or working out will make you perspire, which also helps clean out your system. Anyone in pursuit of a new job should exercise on a regular basis, anyway. Exercise will improve your alertness and physical agility.

Saunas and steam baths can help remove impurities from your system, as well as increase your need to consume more liquids. What's more, they are relaxing, rejuvenating, and good for the complexion.

Finally, you may want to pick up a bottle of B-complex vitamins and take some for the few days preceding your test date. They are good for you, of course, and will leave all sorts of wholesome stuff in your specimen, but they will also give your little glass jar a healthy yellow glow that fairly shouts: "This one is no crack addict!" (Well, appearances do count for something.)

Something New on the Horizon

RIAH (Radio ImmunoAssay of Hair), or hair analysis, is the latest thing on the drug testing scene, with a minimal 1% of the market. This cutting-edge technology is poised for growth. Hair analysis is twice as expensive as urinalysis, but where urinalysis tests for drugs used in the last few days and weeks, hair analysis provides a 90-day drug consumption history and can identify the varying amounts of different drugs taken throughout the period. RIAH methodology, in short, can offer a resume of everything you have consumed in the last 90 days, legal and otherwise, and in what quantity.

An RIAH test requires about sixty strands of hair 1-1/2 inches long, which is taken from the back of your head from just below the crown—hooray for male pattern baldness. The hair is then liquefied and tested. Not much is known about the flaws or risks of this testing method at this point, but there are two areas of concern.

First, RIAH will pick up secondhand smoke, so it's important to keep your hair clean.

The second concern is that RIAH may have the potential for ethnic bias. This is because substances remain sequestered in dark hair longer than in light hair. RIAH testers have stated that their procedures include an additional step that balances the differences between dark and light hair. I was not able to find out from a lab if this step is standard procedure for RIAH testing, whether or not it had to be specially requested, and if not, who makes the judgment call on whether to perform the additional step.

As RIAH is so new, no further information is available at present.

□   □   □

Remember, in the early stages of interviewing, your goal is to generate offers; you want people bidding for your services. Even an offer you don't want can be leveraged into another and better offer elsewhere. I would suggest that you bear in mind that potential employers should be on their best behavior when wooing new recruits. If you have to go through all of this nonsense prior to the wedding, what sort of marriage is it likely to be?

Corporate America is currently wringing its collective hands over the perceived fickleness and lack of loyalty in today's work force; but those in authority really should not be surprised. Loyalty is a two-way street; today, employees and potential employees are sometimes so casually assumed to be guilty before being proven innocent that they cannot be faulted for feeling that loyalty is a function of respect and appreciation. Remember, there is no testing in the boardroom.

26 | How to Ace the Psychological Tests

Careful! Answering these casually can be hazardous to your professional health.

In late 1989, Congress banned most private-sector applications of the polygraph test, voice stress analysis, and other electronic screening methods. While many government personnel (for instance, those involved in drug interdiction activities) are still subject to these tests, many private employers have had to change their ways, and are increasingly turning to psychological testing to weed out what they consider to be undesirable job applicants. These tests may be known as aptitude tests, personality profiles, personnel selection tests, or skills, aptitude, and integrity tests, but in the end they are all the same thing: an attempt to find out if you show signs of being a "risky" hire.

Actually, although the 1989 legislation has led to new popularity for the psychological tests, they have been around for decades. Psychological exams come in two flavors. One is a face-to-face meeting with a psychologist, and the other (far more common) is a written test, often multiple choice.

In any discussion of this issue, we should bear in mind that psychology is, by the admission of its own practitioners, an inexact science; and that few of the tests used in employee selection were designed for that purpose. While the tests cannot yield any definitive litmus test on your potential employability, many companies are grafting the imprecise discipline of psychological testing onto the equally imprecise one of employment selection. The result is easy to administer and relatively cheap. Those seeking employment are often asked to answer "a few routine questions" that end up being anything but routine. The tests, which should not be used as the sole basis for a hiring decision, are nevertheless often used in a pass/fail way and have a huge effect on people's livelihoods. In your case, let's do everything we can to make sure they don't have a negative effect on your job prospects.

It isn't surprising that many of the companies using the tests are concerned about the honesty of prospective employees. Each year American industry loses an estimated $40 billion from employee theft. While honesty is often one of the behavioral profiles examined, the tests can also examine aptitude and suitability for a position. Often, the exams are geared to evaluating the amount of energy a person might bring to the job, how he or she would handle stress, and what their attitudes toward job, peers, and management would be.

Unfortunately, answering a psychological test with complete personal honesty may very well threaten your chance of being offered employment. That's the bad news. Here's the good news: You can ace the tests without having to compromise your personal integrity.

Not long ago, I did an in-house employee selection and motivation seminar for a large corporation. I was asked for my opinion on the subject of psychological testing. I replied that the tests were often used inappropriately as a pass/fail criterion for hiring, and that anyone with half a brain could come up with the desired or correct answers. "The question is," I concluded, "how many people who could have served you well will you miss out on because of a test?"

The managers assured me that they had a test in use that was "virtually infallible" in helping to identify strong hires, and certainly not subject to the machinations of the average applicant. They asked if I would be prepared to take it. I not only agreed, but also promised to prove my point. "Let me take the test twice," I said. "The first profile you get will tell you to hire me; the second will say I'm a bad risk."

I took the test twice that day. "Applicant #1" came back with a strong recommendation for hire. "Applicant #2" came back with a warning to exercise caution.

How was this possible? Well, there is something the tests ignore: None of us is the same person in the workplace as in our personal life. Over a period of time at work, we come to understand the need for different behavioral patterns and different ways of interacting with people.

Sometimes our more considered, analytical, logical approaches pass over from our "professional self" into the personal realm. However, in the world of work, we are not expected to try to override the "corporate way" to do things according to our personal preferences. When this happens, and personal preferences take precedence over existing corporate theories of behavior, we get warnings and terminations. In other words, as professionals, we are inculcated with a set of behavioral patterns that enable us to be successful and productive for our employers.

Did I really "fool" the test? No. I was completely honest both times. The "winning" test was the one in which I viewed myself—and, thus, described myself— as a thoroughly professional white-collar worker in the job for which I was applying. The "losing" test was the one I used to describe myself as the kind of person I see myself as in my personal life.

This was not a hoax perpetrated by a smart aleck. I am that person they would have hired, and I possess a strong track record to back up my claim. I simply learned the behaviors necessary to succeed, adopted them, and made them my own—just as you have undoubtedly done.

Many of the tests simply lack an awareness of the complexity of the human mind. They seem to miss the point when they ask us to speak honestly about our feelings and beliefs. They do not take into account that our learned behaviors in our professional lives are, invariably, quite distinct from the behaviors we display in our personal lives.

The secret of my success—and of yours, if you must take a psychological test—is really quite simple. If you understand what you are likely to face you can prepare and present yourself in the most effective way, and you can do it without compromising your integrity.

How to Prepare for, Read, and Answer the Tests

First of all, understand that there are five different types of tests, designed to plumb different aspects of your doubtless troubled psyche:

- Personality
- Personnel selection
- Aptitude
- Skills
- Integrity

Let's take a look at each of these.

Personality Tests

Are you a people person? Do you get upset easily? Are you quick to anger? Employers are using tests of general personality more frequently these days to screen job candidates. They use these tests because they believe that certain personality traits are required for success in a particular position.

There are two basic kinds of personality tests: projective and objective.

Projective Personality Tests. The projective tests ask you to tell a story, finish a sentence, or describe what you see in a blob of ink. These tests, in some form or other, have been around for decades, and psychologists use them a great deal to help understand how we deal with tough issues.

One popular test shows you pictures of a scene, in black and white usually, and you're asked to describe what's going on. The psychologist may ask you to "tell me more about it." These areas of your mind are also gotten at through the use of incomplete sentences, where you are given the beginning of a sentence and have to fill in the rest of it on your own. So, for instance, you may be asked to complete a sentence such as "When I am at work, I . . ."

In an employment selection context, these tests are generally looking for leaders, achievers, and winners. They search for analytical and system thinking skills, and look at decision-making and consensus-building styles.

Objective Personality Tests. Objective personality tests ask dozens, sometimes hundreds, of questions using some sort of rating scale, like strongly agree to strongly disagree, true/false, or just yes/no. These tests usually have good reliability and validity. But they were not designed to be used for employee screening, although they often are.

Knowing the names of the most common tests can tip you off to the type of screening being done. Tests you might run into that screen personality include:

NEO Personality Inventory: measures adjustment, extroversion, openness, agreeableness, and conscientiousness

16 PF: Measures sixteen personality factors, including a lie scale

California Psychological Inventory: measures twenty personality scales such as empathy, tolerance, responsibility, and dominance[1]

Minnesota Multiphasic Personality Inventory: a very long, heavy-duty test of major psychological problems, often (wrongly) used in employee selection

Personnel Selection Tests

Personnel selection tests are personality tests designed specifically to screen job candidates. These tests measure psychological behaviors such as trustworthiness, reliability, and conscientiousness. Some of them also psychologically screen you for potential alcohol or substance abuse. Tests you might run into that examine these areas include:

- Hogan Personality Inventory
- Employee Reliability Inventory
- PDI Employment Inventory

---

[1] The California Psychological Inventory is a good personality test, but it can be expensive for an employer, so it isn't used as often as some others.

Aptitude

If you don't have the skills it takes to do the job, do you have the aptitude to learn? In a work world where the learning curve for new skill development becomes increasingly interesting to potential employers, we can expect to see the use of aptitude tests on the upswing. Judging your ability to develop skills in general or skills in a particular area is the premise behind these aptitude tests.

Some of the aptitude tests you might run into that examine these areas include:

- Wechsler Adult Intelligence Scale-Revised
- Raven's Progressive Matrices
- Comprehensive Ability Battery
- Differential Aptitude Tests

Skills

If the job calls for typing seventy-five words per minute, then you may be given a typing test. If you are a programmer, you may be asked to take an objective test of programming skills, or asked to debug a program. There are tests to measure every possible skill: filing, bookkeeping, mechanical comprehension, specific computer programs, math, credit rating, and so on. Some of them are typical paper-and-pencil written tests. Newer tests present the information using a software program. Typing tests, for instance, have largely been replaced by keyboarding tests; you are still typing but there's no paper or white-out involved.

It's hard to argue against some of these tests. After all, if the job calls for you to type letters and reports all day, the employer wants to hire the best typist. If you're supposed to use WordPerfect on the PC all day, the employer will look for the person with the best knowledge of that program. As long as the employer is measuring an important skill, testing skills makes sense.

Skill tests you are likely to run into include:

- Wonderlic Basic Skills Test
- TapDance: computer keyboarding test
- Short Employment Test

Integrity Tests

Integrity tests are increasingly popular. Some companies are leery of personality tests, so they turn to integrity tests to screen out the liars, cheats, and thieves. Some tests measure honesty, or integrity, whereas others measure other psychological traits.

The big problem with these integrity tests is that they don't work. A psychologist wrote that in one case using an integrity test would eliminate 2,721 honest applicants so that 101 potentially dishonest applicants would be denied employment.[2] I need to point out that the integrity test actually is okay, it's just that so few people actually steal[3] that the use of the test eliminates a heck of a lot of good applicants. Another major study found that 95.6% of people who take these tests and get a failing score are actually incorrectly classified![4]

Here are a couple of integrity tests in consistent use today:

- Personnel Selection Inventory
- Personnel Reaction Bank

So listen carefully and apply what you learn in this chapter so that you don't become an incorrectly classified statistic.

Getting to Know Yourself and Acing the Mind Readers

Born independently wealthy, very few of us would be doing the jobs we do. But we *are* doing them, and we have learned certain sets of skills and behavioral traits that are critical to our ability to survive and succeed professionally. The first thing you must do, then, is identify and separate the professional you from the personal you.

☐ **Step One: Never consider answering a test from the viewpoint of your innermost beliefs.** Instead, use your learned and developed professional behavior traits and modus operandi. Ask yourself, "How has my experience as a professional taught me to think and respond to this?" To do this effectively (and to understand ourselves a little better in the process), we need some further insights into the three critical skill sets that every professional relies on to succeed:

- Professional/technical skills (whether you're a secretary or a senior vice president)

---

[2] J. William Townsend. "Is integrity testing useful?" *HR Magazine*, July, 1992, p. 96.

[3] In this example, they estimated that 2.5% of employees in the retail business steal from their employer.

[4] U.S. Congress, Office of Technology Assessment (1990). *The use of integrity tests for pre-employment screening.* Washington, DC: U.S. Government Printing Office.

- Industry skills (such as—if you happen to be in banking—your overall knowledge of the world of banking: how things work, how things get done, what is accepted within the industry, and so on)
- Professional behavior traits (the traits, discussed in chapter 14 of this book, that all employers look for, and that will get you ahead once you are on the job)

☐ **Step Two: Look at yourself from the employer's point of view.** (Review "The Five Secrets of the Hire" and "The Other Side of the Desk" for some helpful ideas.) Evaluate what traits come into play that enable you to discharge your duties effectively. Examine the typical crises/emergencies that are likely to arise: What supportive behavioral traits are necessary to overcome them? As you do this, you will almost certainly relive some episodes that seemed to put you at a disadvantage for a time. When it was tough to do things the right way, you had to buckle down and see the problem through, even though doing so did not necessarily "come naturally." The fact is, though, you overcame the obstacle. Remember how you did so, and keep that in mind as you answer the questions.

Conversely, you will want to look at those instances where a crisis had a less-than-successful outcome. What traits did you swear you would develop and use for next time?

Highlighting such traits simply constitutes your acknowledgment of the supremacy of learned behavior in the workplace. It does *not* constitute lying. (Why do you think so many professionals strive to keep their business lives separate from their personal lives? What is the point of such a separation if the two lives are identical?)

☐ **Step Three: Think of people you've known who have failed on the job.** Why did they fail? What have you learned from their mistakes and made a part of the "professional you"?

☐ **Step Four: Think of people you've known who have succeeded on the job.** Why did they succeed? What have you learned from their success and made a part of the "professional you"? Once you have completed this exercise in detail, you will have effectively determined how a professional would react in a wide range of circumstances, and identified the ways in which you have, over time, developed a "professional self" to match that profile.

Getting Ready for the Test

Any test can be nerve-wracking, but when it comes to these tests your livelihood is in the balance, so tip the odds in your favor with these tried and proven techniques:

- The tests instruct you to answer quickly, offering the first response that comes to mind. Don't. Following this path may well cost you a job. Instead, look at the test in terms of the exercises outlined above; provide reasoned responses from the viewpoint of the "professional you."
- Time limits are usually not imposed; on the contrary, those administering the test will often begin the proceedings with a soothing "take your time, there's no pressure." (Except, of course, the minor pressure of knowing a job offer is on the line!)
- If there is a time limit, find out how much time you have. Figure out about how much time per question or section you have. Pacing yourself helps, because then you won't panic when all of a sudden you realize that you've only got five minutes to complete the second half of a fifteen-minute test. Of course, you'll bring your watch.
- When in doubt, guess. Some of the really sophisticated tests you may have taken to get into college nailed you if you guessed wrong, but skill tests usually work differently. They add up all of your right answers to get your test score. So, when in doubt, eliminate any of the obviously wrong answers, and take your best shot.
- With skill tests, you'll want to ask for a warm-up or practice section. One computer typing test has an optional practice session. Ask about it. If the test is on a computer, adjust your chair, keyboard, and monitor before the timer starts.
- For paper and pencil tests, make sure that you have enough desk space and sharp pencils.
- If the test is going to be done with other applicants in a group situation, stay focused on what you are doing. If you have to sit in the front of the room so no one else distracts you, then do it. If the test will be long, and there's no break, make sure that you won't get hungry, have to use the bathroom, or develop a low blood sugar level.
- No matter what, use all of your allotted time! Check your answers, and make sure they are written in the right places. Depending on your remaining time, review every other, or every fourth, question.

- You may not even realize that you're taking an integrity test until the direction of the questions gives it away: "Have you ever stolen anything?" "Have you ever felt guilty?" "Have you ever told a lie?" Avoid the temptation to respond impulsively with something like "Lies? No, I prefer to chop down the damned cherry tree." The truth is, we have all done these things in our lives. When you are asked, for instance, whether there is anything you would ever change about yourself, or whether you think everyone is dishonest to some degree, the overwhelming likelihood is that your own honesty is being tested: The best answer is probably "yes."

In fact, if you never admit to these behaviors, you could be pegged as a faker. While a faker may be kept in the running, they've earned a question mark. Fakers are sometimes viewed as being eager to please or simply a bit out of touch with their true feelings.

Many of the better tests in use today also use lie scales that can detect when someone is faking. How do they do this? One way is to include questions like "I always tell the truth" or "I never have a negative thought about a coworker." When the test is developed, hundreds or thousands of people take it, and the researchers figure out what the typical response is to these questions. Anyone who deviates from the average response on enough of these faking questions is also flagged as a faker.

If you must answer questions about ethics in a face-to-face encounter, you can explain your answer, placing it far in the past where appropriate, and explain what you have learned from any negative experience. If such questions must be answered on paper, the best approach is to follow the dictates of your own conscience and try to bring the issue up after the test. You might say something like this:

> **"Gee, that question about lying was a tough one. I guess everyone has told a lie at some time in the past, and I wanted to be truthful, so I said 'yes.' But I'd be lying if I didn't tell you it made me nervous. You know, I saw a show on television recently about these tests. It told the story of someone who lost a job because of answering a question just like that; the profile came back with an untrustworthy rating."**

This may reduce the odds of your being denied the job in the same way. If the test does come back with a question about your honesty, you will at least have sown seeds of doubt about the validity of such a rating in the interviewer's mind. That doubt, and your disarming honesty, might just turn the tables in your favor.

Be careful, and take a balanced approach as you answer integrity test questions. Honesty is the best policy:

- In a face-to-face meeting with a psychologist, use the same techniques we have discussed throughout *Knock 'em Dead* to qualify the questions before answering them; when you suspect a trap, employ the tricks that will help you clarify things and buy time.
- The written tests may contain "double blinds," where you are asked a question on page one, and then asked a virtually identical one thirty or forty questions later. The technique is based on the belief that most of us can tell a lie, but few of us can remember that lie under stress, and are therefore likely to answer differently later. This is held to show the potential for untruthfulness. The problem isn't that one answer is likely to deny you employment; the questions are asked in patterns to evaluate your behavior and attitudes on different topics.
- Read the test through before you start answering questions! (There's "plenty of time" and "no pressure," remember?) Review the material at least three times, mentally flagging the questions that seem similar. This way you will be able to answer consistently.
- Resist any temptation to project an image of yourself as an interesting person by the answers you select. These tests are not designed to reward eccentricity; think sliced white bread. You are happy at work and home. You enjoy being around people. You don't spend all your evenings watching movies (unless your name is Siskel or Ebert). You don't spend your weekends with a computer or pursuing other solitary pastimes (unless you are a programmer or an aspiring Trappist monk). You have beliefs, but not too strong. You respect the beliefs of all others, regardless of their age, sex, race, or religion.
- Relax. One part of the Wechsler test (a developmental aptitude test) asks you to repeat back a string of numbers to the psychologist. If you're too hyped up, you'll get flustered and blow it. These tests measure intelligence plus your test-taking behavior. And you can certainly improve your test-taking behavior!
- Learn to visualize success in advance. Picture yourself at the test. Go through each step: You hear the instructions, the examiner says to begin. You read the test questions and realize you will do well. You get to a really tough part of the test. Visualize your success, and visualize your setbacks, and realize that you can and you will pull through okay, because you have *a clear vision of the professional you.* When you finish the test, read through your answers a few times; if you don't like any answers, change them.

- Remember to use your professional, working mindset when you take these tests. Answer as you would if you were on the job and your boss was asking the questions.

□   □   □

All of what I have said here takes for granted that the overriding goal of the employer is to determine whether or not you are suitable for the job. If you can give an accurate, affirmative answer to that question, then the approach you take in doing so is—to my way of thinking, anyway—of little consequence. If you have learned and applied what it takes to prosper in your profession, then it is emphatically your right to provide an honest profile of your professional self, in whatever forum you are to be evaluated.

Part V | In Depth

What if things aren't clicking?

On some days, it may look like there are considerably more obstacles to your campaign than anything else. Lethargy and discouragement can set in. What's more, bills maintain a nagging habit of requiring payment, which can be tiresome even if you are still employed—and downright crushing if you're not.

Similar obstacles, of course, can arise on the job. Careers get stalled, promotions fail to materialize, jobs demand change. While there's nothing particularly amusing about career problems, you should bear in mind that your biggest potential asset and/or liability in the search is the person staring back at you from the bathroom mirror each morning. That person is a walking, talking advertisement—pro or con—of your professionalism. If the face you see is drawn, pale, aggravated, or simply tired, you need to stop and take stock. You may be short-circuiting your own efforts.

In this section of the book, we'll look at some techniques for making the financial pinch you may be feeling throughout your job hunt a little more bearable. We'll also examine the best ways to manage your career once you actually get the position you want.

27 | Conducting a Job Search While You're Still Employed

Do whatever is necessary so that you don't get your walking papers before you decide to walk.

Make No Mistake

Looking for a great way to get fired? Leave the original copy of your resume in the office photocopier. It was bad news five years ago, before the downsizing boom. Today it's like signing your own death warrant. Well, who would you lay off, the guy who really wants to work at the company or the one who has demonstrated his intent to leave?

Most prudent people conduct a job search while they're still gainfully employed. In fact, if you suspect a layoff is imminent (see "When You See Clouds on the Horizon," page 270, for some of the early warning signs), you must start looking or get caught in a glut when five hundred others get the pink slip. Maybe you have a dead-end job, are employed in an industry that's doomed in the technological age, or suspect that you have more professional potential than your current employer can tap. Maybe you took a lesser job to put food on the table and keep a roof over your head. No matter what the reason, if your job doesn't seem long for this world, now is the time to start looking around.

Just don't get caught.

Before you start looking for a job while you're still employed, look at your motives.

If you intend to use a job offer from the outside to get a counter-offer from your current employer, forget it. Even if you get a raise, you will likely only benefit in the short term. Sooner or later, the fact that you strong-armed your employer is likely to catch up with you, when the next round of downsizing comes along, as we both know it will.

Home Is Where the Office Is

Use your home rather than the office. You won't be tempted to leave your resume in the photocopier, and you can work with maximum privacy.

For efficiency, set up your home-based office as though you were running a business. Designate a room as yours, and allow no phone calls, TV sets, visitors, or other distractions during work hours.

When job hunting while you're still employed, the last thing you want at your current job is inquiries from potential employers. So you must have a means to take calls from potential employers that will present you in a fashionable light.

You might be able to talk your spouse into taking on the role of receptionist. Or you can have a special hotline installed and give that number exclusively to prospective employers. Keep an appropriate message on your answering machine for the duration of the job search, and make sure that family members and roommates answer the phone professionally at all times.

Stick to It

You might be working for yourself in an informal environment, but there are still some rules. And you're in charge of setting them and implementing them.

Once you've established a plan for your job search, stick to it. Decide what your work-at-home hours will be, whether it's thirty minutes before dinner or two hours before bedtime each night, and then set the schedule in stone.

Since your job search probably won't be a matter of public record, work to keep yourself motivated. Reward yourself for your successes. Decide on a movie you'll see, a restaurant you'll go to, or whatever works for you, to celebrate sending out the twentieth, fiftieth, or hundredth batch of letters, going on your first interview, and so on.

And be persistent. I remember, years ago, my friend Dennis had a hook for his jacket on the back of his office door. When he put it on every evening, the last thing he saw was a message that read, "Keep Writing." It was a reminder for him to continue his job hunting campaign when he got home. When the going gets tough, remember your goal—a more interesting job, better pay, increased job security, etc.—and don't let anything deter you!

Get Organized

Since you have a job already, you don't have the luxury of spending forty hours a week on a job search. So you have to make the most of every moment.

Take some time to research everything you've been wanting to know about the industry you're working in but haven't had time to find out recently. See who the important players are, which companies are prospering, and who's been promoted. Catch up on old contacts. Contact or join trade organizations and associations, and make friends throughout your industry; attend trade shows and conventions. Or, if you prefer, learn all you can about an up-and-coming industry that might make for an interesting career move, and find out how your skills might be applied toward it.

Stretching Your Job Search Hours

To maximize your time, you might want to engage the services of employment agencies. (Use employer-paid services only—see pages 29–30.) That way you can have headhunters do some of the legwork for you—and it always helps to have job search allies.

The key to stretching your job search hours is to make the most of every moment you do have available instead of lamenting about the time you don't have. Use lunch hours, weekends, holidays, personal days, and any other off-the-clock time you have available to conduct research. (If, by the way, you're conducting an after-hours electronic job search—see Appendix A, pages 290–316—your rates will be even cheaper than they would be during business hours.)

Check out job fairs and college or alumni offices for job listings. You might also try your hand at writing (and publishing) magazine articles related to your profession, or securing public-speaking engagements to boost your exposure to large groups of people in your field. The easiest way to get started with either of these tactics is to become an active member of your professional association. That gives you access to trade newsletters, magazines, meetings, and so on.

Market Yourself

Direct mail shots with cover letters and resumes are an effective use of your time when you're looking for a job while you're still employed. Your short-term goal is to turn your home-based office into a direct mail house with one product: You. The selling points? Your skills and experience. And the customers? Any and all prospective employers.

Spend time creating a targeted mailing list composed of the companies most likely to hire you. Then identify the needs of each, so you can market your services appropriately. Use a computer to research companies online (for more information on the electronic job hunt, see Appendix A, pages 290–316). Today, vast amounts of data and contact information are available to you by computer.

Because job hunting while employed is less frantic than the alternative, you will have time to learn about companies and contacts through your research, and you can learn where each company is headed and what each really needs. Then you can use this information to send a perceptive and powerful cover letter with your resume. (For more information about cover letters, see my book, *Cover Letters That Knock 'em Dead.*)

How to Keep Your Job While You're Looking Elsewhere

Do whatever is necessary so that you don't get your walking papers before you decide to walk:

- Don't let anyone in the office know that you're looking for another job, if you can help it. Even if you tell no one besides your best friend, you've told one coworker too many. Word has a way of getting around, and if management finds out, you've had it.
- Make sure everything seems the same. When you're at the office, dress the way you've always dressed, contribute to meetings what you've always contributed, keep the same hours, and so on. Don't let anybody suspect that you're meeting recruiters during lunch hours, losing interest in your job, or taking time off for interviews. Everything should go on as before.
- If anything, do your job better than you have before, and become an even more valuable worker.
- Keep office items at the office. Don't pack up your belongings, even if they're personal things such as photographs, until you're ready to leave.
- The great advantage of job hunting while employed is the relative lack of urgency. You have time to research companies and people, time to rebuild your resume, time to craft *Knock 'em Dead* cover letters, time to become part of your professional resume. You will be more focused and informed.

The result will not always be a better job but will certainly be a more career-buoyant you.

How to Resign

Once you've accepted a job offer and you're ready to resign, do it graciously. Now is not the time to pay back your employer for years of grief; save the bridge burning for your fantasies and go about the business of severing relations professionally. You never know when you'll run into your former employer or when you'll need the old so-and-so again.

Although employees who are terminated are expected to clean out their desks and leave immediately, resigning workers are generally required to give proper notice. Helping make a smooth transition for your remaining colleagues builds bridges for the future. You can even offer to hire and train a replacement—and you can promise to be available to answer questions even after you leave. Be sure and follow through if you do so.

An important tip: It's okay to be happy, but keep your mirth under control while you're in the office. Save the rip-roaring celebration for family and friends. Even your closest colleagues can resent your good fortune, so don't do anything to encourage them to believe you might be gloating. Remember, those you offend on the way up could very well show you the way down sometime in the future.

28 | When You See Clouds on the Horizon

Continued employment no longer depends on company loyalty, but rather on your ability to change with the times.

Yes, it *can* happen to you.

In today's changing economy, any, repeat *any* employee can be laid off. Anytime. Anywhere. And make no mistake about it, if your number comes up it will in all likelihood be time for you to begin looking for another job somewhere else. Despite any delicate layers of euphemism that may accompany your notice, your employer will almost certainly not, as in the past, be calling you back. And in virtually every sector, the competition for available jobs is stiffer than it was a decade ago. So you have to ask yourself: Where would a layoff leave you?

Ten years ago, businesses absorbed employees hungrily and even created jobs based on incoming talent rather than existing need. By the end of that decade, however, the guillotine began to fall, enacting sweeping cuts worthy of *A Tale of Two Cities*. The American Management Association's annual survey on downsizing found that, over a five-year period, fully two-thirds of its sample had downsized at least once; 43 percent had downsized at least twice; and 24 percent had downsized three times or more. In a recent twelve-month period, the average number of positions eliminated in a layoff was more than double that of the previous survey (317 compared to 133).

In other words, heads have rolled—and not solely as a result of the 1989–1991 recession. Today's business climate and technology have changed forever the nature of our work force. Today's markets are ultracompetitive, geared toward sudden technological shifts, and increasingly international in nature. For these and other reasons, all companies—even those showing record profits—are streamlining their organizations. When there are mergers and acquisitions, the elimination of duplicate employees is now the first order of business. An infusion of "new blood" is typically accompanied by a decision to purge the "old blood."

As if that weren't disorienting enough, companies have begun rethinking whether much of the work they do should even require employees in the first place.

More and more, noncore business functions are being contracted out and completely eliminated from the corporate structure. Areas in the direct line of fire include such former "untouchables" as accounting and finance, information systems, and human resources. There is increasing talk of paring down to an "irreducible core" of permanent employees and supplementing cyclical needs with temporary or contract workers.

Yes. All of this is depressing. But for the companies involved, these changes are often unavoidable. In many cases, keeping the guillotine sharpened is the only alternative to shutting the doors and laying *everyone* off.

Your ability to keep your head—and keep yourself employed—will depend on your ability to accept some facts about today's work and world. First, you must accept that the idea that you will work for one employer for the bulk of your career is no longer viable. Check the demographics yourself; employers have shown no hesitation in laying off mid- to senior-level managers short of retirement by a few years, months, or even days. Continued employment no longer depends on company loyalty, but rather on your ability to change with the times.

A Watchful Eye

By continuously assessing the health of your employer, you will be able to make informed decisions about what kind of changes you must make. In some cases, you will find the company so troubled that looking for another job before the ax falls is the best course of action. In other situations, adapting to a new way of doing business may be a sure-fire way to be among those valued employees in the irreducible core. Only you will be able to tell.

While restructuring does not necessarily mean that a company is planning a major layoff, it's a pretty darned good indication. Call it better-than-even odds that the one follows the other. Once you see evidence of unspecified Big Changes on the Horizon, your diagnosis of the situation—and your ability to adapt to it—should come into play. As corporations flatten their structure to become more efficient, employees are asked to work and think in new ways. Those who are unable to adapt to the new structure, or whose roles are found to be untenable in the new organization, will be the first to go.

Unfortunately, many people (and particularly those with a long history at the company) ignore what is going on right under their noses. Witness the case of the flight engineer who worked for a major airplane manufacturer. He saw his own name on a list of people the organization had determined it could do without—and refused to believe it. When he was handed his pink slip, he was speechless with shock.

As an employee, you probably have as much access to information as you need to make an informed judgment about what's on the horizon. When it comes to your own corner of the organization's universe, you know as much as the CEO and probably a good deal more. An accountant can see that revenues are not meeting expenditures. A salesperson knows when quotas aren't being met. Think carefully about the events that affect your department or position, and (discreetly, of course) investigate them further whenever you can.

On the brink of a disaster? Or poised for explosive growth to which you can contribute? You must find out into which category your company falls. But some changes in the company may be difficult to interpret. For instance, your company might use attrition—simply not filling vacated positions—as a way to cut costs. The next step might be to reduce administrative or support staff. You have to determine whether the company is sincerely attempting to improve efficiency and productivity, or whether these actions are leading to deeper staff cuts.

The signs will differ depending on the size of your employer, and you may have to put on your Sherlock Holmes hat to get the type of information you need. Then again, learning more about your company, your industry, and your market will also make you a better and more valuable employee. More important, it will enhance your career buoyancy.

Let's say you work for a publicly held corporation. By watching the price of your employer's stock over a specific period, you should be able to get an idea of the firm's performance and standing in the marketplace. It's simple enough to check the price of your company's stock (and, for comparison, that of its competitors) in a daily newspaper. Your firm's annual report may have similarly useful information, such as long-term plans and recent successes and failures. Has the company consolidated any of its operations? This may be a clue to future downsizing plans.

Many public libraries have CD-ROM services that allow you to access a massive volume of published material in a very short period of time; you can use this resource to scan articles about your company. Are the pieces positive or negative in tone? Do they relate, directly or indirectly, to your work? Read about your employer's competitors as well; you'll be in a better position to understand your company's moves. Trade and business publications are excellent sources of information about your company and its competitors; they will also give you an indication of the overall condition of the market.

During the mid-eighties, one professional woman in the petroleum industry saw the bid rates for consulting work drop dramatically due to an overabundance of workers. Virtually every company in the industry, it seemed, was either laying off employees or going out of business. By understanding the market, she was able to begin her job hunt long before the bottom fell out of the industry in the late eighties. She's now happily employed in another field.

Knowing the strategic advantages your company holds in the market can also be helpful. If you see these advantages disappearing (either because of new technology or other unexpected developments, such as sudden demographic changes or a natural disaster), collapse may be inevitable. If this is the case, you are well advised to start looking for another job *now*. Don't talk yourself into believing that things will eventually get better; they almost certainly won't.

Unfortunately, the downward spiral of a large corporation may be slow and subtle. In many cases, you may have to do more than simply read the trade papers. By successfully building a network of contacts throughout the organization, you may be able to find out exactly what is going on in departments far removed from your own. Developing a strong ally or two in the Human Resources department is often a good first step; people in this area will know in advance about any work force changes. By knowing and understanding what the company's plans are for the next one to five years, you will be better able to judge your employer's stability.

If you work for a large corporation, and you find that the firm is planning for next year, next quarter, or next month, but has no idea where it is going in five years, a red flag should go up immediately. There's a problem somewhere. Either management is simply inept, flying by the seat of its collective pants, or it is in a firefighting mode, living from one day's crisis to the next. You will have to make your own judgment as to whether or not the people at the top will be able to get their act together.

What about a smaller or mid-sized organization? Some clues are bound to be more obvious in a close-knit environment, where people often wear several hats. Look for bills that don't get paid, new work that doesn't come in, and old contracts that end without renewals or new work to take their place. You should also keep an eye on your workload and that of your fellow employees. If the company is shuffling people around more than usual, or if job responsibilities are changing significantly or frequently in a short period of time, there may be trouble ahead.

With work wrapping up on the two key projects in which he was involved, a highway engineer found himself shuffled between southern California, Milwaukee, and his home office in Phoenix several times in one year. He knew that, when things were going well, he rarely traveled, because he had enough work to keep him in the office. From these clues, he deduced that his number was up. Not long after the new travel pattern emerged, his employer asked him to take early retirement.

Dramatically increased or decreased travel can be one sign that new initiatives affecting you may be on the way; there are others. A sudden change in your performance evaluations may indicate some behind-the-scenes politicking—or a more straightforward attempt to discredit you and justify your dismissal.

Similarly, any indication that your boss's position is shaky may mean that your job is at risk as well. Changes in top leadership often mean a shakeup of philosophies, standard operating procedures, and staffing levels. Your value to members of the "old guard" may prove to be of little consequence to the incoming "new guard." However, proving yourself valuable to the organization in general may help stall your demise—and buy you the time you need to look for another job. (It may also provide you with better referrals, or a chance to be redeployed elsewhere in the company.)

The Hammer Falls

Some layoffs are completely unavoidable. Perhaps the company is no longer involved in the part of the business in which you have worked, or it cannot support more than the most elementary operations.

If you are asked to leave, it's in your best interest to keep your cool. Resist the temptation to blow up at your employer. Sure, it's unlikely you'll ever be asked back to your job, but there is that saying about burning bridges, remember? Concentrate on getting the best severance package (and future references) you can.

Ready for a surprise? You might be in a good negotiating position when it comes to that severance package. There are a number of reasons for this. First, it's likely that the employer is feeling guilty about the layoff. Second, other employees will watch how you're treated when you leave. It's bad for company morale if you're treated unfairly at this stage, and the employer knows it. Finally, there are pragmatic reasons to be fair. Who knows where you'll find yourself after you leave the company? Someday, when you make it to the top, your former boss may even approach *you* for a job!

When a severance package is presented to you, listen calmly. Once the details have been laid out, you will probably want to ask for more. Unless the company's employee handbook clearly details the benefits you are entitled to, it is almost certainly to your advantage to attempt to negotiate a higher severance figure. But how and when you ask are the key.

You may want to take more time to think about a severance package before signing anything. By then, you will have had time to think clearly, assess your situation, and figure out your financial needs. (See chapter 29, "Keeping the Financial Boat Afloat," for more details on this.) Taking a little extra time also allows you a "chill-out" period, which will reduce the likelihood that you will come across as angry and irrational when you present your arguments.

Whether or not you decide to ask for time to think about the severance offer, you should approach any attempt to increase the severance package in a nonthreatening manner. Be sure to begin by saying, "I'm certain that you're making every effort to be fair." Then summarize your contribution to the company so the employer knows exactly why you deserve the increased consideration.

Try for benefits that are already in the company's budget, such as magazine and newspaper subscriptions or professional association membership renewals. You might even be able to talk your former employee into continued use of a company car for a time.

As helpful as it may have been in helping you forecast the rough weather you are now negotiating, the Human Resources department, with its rulebooks and set policies, is unlikely to be your greatest ally in this cause. You should try to avoid negotiating your severance package solely through this office. Instead, co-opt your former supervisor, who is likely to feel much more guilt. Granted, the meeting may not be one you look forward to with great enthusiasm, but then again, this is not about getting mad or becoming vindictive; this is about survival. The best recipe calls for generous amounts of calm objectivity and carefully measured doses of despair.

The Emotional Costs

Take time to mourn the loss of your job, as you would any other loss. Don't tough it out. Admit that this hurts. The degree to which you effectively work through the shock will determine how quickly you can get back on your feet and mount a successful job search.

The aftereffects of job loss are similar to the stages of grieving that follow divorce or the death of a loved one: denial, bargaining, anger, depression, and acceptance. Dealing with these can be difficult, and may require more time than you would think.

Finding support is crucial to your success in landing another job. Consider joining community job search clubs or meeting with an ad hoc group of other people in your situation. (Perhaps there are others who were laid off at the same time you were at your old firm.) By following these steps, you will expand your opportunities and maintain some perspective on the situation.

When you're ready, turn this horrible experience into a growth opportunity. Assess the experience and be honest with yourself. Did you inadvertently contribute to the situation? Was there anything you might have done differently? Did you learn anything that you can apply in your next job?

29 | Keeping the Financial Boat Afloat

How to make the best choices in tough times.

For too many of us, it actually takes losing a job in tough times to illustrate how close to the economic edge we usually live. To be sure, we take on financial obligations of our own free will—but the media, the society we live in, and, yes, our erstwhile employers all encourage standards of consumption we quickly learn to take for granted.

If you are reading this in a state of shock because you have recently been terminated, have a seat and take a deep breath. Things are probably not as bad as they seem right about now, but even if they were, you would need to keep your wits about you. Rash decisions, decisions made in desperation, are the ones we end up regretting. Take some time to decompress.

When Still Inside the Building . . .

If, on the other hand, you are lucky enough to be reading this before your termination has been finalized, you should be very careful how you approach matters. It goes without saying that you should check your instinct to settle old scores or to lash out at the firm that is letting you go, but there are other important pieces of advice you should follow as well. Most of what follows is meant for those who have fallen victim to staffing cuts, but some of the ideas can be adapted to those who are terminated under less than favorable conditions—especially Rule Number One.

Rule Number One is simple: *Don't sign anything* until you are convinced you have everything the law, ethical considerations, and good old-fashioned guilt can elicit from the employer.

Ask about outplacement services. Outplacement firms are companies that provide you with job hunting assistance ranging from a one-day seminar to "as-long-as-it-takes" counseling. This type of program is increasingly common; don't feel guilty about asking for it.

Negotiate the best possible severance package. A week's severance pay for every year of service is the standard, inadequate though it is. Whatever you are offered, try to wheedle a little more. Point out that times are tough; if the unemployment rate is high, say so, and use actual numbers if you can. Remember, guilt works. Those that don't ask, don't get.

Find out what your benefits will be over the next months. Murphy's law, which states that whatever can go wrong will, applies with double force to the unemployed. Under the current insurance laws, you can continue the health plan your employer provided for you at a subsidized rate for up to eighteen months, after which time you can continue on the same plan at a (much higher) personal rate.

Determine the company policy on providing references. Sometimes companies will give no more than salary and dates of employment to those who call asking about your tenure there, regardless of your level of performance; this can adversely affect your job hunt. If you learn that this is the policy in your case, get a written letter to that effect to show to potential employers. If at all possible, you should obtain a written testimonial from your manager before you sign anything or leave the company.

You and I know, of course, that a reference is essentially the same thing as a letter testifying to your character. It is gratifying, however, how many superiors bidding a reluctant adieu to a team member are willing to forget this point. If you run into "company policy" trouble here, you can point out that you are not asking for an official reference, but the supervisor's personal evaluation of you as one professional discussing another. The fact that the personal reference need not appear on company stationery is usually a plus in obtaining the letter.

Request that the employer tell callers that you are unavailable, rather than unemployed, and that you will return all calls. Obviously, you won't be able to make this last forever, but you may be able to maintain at least the appearance of gainful employment. Every little bit helps.

If it isn't part of your outplacement package, try asking for desk space and telephone cost reimbursement for your job hunt. Of course, this is only feasible if you work in an appropriate office environment. Asking for desk space and telephone time in, say, a retail setting will do nothing but brand you as a head case. Assuming the circumstances are favorable for such a request, you may be able to get two or three months worth of help, or perhaps a flat cash payment. You certainly shouldn't rely on this, but it could be worth asking about.

Ask for professional financial counseling. In case the employer hasn't thought of this (a good bet), call an accountant for an estimate of the amount of money involved; the *Yellow Pages* are a good resource to use if you don't already know of a reputable accountant. Say, "I've just been laid off; I'm married, with two kids and a mortgage. I want to know how much you'd charge to help me create a liveable, pared-down budget." Then go to the employer with the figure. If a number of people are being let go, you may be able to get the employer to spring for a seminar for everyone.

Once You've Left the Building . . .

The time for all of the above has passed. You and the employer have parted company, and you must make some sense of the financial picture before you. If you don't face up to the financial problems of unemployment in a timely fashion, you may end up losing everything except the shopping cart. So face the facts early—and if you didn't do it early, do it now. Immediate action will only help you reach the point where problems are rectified all the sooner. Procrastination can only worsen your situation.

If you have stocks or stock options, you may want to consider cashing them in. However, you should be prepared to pay a capital gains tax on your profits. If you have a vested company-sponsored pension plan, this will merit your close attention, as well. I have heard of employees who had to sue to get monies owed them through these plans, but this problem generally arises only with smaller employers. Check with an accountant or financial advisor for all the details.

You may have the option of having your severance moneys paid out to you on a regular basis, approximating the payment pattern of your wages, or in a lump sum. Arguments run in two directions on this. Some feel that it is to your advantage to have the payments spread out because this realistically defines you as being on the payroll and, therefore, at least technically employed. Others argue, though, that such a ruse is often of marginal aid, and point out that in a time of severe financial stress, you should at least earn some interest on your money.

Your best course is probably to ask to have the money paid out over a period, if you see a realistic prospect of an offer on the horizon, and if that offer will be aided by your being able to claim, legitimately, that you are still on someone's payroll. Otherwise, bank it all. If you do choose to deposit all the money, look at your calendar before the check is cut; for tax reasons, you will almost certainly want to avoid receiving huge sums late in the year.

That lump sum can be dangerous if you're not used to dealing with large amounts of cash; beware of the Payday Millionaire Syndrome. Now is not the time to use "all that money" to refinish your basement or get a new car. Be prudent with

ONLINE RESOURCES

Debt Counselors of America
http://www.dca.org
An excellent site for people who find themselves in financial hot water because of credit card overuse. This website offers free advice on how to reduce and eliminate credit card debt. This organization also offers two special debt repayment programs.

National Foundation for Consumer Credit
http://www.nfcc.org
This organization provides excellent information for people who need help managing their credit. The National Foundation for Consumer Credit also shows you how to get your credit report, how to fix mistakes on your credit report (legally and cheap!), and offers free advice on buying a home.

National Center for Financial Education
http://www.ncfe.org
Another good site with free advice on how to manage credit problems. The information on this site also branches out to include more general financial matters including developing a monthly spending plan; teaching children about money matters; and learning how to plan, save, and invest for the future.

your cash. Strike that: Be *miserly* with your cash. Bear in mind that some authorities estimate it will take you, on average, one month of job hunting for every ten thousand dollars of yearly salary in your desired job. Whether or not that is accurate, you should prepare yourself for quite a wait between paychecks!

No matter how bad things get or how tempted you may be, avoid cashing in any IRAs you have—you will pay huge tax penalties. Instead, look into a loan against your IRA or any other tax-deferred annuity.

If you consider refinancing your home mortgage, take into account not only the new interest rates you will pay and your likelihood of moving within five years, but also any closing fees you will encounter. Closing costs on refinanced mortgages typically run between three and six thousand dollars as of this writing. There may also be tax issues to consider, and these could add to the cost of refinancing as well. You may end up pursuing savings that are illusory; check with a qualified financial adviser before refinancing.

Get a handle on your credit card use. *This is a vitally important point.*

It is natural to avoid the unpleasant, and no one enjoys the business of downgrading one's lifestyle expectations. But as bad as the picture may be, it can't be half as depressing as turning a blind eye to your problems. Avoid, at all costs, maintaining a false standard of living by pushing your credit card limits to the upper ionosphere. As will be detailed later in this chapter, your best course for now is simply to cut all existing cards (but one) in half.

Getting into credit difficulties will undermine your confidence, strain your personal relationships, put a big dent in your morale, and, most important of all, *stop you from getting hired!* You will remember from past experience, no doubt, that virtually all professional interviews these days are preceded by an application form with a space for your signature beneath a block of minute type. In that unreadable thicket of words, required by the Fair Credit Reporting Act of 1972, is an authorization for the employer to check your references and your credit history. Employers are usually quite content to process your application if they have your resume, your name, your address, and your signature on the application form. This signature, they will tell you, is simply something they "need for their records."

Uh-huh.

Credit agencies make a business of marketing their files to corporate employers, who use them as tools for evaluation of potential employees. The service is popular because credit information is seen as an indicator of future performance. This, of course, is based on the premise that knowing how a potential employee handles fiscal obligations provides a preview of that person's likelihood of stealing from the company, acting irresponsibly, or otherwise compromising the employer. Whether or not you agree with this idea, you should know that a bad credit rating has the potential to blow your candidacy right out of the water—and that it can do so even if *all* the other variables point to a successful outcome for your job search.

You can find out more about your credit rating by contacting the major national credit rating bureaus:

CSC Credit Services, Inc. (Houston, Texas): 713/878-4840
TransUnion Credit Information (Chicago, Illinois): 312/408-1050
CBI/Equifax (Atlanta, Georgia): 1-800/685-1111
Experian (formerly TRW Information Systems and Services) (Allen, Texas): 1-888/397-3742

Credit bureaus are legally obligated to update reports containing factual errors, so be sure to notify the appropriate companies immediately if you find any mistakes. Even if you do not find outright misstatements on your report, you have some options. Many experts recommend that you send the credit bureau a letter explaining that your late or incomplete payments resulted from the loss of a job—a temporary state of affairs that is a world away from simple fiscal irresponsibility.

ONLINE RESOURCES

Equifax
http://www.equifax.com
You may want to look at your credit report before potential employers do. This website contains information on how to obtain your report from Equifax, one of the three largest credit reporting agencies in the nation.

Experian
http://www.experian.com
Formerly TRW Information Systems and Services, Experian is one of the three largest credit reporting agencies in the country. This website contains information on how to obtain your credit report from Experian, and a helpful advice column called Ask Max.

Starting Over

If you are in or are getting into debt as a result of losing your job, you should by all means face the problem squarely.

Sit down (with your family, if this is applicable) and review the situation. Air any unresolved issues and thoroughly examine your situation. Then work out your current monthly financial picture with a form something like the one reproduced on the facing page.

Once you know where you stand, there comes the dreaded task of taking action.

I said a little earlier on that you should, if you find yourself in financial difficulties while conducting your job search, simply cut your credit cards in half—all but one of them, at any rate. The one exception is to allow the member of the family who is conducting the job search to have some flexibility in obtaining stationery supplies, strategically selected interview wear, printing services, and the like. But even this carries with it a warning: Make your plastic job search purchases prudent ones! This is not the time to update your entire wardrobe on the vague idea that you'll be going on *lots* of interviews and will therefore need *lots* of great clothes.

Treat your remaining credit card with the wary respect you would accord an adversary who has become a temporary ally—that is, someone who still very much bears watching. Bear in mind that it is misuse of credit cards, more than anything else, that is responsible for plunging the professional into hopeless levels of debt.

If your financial situation is giving you cause for concern, you might consider contacting the nonprofit National Foundation for Consumer Credit at 301/589-5600. They have been providing free and low-cost counseling to people in financial hot water

MONTHLY INCOME

Earnings	_____
Severance	_____
Spouse's salary	_____
Unemployment benefits*	_____
Withdrawal from savings	_____
Dividends	_____
Interest	_____
Gifts	_____
TOTAL INCOME:	_____

MONTHLY OBLIGATIONS/PAYMENTS

Rent/mortgage	_____
Taxes	_____
Groceries	_____
Clothing	_____
Household	_____
Loan repayments	_____
Car expenses	_____
Insurance	_____
Recreation	_____
Charitable contributions/dues/gifts	_____
Medical expenses	_____
Auto-related expenses	_____
Credit card repayments	_____
Job-search-related expenses	_____
Mortgage	_____
Home-equity loan	_____
Miscellaneous	_____
TOTAL OUTGOING:	_____

* If you have worked and received unemployment benefits in the same tax year, those unemployment benefits will be regarded as taxable income.

for over thirty years. With branches throughout the country, they can assist you in creating a workable budget and realistic plans for debt repayment, and they can even contact creditors on your behalf. Another good organization to contact is the National Center for Financial Education, which can be reached by calling 619/232-8811. They can advise you on a wide range of financial issues, including repairing your credit.

If Things Don't Look Good . . .

You might want to consider a debt consolidation loan. This is an arrangement whereby a loan is taken out to pay off all debts, giving you just one simple bill to deal with per month.

Such a loan looks like a great hassle eradicator, but it can cause more problems than it solves if you're not careful. Some people have taken out consolidation loans and gotten everything ship-shape—only to use the new "breathing room" they've won to charge their credit cards back up to the limit and push their home equity lines to dangerous levels. The result is not a reprieve from financial woes, but a doubling of their severity.

Whatever you do, watch out for the "credit repair" companies that offer to "fix" all your credit problems for a substantial but (considering the stakes) seemingly reasonable fee. The Federal Trade Commission has been all over these fly-by-night outfits, and with good reason. The overwhelming majority do nothing but take your money, dazzle you with words, and baffle you with B.S.—and I'm not talking undergraduate degrees here.

If the situation deteriorates to the point where bankruptcy seems to be a realistic prospect, I recommend that you contact creditors to negotiate even smaller payments than the ones you've been making. You may be surprised at their eagerness to work with you. Tell them what you can pay; if it's interest plus something, there is probably a deal to be worked out. Using the legitimate threat of bankruptcy to get creditors to offer you more favorable settlement arrangements is a powerful tool; credit card companies have been known to accept a fraction of what is owed them under these circumstances. The reason is simple: Once you go into bankruptcy, the creditors are likely to get nothing whatsoever from you. (By the way, this maneuver is one you can use but once in a lifetime. Sadly, it cannot be employed as an annual cost-cutting measure.)

For more information on personal bankruptcy, consult your attorney or contact the local bar association, which is listed in your phone directory and can refer you to a bankruptcy specialist in your price range.

ONLINE RESOURCE

The Money Store
http://www.themoneystore.com
If you need a loan, this is a good place to start. The Money Store offers mortgage/home equity loans, small business loans, student loans, and home improvement loans.

On a more positive note, remember that there are many steps you can take to generate some interim cash that will see you through the tough times. You can:

- Rent out a room in your house.
- Get a part-time or temp job.
- Take out an ad in the local penny saver promoting your services as a repairperson (if you've always been good with your hands).
- Sell your professional services as a consultant.
- Turn a hobby into a profitable occupation. (A friend of mine lost her income and, being an artist, started an after-school art program for kids. Now she has three employees, is looking for more space, and is making over $60,000 per year. Very wisely, she contacted SCORE, the Service Corps of Retired Executives, for free counseling on how to start and operate her business. SCORE is sponsored by the Small Business Administration and has offices just about everywhere. For women and minorities, there are numerous low-interest loan programs available through the Small Business Administration. Contact your local office.)

Debt Collectors

If you're seriously considering talking to an attorney about filing for bankruptcy, chances are you are also being dunned by debt collectors, a fearsome species to say the least. People in this profession generally do not attend charm school as part of their training, so don't be surprised if you are addressed in a way that oversteps the *social* niceties. On the other hand, you should know when these people overstep their *legal* bounds.

The Fair Debt Collection Practices Act of 1977 protects you and your loved ones from illegal, rude, unfair, and unreasonable collection practices. Some of the specific limitations under which the debt collection industry must act are listed below:

- Debt collectors are forbidden to ask you for your telephone number, salary, payment dates, or place of employment. (But they may still use their own best efforts to locate you, and they can be depended upon to come after you when you find a new job.)
- Debt collectors can only speak to others about you in the context of determining your whereabouts. They cannot discuss with anyone the nature of their business with you unless you give them permission to do so.
- Debt collectors can contact you in person, by phone, or by letter—but only at times and places convenient to you.
- Debt collectors cannot harass or abuse you or anyone connected with you (such as a spouse or other family member) about the collection of your debt. This means telephone harassment, abusive language, and threats of violence are all out.

ONLINE RESOURCE

Federal Trade Commission
http://www.ftc.gov
The Federal Trade Commission's site provides good information on credit card fraud, managing your credit cards, and protecting your rights as a consumer, as well as a wealth of information on consumer laws in general. If there's a scam or fraud going on, you'll probably find something about it at this site.

In all fairness to debt collectors, they have a job to do and bosses to pacify just like everyone else. Treat them with respect and they will probably return the favor. If you keep the channels of communication open, you probably won't have to worry about any of the above-mentioned horrors. But if you do have problems in any of these areas, don't hesitate to talk to a lawyer.

The Second Time Around

Time passes. (It always does.) Life continues, crises recede. This is a tough stretch, but it won't last forever. Once you make it through to the other side—and you will—take a look around and prepare yourself for a surprise. You will probably be a better person for all of this. The next time you're on a career roll, you will likely find it easier to forget the myriad admonishments we all receive to "live up to our income." The next time, you might be perfectly positioned to live up to your dreams instead.

Conclusion: The Glittering Prizes

All victories have their foundation in careful preparation, and in finishing *Knock 'em Dead*, you are loaded for bear and ready for the hunt.

Your winning attitude is positive and active—dream jobs don't come to those who sit and wait—and you realize that success depends on getting out and generating interviews for yourself. At those interviews, you will maintain the interviewer's interest and attention by carrying your half of the conversation. What you ask will show your interest, demonstrate your analytical abilities, and carry the conversation forward. If in doubt about the meaning of a question, you will ask one of your own to clarify it.

The corporate body recognizes that its most valuable resource is in those employees who understand and contribute toward its goals. These people have something in common: They all recognize their differing jobs as a series of challenges and problems, each to be anticipated, met, and solved. It's that attitude that lands jobs and enhances careers.

People with that attitude advance their careers faster than others, because they possess a critical awareness of universally admired business practices and value systems. They then leverage their careers by projecting the personality traits that most closely complement those practices and values.

As I said at the beginning of this book, your job search can be seen as a ritualized mating dance. The name of that dance is "attitude." Now that you know the steps, you are ready to whirl away with the glittering prizes. There is no more to say except go to your next interview and knock 'em dead.

Appendices

APPENDIX A | You're Not in Kansas Anymore: The Joys of Online Job Hunting

About four years ago, job hunting electronically meant that you could download lists of potential employers from about twenty databases. Suddenly, you could do in an hour online what might have taken you two days in a traditional library. Nevertheless, these databases still weren't much more than electronic reference books.

My, how times have changed. Today, when you log on the Internet and tap out a search on simple keywords such as "jobs" or "employment" or "careers," you're likely to find over eighty-one thousand listings. So for future years, let's just agree that there is a bunch of stuff out there that has some relevance to your job search.

Practical Considerations

This rapid proliferation of employment resources now provides a daunting challenge: "How do I make my online job hunting efficient and economical?" These two concerns have become far more pressing—unlike the earliest days of electronic job hunting, there are literally hundreds or even thousands of providers of far more comprehensive services than before. In a world where (connect) time is money, stumbling around blind in this forest of opportunities could cost you the farm, and what's left of your youth.

Electronic job hunting can be effective, it can sometimes be fun, and it can certainly be time-consuming. As both time and money are important dimensions of your job hunt, you will want to integrate electronic job hunting into your overall plan in a prudent manner. If you drop all of your other approaches and focus solely on exploring the World Wide Web, for example, you won't be acting in your own best interests.

Dedicate some time to learning about electronic job hunting, load your resume onto the various resume banks (see *Resumes That Knock 'em Dead* for a detailed discussion on scannable and electronic resumes), scan the jobs listed on the job banks, network with your professional peers, and ask questions of the resident experts in the discussion groups and chat sessions, but don't let your other, more traditional, job hunting activities fall by the wayside.

How to Get Started

Of course, this electronic information is available only if you can go online. Given how much job and career information is available and how fast these resources are growing in size and scope, this may be one of the best reasons yet to get yourself set up with some kind of online access. I won't bore you with the messy technical details of getting hooked up—obviously, you'll need a computer with a considerable amount of free memory, a (relatively) fast modem, and an online account. Here, you have two choices. For direct Internet access, look in your business telephone directory for Internet Service Providers (ISPs, in Netspeak). These companies are in the business of hooking individuals or businesses up to the Net—they'll let you know what you need to do to set up your own account. Or you can access this online career info through a commercial online service, such as America Online or CompuServe, that offers Net access—including access to the World Wide Web (an international hyperlinked database)—as part of its services. Alternately, you may be able to access the Internet through a local school or library.

Internet Access Providers

There are a number of online services, but as of this writing only four really qualify as major consumer-oriented online service providers: CompuServe, America Online, Prodigy, and Microsoft Network. True Internet surfers look down on these services as being big, slow, and, well, *commercial*. The services, on the other hand, try to make online access (including Internet access) easy for even the most technophobic user. In all four cases, there are monthly or hourly connection fees to be paid. You would be prudent to ensure you are on a flat rate plan with both your service and your phone company to keep costs down. Practically speaking, you might want to start with AOL; then once you know what you are doing switch to the far cheaper ISPs.

America Online

AOL, the source for those ubiquitous "trial offer" diskettes you get in the mail, offers a broad range of services for job hunters, including their career center (named, originally enough, the Career Center) and the "Help Wanted USA" jobs database. America Online also offers users access to a whole range of Internet services: Gopher (don't ask), Usenet, and the Web. As of 1997, AOL offers a flat monthly rate for unlimited use. AOL has recently purchased the huge and venerable CompuServe, and thus becomes the dominant player in this sector.

Prodigy

This service, while not as comprehensive as CompuServe nor as well advertised as AOL, offers many of the same resources—including Internet access.

Microsoft Network

Microsoft Network offers the same type of services as AOL and CompuServe, with one drawback . . . it only works with Windows 95.

Navigators/Search Engines

Your online search will be a much more satisfying experience with the aid of a good browser. Most service providers such as AOL and CompuServe provide you with one, but it is worth your while if you have eight megabytes of available memory to download Netscape Navigator, the best and brightest. You will then have easy access to the best search engines such as Alta Vista, AOL NetFind, Electronic Library, HOTBOT, and Webcrawler, and the Web Guides such as Excite, Infoseek, LookSmart, Lycos, CNet Search.com, and Yahoo.

Where to Start Looking

Unless you want to emulate a blind pig snuffling through a forest in hopes of unearthing the occasional acorn, you need to create a short list of places to visit out of the tens of thousands of options available. You can develop your own short list by visiting one of the online equivalents of a book's table of contents, often referred to as *resource lists*, *link lists*, or *meta-lists*.

Resource lists are online "sites" that offer links to other sources of information for job seekers—typically listing a given source's electronic "address" along with a brief description of the resources available at that site. In most cases, these lists are set up so that you can transfer to the destination of your choice by clicking on the underlined (or otherwise highlighted) name of the source. This feature is a great improvement on the time-consuming process of typing out the multi-character "dot com" addresses (properly known as URLs, or Uniform Resource Locators).

On America Online, for example, you can access these links through the Webcrawler search engine. ("Go to" the keyword "Webcrawler"—or if you have direct World Wide Web access, type the URL "http://www.webcrawler.com.") Once you've started up Webcrawler, type in the keywords "jobs," "employment," and/or "careers." You'll instantly get a list of the first twenty-five of over thirty-eight thousand career listings. You can get a quick summary of each listing, and then choose to go into the listings that seem most relevant, just by clicking on them!

These listings can include everything from job listings to full-service "career centers" (more on these later). But the most important entries, at this point in your job search, are the resource lists. Here are my favorites as of the time this section was written.

AltaVista Careers
http://www.careeraltavista.com/

Not only does this resource list include links to other major career sites like Monster Board, Career Mosaic, and CareerWeb, but it also includes helpful features, including a salary calculator, a Career Coach, and a resume posting service. AltaVista Careers also lets employers post job listings and search resumes. This site looks promising for the future.

Job Search and Employment Opportunities: Best Bets from the Net
http://www.lib.umich.edu/chdocs/employment/

This list from the University of Michigan, only three years old in 1998, is a tremendously helpful starting place for any electronic job hunter, especially the majority who are new to the Net. The career services and placement gurus at the U of M, long respected for their career know-how, have really done their homework this time! You can link to job banks, resume banks, and career information resources, as well as find some sensible tips on navigating through the career network.

Their "best of the best" list identifies sites that they feel are comprehensive, high quality, easy to navigate, and cover the needs of both recent graduates and seasoned professionals. The list is not extensive, but in a world where quantity is often erroneously seen as the benchmark of excellence, the brevity and quality of this list make it a real standout. The site has been reviewed favorably by many sources, including *U.S. News and World Report* and the *National Business Employment Weekly*—two of the most knowledgeable commentators on the employment and careers scene.

Career Paradise—Colossal List of Career Links
http://www.service.emory.edu/CAREER/Main/Links.html

The Colossal List of Career Links is a link of Emory University's comprehensive career center "Career Paradise." This is one of my personal favorites, because it's so well organized and because of its upbeat tone. It categorizes sixty resources into sections such as "prime sites," "career & job search web sites," "graduate & professional schools," and "specialty sites." These listings include all of the best-known sites, but also include some great treasures, such as sites that serve minorities and a great site that calculates salary equivalencies for various cities across the country: (http://www2.homefair.com/calc/salcalc.html/). It rates each site for content and artistic appeal.

The Gordon Group: Job and Career Information; Links
http://www.owt.com/jobsinfo/jobsinfo.htm

This plain and simple list of nearly two hundred career links is a goldmine. From A to Y (from A Survival Guide for College Graduates to Yahoo Employment), you won't find a more direct and comprehensive list online.

Nerd World Media: Jobs and Related Links
http://www.nerdworld.com/users/dstein/nw102.html

This is a comprehensive alphabetized listing of resources, with summaries so that you don't waste your time browsing through sites that prove to be of no interest. This site also includes a list of related newsgroup links that make for easy access.

JobHunt: Outstanding Job Resources
http://www.job-hunt.org

This is a highly regarded source list of recommended starting points for job seekers, including sources for general job listings, newsgroup searches, other lists, recruiting agencies, reference materials, resume banks, and more. The complete list offers nearly one thousand links to career-based sites, but the cream of the crop are noted with a smiley face and can be viewed exclusively, giving you forty-five of the best links on the Internet in a neat little package. You probably will not need to go to their extended list unless you're specifically looking for such unique gems as *Carbonate Your Brain: Job Pool*, which specializes in job opportunities for students in the music industry.

Yahoo! Internet Life: Employment Resources
http://www3.zdnet.com/yil/content/profit/profess/empl1.html

I highly recommend that you just get into Search mode, find Yahoo and click on the link rather than type in that ridiculously long URL. However you do it, this is a great site as it gives a comprehensive review of about thirty of the best sites, rated from 4 down to 2 stars for content and practical application.

But enough of these lists! I'm sure you've gotten an idea by now of just how much information is available even at this first stage of the game. There are literally thousands of these lists online. There is a lot of duplication, but each offers a unique personality, and usually a unique focus. Let me know if there are resources you couldn't find through these lists, and I'll try to make up for it in future editions.

Career Centers

The next major category of useful sites is made up of what are loosely defined as "career centers." Career centers are the job hunter's equivalent of the local mall. These are multifunctional sites made up of an assortment of career advice and resources job listings, collections of resumes submitted by job seekers, resume design services, reference libraries, company profiles, salary information, discussion groups, and more. Each site is different and offers a unique blend of these elements, but you can count on a few standard elements.

As with the "lists of links" above, each of these sites is different and offers its own blend of career assistance. You're sure to find some of the sites that follow interesting and useful. There are hundreds of these little darlings, and more are being created on a daily basis.

CareerCity
http://www.careercity.com

This site has been set up by Adams Media Corporation, one of the most successful publishers of career and job search-related books (and—truth be told—

the publisher of *Knock 'em Dead*!). It includes an impressive array of features for job seekers, including:

- Links to the *Knock 'em Dead* website, which features excerpts from this bestselling book and other *Knock 'em Dead* books in the series
- Access to over 130,000 current job listings
- Links to job openings for major employers
- Job searches by state, country, job category, description, title, or company name
- An employer database with profiles of over 27,000 companies
- Electronic resume posting directly to potential employers

CareerCity also supports an extensive resume database with over 15,000 resumes on file. An easy-to-use password system allows users to view, edit, or delete an existing resume. If you're not sure what to include, this site also offers advice on creating a great resume.

CareerCity also contains special sections for computer/high-tech, health care, education, and government jobs; salaries and job searching; career planning; and unique diversity and women's centers.

The Riley Guide
http://www.dbm.com/jobguide/index.html
e-mail: Riley Guide@dbm.com

Let me start by saying that this so-called grandmother (of the Internet job search) is a mensch. Her aim is pure: to make the job search simple, purposeful, free wherever possible, and practical. She gives you all the basics; reasons to use the Internet for a job search, how to prepare, where to start, resource choices, netiquette, and time management. You can link onto any of these general titles for reams of details on each area.

The Site Map will take you to:

- Work opportunities—a list of eight subgroups of job opportunity sites arranged by topic, i.e., large overall job sites, local employment sites, non-U.S. sites, sites for women and minorities, online resume databases, summer, self-employment, and volunteer opportunities, other meta sites, etc.
- Resources by specific occupation—fourteen categories
- Career guides/planning/salary information

- Help with Internet job searches: For newcomers, this link alone is worth the visit at **http://www.dbm.com/jobguide/net-help.html**

I went into Resources for Specific Occupational Areas and linked into *Sales & Marketing*, which took me to a list of six links in that area. I chose American Marketing Association Marketplace, which spat up sixty-four very detailed and fascinating job opportunities.

Next I tried *Arts, Humanities, Recreation, and Hospitality* which took me to ONLINE Sports Career Center where I clicked onto the job bank where thirty-two positions in sports-related positions were listed, from tennis instructor to a sales executive for an athletic apparel company in Toyko at a respectable $125,000 per year.

I searched under *Engineering, Technology and Mathematics* and was faced with twelve subcategories, including *Computing & Technology*, which was further broken down into three categories, General Resources, Recruiters and Recruiting Sites, and Trade Publications and Professional Societies. Guess what! Each of these categories had multiple subcategories, but I kept on truckin'. I thought *Computer Jobs* sounded most direct, and there I found over 8,000 job openings advertised. Most of these are computer positions in the Atlanta area, though there is a specific area for the Carolinas, Chicago and the Midwest, Texas and the Southwest, and Other Regions. This is a fabulous link for computer career job-seekers. The jobs can be searched by system expertise or specific job title. You can also do a keyword search or look at jobs listed in the last three to five days.

The job search at the Riley Guide was a marathon, but well worth it. I ended at *Something to bring a smile to your face...*, a delightful spoof on a rejection letter, which definitely brightened my day.

Gonyea Online Career Center

You must be a subscriber to America Online to access these services. For $19.95 a month (at this writing) and the cost of the phone call, you have access to a very impressive array of job search tools. To get to this site, search AOL by keyword and type in either "career" or "career center." You'll see the Gonyea Online Career Center as one of the search results. Formerly the America Online Career Center, the Gonyea Online Career Center was the power behind that throne, and still offers a good selection of career-related services, including:

- Help Wanted-USA
- Worldwide Resume Bank

- Career Guidance Services
- Government Jobs Central
- Career Resource Mall
- Occupational Profiles
- Employment Agencies
- Online Job Hunting.

One service that will be of primary interest is Help Wanted—USA, where you can key in a preset job code and location for job categories and receive a list of matching job openings. I ran the same test on every set of job listings I encountered. I searched for three distinct jobs: a systems analyst and a retail merchandise manager, both located in New York, and a swim team coach located in California. I chose the first two jobs because they are both growing careers in growing industries, and added the swim coach as a wild card—because it would be a dream job!

In Help Wanted—USA I found ninety-seven listings in the computer category for New York, about one-third of which were for systems analysts or something closely related. There were absolutely no listings for retail trade (which I found odd) and none under the sports/recreation category either. This isn't meant as a criticism, since these sites are growing and changing all the time, and no one can keep track of all of the jobs or careers. It is meant as a caution for you. Just because a site is big or well known doesn't mean it has what you need, or that what you need isn't out there somewhere. By the time you read this, there may be dozens of retail merchandise managers popping out of Help Wanted—USA.

This site claims to have ten thousand new job listings per week, updated weekly. It recommends that the best time to check for new listings is Wednesday morning.The Gonyea Online Career Center also boasts over 1 million users a month. This makes it one of the most visited career sites available today.

The Internet's Online Career Center
http://www.occ.com
e-mail: occ@ooc.com
phone: (317) 293-6499

Go to this site and you'll be faced with far more choices than you could ever examine. The company that created this site intends to be all electronic things to all electronic people. It works with all of the online networks to provide the most economical and efficient methods and services for employers and employees who are making use of these high-tech job search tools.

The OCC also claims to be the first and most popular online career center—it boasts of having over thirty million users! The site features:

- A recruiting center database
- A bank of job listings with keyword searching
- A resume bank with keyword searching
- A database of company profiles
- Links to other relevant Web sites
- A relocation guide which links you to an apartment guide, maps, local newspapers, chambers of commerce, weather, TV, schools, cost of living guide, and even the local phone directory

Inquiries are free for job seekers—and the keyword searching mechanism is easy to use. You simply type in the job title you're interested in and narrow the search by the location you desire. Initially, I keyed in systems analyst without designating a location and got 632 listings that had been posted within the last seven days; 276 were posted that day. This site truly seems to have mostly technical-type job listings. There were no listings for retail merchandise managers in New York, but there was one nationwide.

E-Span
http://www.espan.com
E-Span is well worth a visit. It can be accessed directly through the Net or through CompuServe and AOL. Since 1991 they have been pioneers in the online job search market, but they have recently taken on a whole new look with two very simple headlines: "The Right Person for the Job" and the "Right Job for the Person." The former offers job seekers a wide range of services in a unique format:

- Employer profiles for at least one hundred and twenty companies, with featured employers
- Tips for resumes, interviews, motivation, networking, references, salary guidelines, etc.
- Both a job database and a resume database
- Relocation Pro—you indicate a target state and fill out a profile to receive specific information
- A "Hot Job" feature which lists forty of the best jobs available around the country

- A salary calculator that gives equivalent salaries for cities across the country
- A career library

The job bank features a comprehensive search function that allows you to specify up to six variables in your research. You can search by education, experience, current position, and location. Within a few short minutes, your search will generate a highly specific set of matching job openings.

In my test, there were ten job matches for a computer systems analyst in New York. There were no matches for the retail merchandise manager, and no matches for the swim coach. E-Span now has a link to the Wall Street Journal site, with its 100,000 plus job listings and host of other offerings.

The Job Center
http://www.jobcenter.com
e-mail: info@jobcenter.com
phone: (800) 562-2368

The Job Center was one of the first to offer an active database that automatically matches candidates and employers and notifies both (via e-mail) of any and all matches—sending the matching resumes to the employer, and the job description to the job seeker. Job seekers can "protect" their resume—so that their current employer doesn't accidentally pick up their resume as a match—and can specify which Usenet newsgroups they want to be listed on. The database automatically discards job listings/resumes you have already reviewed, so that you don't constantly have to go over the same material when you check in. If you're not happy with the results, you can adjust your profile with more or less information at any point. And you have the option of independently searching the database just like on the listings systems. It costs $20 to post your resume for six months. You can also do a keyword job search, which gives you an idea of what they have to offer . . . twenty-seven systems analysts and one merchandise manager nationwide.

Aside from the above, this site also offers goodies such as tips on resume writing and corporate profiles, and information on scholarships from educational institutions. The system is really quick, the information is well organized and comprehensible, and the Job Center seems very service-oriented. I like these guys— they're well worth the visit.

Career Mosaic
http://www.careermosaic.com/

This is definitely one of the larger employment sites around, and another that claims to be the firstest, biggest, and bestest. Career Mosaic offers a multitude of great services, including:

- A career resource center, containing advice for job seekers and links to other services
- Free resume posting!
- The College Connection—for students or first-time job searchers
- Online job fairs
- Employer profiles
- A special area for health care jobs
- USENET jobs offered featuring 60,000 postings daily, rebuilt daily, cleared weekly
- J.O.B.S. database featuring "thousands of up-to-date job opportunities"

The job database is free. You enter the position or title you're looking for, and specify a company or state if you'd like. I asked to see postings for systems analysts in New York, and received a list of fifty jobs. There were two listings for retail merchandise managers and none for swim coaches, alas!

This site is all business, and has expanded rapidly. Their international gateway features Career Mosaic for Japan, Canada, the UK, Australia, Asia, France, Hong Kong, Korea New Zealand, and Indonesia.

The Monster Board
http://www.monster.com

This is another well-established and exceptionally popular site. Monster Board features an enormous job bank, and:

- Career Insight & Advice—including links to other career sites and career advice columns by renowned employee advocate Joyce Lain Kennedy
- A resume builder
- A resume database
- Relocation services including apartment search, moving services, housing, and international rentals. You can see photographs of the area, see a floor

plan, and (with a little download capability) you can actually do a 3-D tour of your potential digs online!

- Personal job search agent—you fill in a profile with details of the job you seek and all matches are displayed each time you log on.

The jobs listed here seem to be primarily located on the East Coast and are mostly in technical fields. You can search the database by discipline (almost 300 very specific titles), location (over 200 towns/states), or keyword, and get a list of available positions.

A search in New York for systems analysts brought up twenty-nine postings, none for merchandise managers, and none for swim coaches (what a surprise!).

They seem to have resolved their previous traffic problems and the response time is now very good. The Monster Board has gone through a lot of changes recently, and continues to grow at a staggering pace.

CareerWeb
http://www.cweb.com
e-mail: info@cweb.com

This site is the only career site included in *PC Magazine*'s list of Top 100 sites on the Web. It has won numerous awards, so it must be great, right? It does have great resources, too numerous to list except by category:

- Articles and essays (The Career Doctor)
- Associations
- Books, publications, and news articles
- Career advice
- Career fairs
- Consulting and counseling services
- Directories
- Future societies
- Healthcare and human resource, professional information, opportunities, and organizations
- Internships and career advice
- Networking
- Professional training and career development
- Salary calculator

- Career assessment
- Resume bank
- Job Bank
- Job hunting tips

A search in any of the above will inspire you to mind-boggling new levels of employment nirvana. But control yourself and concentrate on the here and now. To execute a job search, you select from fifty preset job categories and then fine-tune with keywords. I asked to see systems analyst positions in New York, and got seventeen of them. There were no retail merchandise managers, and still nary a swim coach. This site is heavy on resources and advice, but a little light on the actual job listings.

This site also offers a job matching service which will notify you by e-mail anytime a job matching your preset requirements is posted on CareerWeb.

CAREERMagazine
http://www.careermag.com/
e-mail: editor@careermag.com

You will never have time to peruse all of these sites thoroughly and ultimately first impressions do count. If a site appeals to your aesthetic senses, you're more likely to stick to it. This site is fun because it is formatted just like a magazine, so you periodicalholics will feel comfortable here.

CAREERMagazine has all the essentials of a thorough Career Site, a keyword-based Job database, employer profiles, a resume bank, a career forum, job fairs, a recruiter directory, relocation resources. It also features articles on employment, employment book excerpts and reviews, a bookstore where you can order books, On Campus update, the thirty fastest growing occupations, and areas covering such subjects as diversity and self-employment.

This does not appear to have the most comprehensive job database; there were only ten systems analyst positions on file for New York, twenty-six merchandise managers in America, and no swim coaches. Perhaps I need to be more precise in my search, but I got too distracted by all the other features on this site. Try it, you'll like it!

Like all career websites (and there are now thousands of them), CAREERMagazine is becoming more commecially oriented. They are adding banner advertising, more links, and information on advertisers. Most interesting is their addition of information on the legal aspects of employment.

Job Web
http://www.jobweb.org
e-mail: webmaster@jobweb.org

The first Internet site developed by a human resources organization, this one is owned and maintained by the National Association of Colleges and Employers (NACE), a nonprofit organization comprised of over 1,700 colleges and universities and over 1,400 business organizations. It caters to the college-educated work force, including students, recent graduates, and experienced professionals.

Winner of the 1997 Gutenberg award for the Best HTML Career/Employment Publications, the features of Job Web are impressive, including:

- Jobs—a keyword search database, free for job seekers
- Employer profiles, hundreds of companies listed alphabetically
- A database of U.S. school districts (representing 16,588 schools)
- Job search and industry information
- Career planning resources
- Career services professionals
- Catalogs for job seekers
- Minorities/disabilities resources
- Relocation resources
- International resources
- The Catapult—a resource gem for grads

The Jobs database accepts your qualifications and spits out any matches. There were two listings for computer systems analysts in New York, none for merchandise managers, and as you might imagine, none for swim team coaches anywhere.

This site is especially worth visiting if you are in the human resources field or if you are a college graduate looking for your first job. This job site is likely to be a winner because of all the campus recruiters who belong to the sponsoring organization. Expect it to achieve greatness!

Job Banks

The sites that follow are primarily job banks. Rather than focusing on career planning issues, these sites stick to matching people with jobs. They are made up of listings of available jobs, which work much like the Help Wanted section in your local newspaper.

In fact, newspapers, recruiters, career centers, professional organizations, or other special-interest groups usually set up these sites. Some of the sites are more active than others, specifically matching your qualifications and experience with an employer's needs. For these sites, employers fill out specification sheets that describe job openings, and you fill out a form that describes your qualifications. When a sufficiently close match occurs, both you and your potential employer will be notified. More commonly, job banks consist of long lists of available jobs. You can choose between different job categories, then scroll through the job listings until you find a job that fits your interests.

CareerPath
http://www.careerpath.com
e-mail: webmaster@careerpath.com

This high-profile site was cited as one of four "Best of the Best" in the University of Michigan's well-respected guide to job search and employment opportunities on the Net and claims to be the most visited job-related site on the Internet. It is a compilation of advertised jobs in thirty-five of the top newspapers across the country. The ads are updated daily by 6 a.m. Eastern Standard Time. They also post each day's number of ads—when I searched they boasted 278,551 ads for the week!

You can search this site without registering to get a feel for what's available, but I guarantee that you will ultimately register. For one thing, the price is right; registration is free. Registering involves filling in your name and e-mail address (if applicable), and choosing a password and a screen name. (Your choice of online moniker must be really unique—I resorted to "Battlerager" when all else failed. Dinner for two to the first reader who gets the reference! Send me a note in care of the publisher.) The security for this site is very tight, but the administrators claim they're just keeping track of how people use the site. They are quite adamant that they are not trying to sell you something!

Once you begin your search, the site is responsive, and easy to use. You simply select a newspaper from a scroll list, then select a job category you're interested in from a list of 110, including such unique ones as activism, gardening, pest control, modeling, and yes, merchandising. You can also enter additional keywords that the database will use to narrow your search.

The *New York Times* had 775 ads under the preset computer category. When I keyed in systems analyst, there were 282 matches. But remember, this reflects ads that have either the word systems *or* analyst. The *San Jose Mercury News* (CA) had only 194 computer ads, but 61 were for systems analysts. The *New York Times* had

24 ads under the fashion/apparel category, none of which were for merchandise managers. But I got really excited when I clicked on the "recreation" category in the *San Jose Mercury News* and my search turned up one match for swim coach! Of course, the database had scanned for "swim" and "coach" and the match was for a lifeguard/swim instructor at a day camp. Pretty close though!

JOBTRAK
http://www.jobtrak.com
e-mail: www@jobtrak.com
phone: (800) 999-8725

Established in 1987 as a service for college students, graduates, and alumni, this has developed into one of the most critically acclaimed sites on the Web. Also chosen as one of the University of Michigan's top four "Best of the Best" in job search sites, JOBTRAK was distinguished in 1992 as Entrepreneur of the Year by the state of California, semifinalist in the 1997 National Information & Infrastructure Awards as well as earning ten other online awards. It is said to be the third most-visited job-listing site on the Web, having been visited by over 300,000 employers. There are 250,000-page viewers daily and over 2,400 new job postings each day from a wide variety of industries and occupations. This service is completely free to job seekers. There is only one prerequisite. You must be a college student or an alum, since the only way you can get a password is through your campus or *alma mater*.

You can see why employers would register with and frequent this site! It is also user-friendly for employers: They can phone in their ads rather than have to master the Net in order to get access to this wonderful pool of talent. You begin by choosing a college from a scroll list (I went into the UCLA database). This brings you to a menu from which you choose how you would like to conduct your search: by type of work, location, keyword, company name, or date of job listings.

I started by searching under "type of work," for which there are thirty standard choices. You then choose whether you are looking for full-time, full-time experienced, part-time, internship, or summer work. There were 185 job listings under the "computer" job category, twenty-six of which were in New York. Almost all the rest were in California, which makes sense for a UCLA (southern California) database. No merchandise managers or swim coaches were to be found, but there was a very diversified range of jobs listed. If you've registered a resume with JOBTRAK, you can send it to potential employers online merely by entering your resume number and password.

This extremely diverse and comprehensive list is organized alphabetically. I was intrigued by an offering from MTV for internships on a program called *Buzzkill*. For no pay and mandatory college credit, applicants have the opportunity to help in areas of production and cataloging as well as gaining exposure to brainstorming and writing sessions. What a great opportunity for a college student looking for a future in entertainment! This site is a gold mine!

In the past year Job Track has continued its regular launch of new features, including salary calculators, Career Fair calendars, more relocation information and an expanded resource center.

Career Shop
http://www.careershop.com
e-mail: webmaster@tenkey.com

One of Careershop's strengths seems to be its online jobfairs. There are jobfairs for over fifty cities and states listed, plus a list of hot employers. Careershop also lets you post your resume or search their job database. You can search the job postings by category, state, how long the job has been posted, or keyword. I found no listings for merchandise manager or swim coach and only one for systems analysts in New York. Careershop's search method can be a little tedious if you can't match up your desired position with one of the preset categories. This site also includes special employer profiles, advice on interviewing, and salary surveys.

America's Job Bank
http://www.ajb.dni.us/

This company, a subsidiary of the public Employment Service, was originally established in 1979 as the Interstate Job Bank. It lists over almost 700,000 jobs, representing a broad spectrum of professions, that have been registered at the 1,800 state-level Employment Service offices. The site was accessed by over fifteen million people in the past six months. The payoffs for both the state and the public are obvious. In 1993, the company was renamed America's Job Bank. The service is free to all job seekers and employers; it is funded through state unemployment taxes. (Gee, it's nice to know your taxes are going to a good cause!) Aside from an enormous job database, America's Job Bank offers access to the government's Occupational Outlook Handbook, Employment Service's Websites, employer Websites, and private placement agencies. There is a page of Occupational Employment Trends that lists the fastest/slowest growing occupations.

You have three choices once you get into the Job Bank: menu search, keyword search, or code search (for those savvy individuals who know the D.O.T.—Dictionary of Occupational Titles—code for their profession). Menu search gives you a scroll list of twenty-two standard job categories. The 3,326 computer jobs on file for New York came up onto the screen in less than thirty seconds. I was impressed, having done so much waiting for so much less at other, more self-important sites. Each listing shows job title, location, salary, education required, experience required, and whether the job is full-time or part-time. I was even able to learn which industries the jobs were in. Jobs are listed alphabetically so it is easy to sort through them. New listings are asterisked to save regular users' time. The really neat thing about this site is that once the jobs are on screen, you can re-sort the order they are listed in by state, city, job title, salary, or new jobs. America's Job Bank is one site that lives up to its claims. It's friendly, flexible, fast—and it delivers.

In the last year they have added a straightforward resume builder and a resume database.

Jobs MetaSEARCH @ JobBank USA
http://www.jobbankusa.com/search.html

Let's say by now you've been around the cyber block a few times and you just want to get down to business and search through all the possible job listings without all the hullabaloo and advice. Jobs USA created the jobs MetaSEARCH just for you. At this one-stop shopping site over twenty career search engines are at your service, all in a row, one after the other including most of the biggies such as Monster Board, Career Mosaic, E-Span, etc., and including almost every one I have reviewed here. Most of the searches are keyword job title/location. You can also search by position type (e.g. permanent, contract, temporary, internship, or summer job) or location. This is a great wham-bam-thank-you-ma'am experience.

Exec.U.Net
http://www.execunet.com
e-mail: Canada@execunet.com

Exec.U.Net has been in business since 1988, serving over fifteen thousand members. This is one site executive search firms always check. Over 2,500 companies and search firms access this site. By the middle of 1998 (when the editor demands my copy) it had posted over twenty thousand jobs from the hidden job market.

Exec.U.Net publishes a jobs lead report every two weeks covering 350–400 new and unadvertised opportunities nationwide in the functional areas of general management, finance, sales, marketing, human resources, operations management, research & development, engineering, and MIS. Information is collected by e-mail or U.S. Post.

You can sample a list of the job opportunities members have access to when you visit the site. Membership is completely confidential and costs $110 for three months (six issues), $170 for six months (twelve issues), or $290 annually (twenty-four issues). There's a money-back guarantee if you're not satisfied (although you should check the site for current policies). Other career resources, including a career management library (books are offered at a 10% discount—including those by that truly outstanding *New York Times* bestseller Martin Yate!), a newsletter with up-to-date management strategies and techniques, information on networking opportunities through regional meetings, and workshops and seminars, are available online.

Exec.U.Net continues to ad useful information, including more data on market trends, and resources for job search and career management. A great specialist site, this is where you'll get the best chance to meet and be wooed by the headhunters.

This site has been acclaimed by *Business Week, Fortune, Money, Investor's Business Daily, ABC Nightly News,* and the *New York Times*. Perhaps even more important, it now gets a top rating from *Knock 'Em Dead*. Go and visit—it will elevate your career. Great site, run by good professional, and conscientious people.

Med Search America
http://www.medsearch.com

There is no better site for health care professionals to find the perfect job. Thousands of job opportunities from all over the country are accessible to job seekers for *free!* It is powered by Monster Board and features a similar format. When you see a Website that says "powered by" it means the site has reached a commercial agreement to use products and services of another vendor under their own banner. As time goes by you will see more and more of such announcements.

Academe This Week
http://chronicle.merit.edu/.ads/.links.html

This site is a service of the prestigious *Chronicle of Higher Education*, a weekly publication for college and university faculty members and administrators. The magazine is a fascinating read, but we need to concentrate on the service itself here. On this site you can browse through a list of available positions within these categories: humanities, social sciences, science and technology, and professional academics. Each of these categories offers more selections. In science and technology, for example, there were fourteen subcategories starting with agricultural science.

There were twenty-eight positions worldwide for teachers and professors of computer technology, most of which required a Ph.D. Most of the jobs listed here last year are no longer available.

The Business Job Finder
http://www.cob.ohio-state.edu/dept/fin/osujobs.htm

I originally got to this site via Career Paradise, Emory College's very humorous and innovative site, which I did not review here simply because it is available only to Emory students.

The Business Job Finder, as its name suggests, focuses on jobs in the world of business. It is geared toward recent graduates and includes lots of advice and information on career planning, but it is also an excellent resource for business professionals who are looking for a new position. The site features "Explore Business Careers," a thorough look at the world of employment in finance, accounting, and management—and "Career Reference," a center for job searches, employer profiles, education, and links to some of the best career sites for business professionals.

To search for a job, you click onto "Business Job listings," and you will be presented with a list in three sections: "Business jobs at this Site" (twenty-three categories of companies and/or industries with multiple listings), and "Other Sites with Business job listings" (twenty links to sources with business job listings such as newspapers and other career sites). This site is somewhat overwhelming.

FedWorld
http://www.fedworld.gov
e-mail: webmaster@Fedworld.gov

The FedWorld Information Network is a service designed to give the general public access to government information. FedWorld provides access to 100-plus dialup bulletin boards that are not otherwise available on the Internet.

FedWorld's Federal Job Announcement search capability allows you to search a database of about 2,000 U.S. government job announcements that are updated daily from Tuesday through Saturday at 9:30 a.m. Eastern Standard Time. From the initial home page key in "Job Announcements," which brings you to a keyword search that allows you to enter one or two relevant job field words, you can choose to scan alphabetically, reverse alphabetically, or in the most relevant job order. You can narrow your search by location and start to search. I found that most of the jobs with the government were in Washington, D.C. (Gee, don't you just love learning something new every day!)

Resume Banks

Resume banks are the reverse of job banks. Instead of employers listing available jobs to be scanned by job hunters, resume banks are made up of resumes supplied by job applicants, intended to be scanned by prospective employers. In most resume banks, you either upload your resume in file or HTML form into the site, or fill out an online form, which will generate a resume-like document for employers to scan. You can find out how to build a powerful yet painless HTML resume in *Resumes That Knock 'em Dead*.

It used to be fashionable for job search experts to advise job hunters to take out newspaper ads announcing their abilities. I never endorsed this approach because I'd never met an employer who saw it as a viable avenue for finding quality employees. Even though resume banks are, in effect, an electronic version of these ads, they seem to be working. I think the reason is twofold. First of all, these banks are set up so that a computer, not a person, is doing the initial searching for candidates, and second, people who are active online are, *ipso facto*, computer literate, and therefore more desirable as employees.

An employer requesting a search from a resume database will describe the available job with a number of descriptive words and/or phrases. The computer then searches for those words and phrases in all the resumes in the database. An employer can typically search for up to twelve keywords or phrases. It isn't necessary that you match all twelve keywords—just one match is usually all it takes. If the keyword or phrase is not in your resume, the computer won't retrieve it for the employer.

If you are going to post your resume online, follow these guidelines:

- Use 14 point (size) Courier type, or a similar plain font.
- Avoid italics, script, underlining, and boldface, along with two-column or other nontraditional formatting.
- Use upper/lower case to differentiate headings.
- Use plenty of white space.
- Do not include large paragraphs of text.
- You can use bulleted lists, but use a dash as your bullet "point."

If you are an experienced professional with qualifications for more than one job, you may want to post additional resumes under appropriate job titles, including the appropriate keywords and phrases for that job. Some people are concerned about confidentiality. If you upload your resume into a resume bank, theoretically your employer may find your resume online. Practically speaking, most active resume banks have ways to protect your confidentiality. You can try to improve your odds by replacing the name of your current employer with a generic name. For example, you could change "The First International Bank of Last Resort" to "A Major Bahamian Bank"; headhunters do this for their clients all the time.

Resume banks are new for employers and employees alike. A resume bank with a thousand resumes on it is currently considered quite a respectable size. However, I have this sneaky feeling that in a couple of years we'll have banks with fifty thousand–plus resumes, and they'll have become an integral part of many corporate recruitment programs. My advice is to get used to maintaining your resume online on a permanent basis—it's better to find out about available jobs (no matter how) and have the opportunity to turn them down, rather than never having heard about them at all.

Most resume banks are free (at present). The few who do charge typically offer special additional services, and the fees for these are usually quite reasonable.

Yahoo Resume Bank
http://www.yahoo.com

Good old Yahoo—one of the Web's most popular search engines and most visited sites—really comes up roses here. When you get into Yahoo, just type in "individual resumes" and you will be presented with ninety-one headings you can link to, covering all major industries. The categories at the time of writing was somewhat scattered; for instance, there are six listings for "Computers and Internet" randomly interspersed amongst science and art and business. Click onto any one of these and a plethora of resumes are at your fingertips. This is a gold mine for computer graphic artists, both to show off your capabilities and to check out the competition . . . there are a lot of very talented people out there looking for work; just scanning their resumes is like walking through a cyber museum!

This bank has a growing roster of thousands of professional resumes. When you check on a category (in some areas there are also subcategories within job categories) you are instantly presented with a list of names, each annotated with a quick quip designed to attract your attention. One of these "headlines" read, "will bring you a smile." Now, on a resume, this might make a hardened HR pro vomit and move on. (I would have been put off by the coyness in a flash.) Online, as you'll soon see, things are different. Here, that human touch didn't seem to offend so much; in fact, I checked out the resume!

Once you click on a name, you get a full resume with all the details: experience, education, activities, references, etc. For an employer, the Yahoo resume bank is accessible, easy to use, and fast; for you, it is free. Go on, post your resume!

A+ Online Resumes
http://ol-resume.com/
e-mail: webmaster@ol-resume.com

This is a professional resume service that will convert your resume to HTML (Hyper Text Markup Language) and post it on the WWW, where HR professionals and business owners can have access to it around the clock. Employers can find your resume either by job category or location. Resumes are registered with the most popular Web search engines, such as Yahoo, Webcrawler, etc. You are given your own home page with a URL. Postings cost $40 for three months, $60 for six months, $80 for nine months, and $100 for a full year. A+ aggressively promotes the site throughout the Internet on highly targeted hyperlinks to ensure that it maintains a high profile.

You can view the guest book, which contains a list of employers who use the site. These companies are listed by state. California had 127 companies listed, Alabama had nine, and Hawaii had one.

America's Employers Resume Bank
http://www.americasemployers.com//resume.html

This subsidiary site of the America's Employers Career Center caters primarily to executives who have been prescreened by America's Employers career counselors. The resume database has grown by leaps and bounds since last year. When I searched this site for the 1998 edition, I found seventeen resumes in accounting and finance, eleven in health care, and twenty-six in information systems. This year I found several hundred resumes in accounting alone. Member companies are able to access contact information on the candidates directly. If a company who is not a member of America's Employers is interested in contacting you, the service will notify you.

Resumes on the Web
http://www.resweb.com
e-mail: sdas@ifu.net

This service offers resume postings with an e-mail link and Usenet cross-postings for $10.50, a home page link only or resumes supplied in HTML for $7.50, and full Internet resume publicity (includes at least three leads) for $100 to $250.

There is no fee for searching the site, making it attractive to recruiters and employers alike. You simply click onto the job category and the names of candidates appear. Click again and a complete resume with contact information appears—very straightforward. This is not a huge resume bank as yet, but the resumes I looked at had impressive credentials, making this site a place that employers and recruiters could well come to respect.

Shawn's Internet Resume Center
http://www.inpursuit.com/sirc/

For a one-time fee of $30 you can post your resume on this very heavily visited site, which caters to high-end management. Check out the guest book, and you'll be impressed by the employers and recruiters who are searching the site. Check out your competition by doing a resume search on others looking for work in your field—an idea of what kind of qualifications they have and how they're presenting themselves to employers could be time and money well spent.

Headhunters and Recruiting Firms

More and more employment agencies, recruiters, and headhunters are also establishing an online presence. They typically recruit in specialized areas—for example, health care or insurance—and use their sites both for recruitment and as public relations tools. At a site belonging to a recruitment firm you may find a job bank, a resume bank, and a newsgroup where you can post questions and join discussions. As time goes on, it will become harder to determine what makes a career center (a site that makes its money largely from advertising revenues) different from a site offered by a recruitment firm (which makes its money from its clients). From the job hunter's point of view, these distinctions aren't always that important. As I said earlier in the book, there is no one right way to dig up job leads, except to pursue every way to dig up job leads.

Another Internet Resource: Usenet Newsgroups

The Usenet newsgroups offer a bonanza of job searching information on the Internet. The newsgroups are made up of thousands of discussion areas covering about any topic you can imagine. Within these areas, anyone with access to the Internet can either read or post a message. Several of these areas focus on employment-related topics. These newsgroups are accessible through every major online service. Among the largest:

Misc.jobs.offered is a place for employers to list open positions. The volume of job openings is enormous. Because of this, you will want to check this newsgroup frequently.

Misc.jobs.misc is an open discussion group for anything related to jobs. You never know what you'll find in here, so check it often.

Misc.jobs.contract lists only contract positions, but there are quite a few of them. Check this group often.

Misc.jobs.resumes gives you a place to list your resume. Be sure to send only an ASCII version, and be sure to visit at least every few weeks. Much like the *misc.jobs.offered* newsgroup, sheer volume can overcome a potential employer. Remember that when posting your resume, your message title is all users will see unless they choose to view your entire resume. This means you should give careful thought to the title your resume will carry, because it will determine how many people actually choose to view your resume. Take a look at previous postings to the group to get an idea of what works and what doesn't.

The Internet is huge and the resources it offers are vast. Many specialty newsgroups exist, and new ones are being created all the time. For example, if you live in the San Francisco Bay Area you should check *ba.misc.jobs* (Bay Area). If you live in New England, you may check *ne.jobs* or *ne.jobs.contract.* Look around on the Internet—there may be a newsgroup that fits your needs.

Knock 'em Dead Electronic Resources

If all of this discussion of URLs and .COMs has left you a little intimidated about starting the online part of your job search, try this simple three-step approach.

Search the lists. Start by searching the resource lists described at the beginning of the appendix. These lists will help you identify those sites that are most likely to be relevant to your specific needs. Use the search capabilities built into some of these sites to search by job title, profession, education, and geographic area to pin down the right resources for your job hunt. To find recruiters who handle your area of expertise or specialty, you might try a keyword search along the lines of "[medical secretary] (insert your specialty here) recruitment."

Research the career centers. Visit some of the career centers listed here to gather information that will help you in your search. The career centers tend to have a range of different resources conveniently located together, under one roof. These may not be the best of their kind, or contain the answer to all of your questions, but they can't help but provide information that you'll find useful and, more important, will point you in the right direction.

Remember that career centers typically include job and resume banks, special-interest databases, advice and tips on resumes, cover letters, advice networking, and other aspects of job hunting, as well as opportunities to communicate with other job seekers and job hunt experts.

Narrow your search. Now that you have a good idea of what's available online that suits your purposes, you can begin to concentrate on more specific targets—company sites that list jobs or resumes in your industry, sites set up by headhunters and recruiters that cover your field, or professional association sites that contain specific information you can use.

□   □   □

You'll notice, as you use more and more of these sites, that the online world is continually and rapidly evolving, with everyone trying their best to offer the services that are in highest demand. In the process, the amount of information available to you can only increase in quantity and quality.

This year's prime site may become last year's also-ran, so keep your eyes open for new sites that help you in your job search. I'll update this section of *Knock 'em Dead* on a yearly basis, and I'd appreciate your sending your discoveries along to me care of the publisher.

HEALTH CARE

Publications

Hospital Phone Book
U.S. Directory Service, Miami, FL
Provides information on over 7,940 government and private hospitals in the U.S.

National Association of County Health Officials Sustaining Membership Directory
National Association of County Health Officials, Washington, DC
Lists national health officials for almost every county in the U.S. Published annually. $10. Call 202-783-5550 for more information.

National Jobs in Dietetics
Jobs in Dietetics, Santa Monica, CA
Lists jobs nationwide in the field of dietetics. Published monthly; an annual subscription is $84. Call 310-453-5375 for more information.

U.S. Medical Directory
U.S. Directory Service, Miami, FL
Over one thousand pages of information on doctors, hospitals, nursing facilities, medical laboratories, and medical libraries.

Associations

HEALTH CARE ADMINISTRATION

American Association of Medical Assistants
20 North Wacker Drive, Suite 1575
Chicago, IL 60606-2903; tel: 312-899-1500

American College of Healthcare Executives
1 North Franklin, Suite 1700
Chicago, IL 60606-3491; tel: 312-424-2800
http://www.ache.org/

American Health Care Association
1201 L Street NW
Washington, DC 20005; tel: 202-842-4444
http://www.ahca.org/

American Health Information Management Association
919 North Michigan Avenue
Chicago, IL 60611; tel: 312-787-2672
http://www.ahima.org/

American Medical Technologists
710 Higgins Road
Park Ridge, IL 60068; tel: 708-823-5169

Healthcare Financial Management Association
Two Westbrook Corporate Center, Suite 700
Westchester, IL 60154; tel: 708-531-9600
http://www.hfmawny.org/

National Association of Emergency Medical Technicians
102 West Leake Street
Clinton, MS 39056; tel: 601-924-7747
http://www.naemt.org/

Nuclear Medicine Technology Certification Board
2970 Clairmont Road, Suite 610
Atlanta, GA 30329-1634; tel: 404-315-1739
http://www.nmtcb.org/

NURSING

American Association of Nurse Anesthetists
222 South Prospect Avenue
Park Ridge, IL 60068-4001; tel: 708-692-7050
http://www.aana.com/

American Association of Occupational Health Nurses
50 Lenox Pointe
Atlanta, GA 30324; tel: 404-262-1162 or 800-241-8014

American Hospital Association
1 North Franklin
Chicago, IL 60606; tel: 312-422-3000
http://www.aha.org/

American Nurses Association
600 Maryland Avenue SW, Suite 100 W
Washington, DC 20024-2571; tel: 202-651-7000
http://www.ana.org/

National Association for Home Care
519 C Street NE
Washington, DC 20002; tel: 202-547-7424
(send SASE for general information)
http://www.nahc.org/

National Association for Practical Nurse Education and Service
1400 Spring Street, Suite 310
Silver Spring, MD 20910; tel: 301-588-2491

National Association of Pediatric Nurse Associates and Practitioners
1101 Kings Highway N, Suite 206
Cherry Hill, NJ 08034-1921; tel: 609-667-1773
http://www.napnap.org/

National Federation of Licensed Practical Nurses
1418 Aversboro Road
Garner, NC 27529-4547; tel: 919-779-0046
http://www.nflpn.org/

National League for Nursing Communications Department
350 Hudson Street
New York, NY 10014; tel: 212-989-9393

National Rehabilitation Association
633 South Washington Street
Alexandria, VA 22314; tel: 703-836-0850

Medical Economics Publishing
5 Paragon Drive
Montvale, NJ 07645-1742; tel: 201-358-7200

PHYSICAL HEALTH

Accreditation Council for Graduate Medical Education
515 North State Street, Suite 2000
Chicago, IL 60610; tel: 312-464-4920
http://www.acgme.org/

American Association for Respiratory Care
11030 Ables Lane
Dallas, TX 75229-4593; tel: 214-243-2272
http://www.arc.org/

American Association of Colleges of Pediatric Medicine
1350 Piccard Drive, Suite 322
Rockville, MD 20850; tel: 301-990-7400
http://www.aacpm.org/

American Board of Preventive Medicine
9950 West Lawrence Avenue, Suite 106
Schiller Park, IL 60176; tel: 847-671-1750

American Medical Association
515 North State Street
Chicago, IL 60610; tel: 312-464-5000

American Occupational Therapy Association
4720 Montgomery Lane, P.O. Box 31220
Bethesda, MD 20824-1220; tel: 301-652-2682
http://www.aota.org/

American Physical Therapy Association
1111 North Fairfax Street
Alexandria, VA 22314; tel: 703-684-2782 or 800-999-2782
http://www.apta.org/

American Podiatric Medical Association
9312 Old Georgetown Road
Bethesda, MD 20814-1621; tel: 301-571-9200
http://www.apma.org/

American Society of Radiology Technologists
15000 Central Avenue SE
Albuquerque, NM 87123-4605; tel: 505-298-4500
http://www.asrt.org/

Society of Diagnostic Medical Sonographers
12770 Coit Road, Suite 508
Dallas, TX 75251; tel: 214-239-7367
http://www.sdms.org/

DENTISTRY

American Association of Dental Assistants
203 North LaSalle Street, Suite 132
Chicago, IL 60601-1225; tel: 312-541-1550

American Association of Dental Schools
1625 Massachusetts Avenue NW
Washington, DC 20036; tel: 202-667-9433

American Association of Orthodontists
401 North Lindbergh Blvd.
St. Louis, MO 63141-7816; tel: 314-993-1700

American Dental Association
211 East Chicago Avenue
Chicago, IL 60611; tel: 312-440-2500
(for Commission on Dental Accreditation, direct correspondence
to Suite 3400; for SELECT Program, direct correspondence to
Department of Career Guidance, Suite 1804)

American Dental Hygienists Association
Division of Professional Development
444 North Michigan Avenue, Suite 3400
Chicago, IL 60611; tel: 312-440-8900
http://www.adha.org/

National Association of Dental Laboratories
555 East Braddock Road
Alexandria, VA 22305; tel: 703-683-5263
http://www.nadl.org/

National Board for Certification in Dental Technology
555 East Braddock Road
Alexandria, VA 22305; tel: 703-683-5263

MENTAL HEALTH

American Association for Counseling and Development
5999 Stevenson Avenue
Alexandria, VA 22304; tel: 703-823-9800

American Association for Marriage and Family Therapy
11331 5th Street NW, Suite 300
Washington, DC 20005; tel: 202-452-0109
http://www.aamft.org/

American Association of Mental Retardation
444 North Capitol Street, NW, Suite 846
Washington, DC 20001-1512; tel: 202-387-1968 or 800-424-3688
http://www. aamr.org/

American Psychiatric Association
1400 K Street NW
Washington, DC 20005; tel: 202-682-6000

American Psychological Association
750 First Street NE
Washington, DC 20002; tel: 202-336-5500
http://www.apa.org/

National Board for Certified Counselors
3 Terrace Way, Suite D
Greensboro, NC 27403-3660; tel: 910-547-0607
http://www.nbcc.org/

BIOTECHNOLOGY AND ENVIRONMENTAL TECHNOLOGY

Publications

Corporate Technology Directory
CorpTech, Woburn, MA
Lists over 35,000 businesses and 110,000 executives. Describes products and services in such fields as automation, biotechnology, chemicals, computers and software, defense, energy, environment, manufacturing equipment, advanced materials, medical, pharmaceuticals, photonics, subassemblies and components, testing and measurements, telecommunications, and transportation and holding companies. Published annually.

CorpTech Fast 5,000 Company Locator
CorpTech, Woburn, MA
Lists over five thousand of the fastest-growing companies listed in the Corporate Technology Directory, but includes addresses and phone numbers, number of employees, sales, and industries by state. Published annually.

Directory of Environmental Information
Government Institutes, Rockville, MD
Lists federal and state government resources, trade organizations, and professional and scientific newsletters, magazines, and databases. Published every other year.

Environmental Telephone Directory
Governmental Institutes, Rockville, MD
Lists detailed information on governmental agencies that deal with the environment. The directory also identifies the environmental aides of U.S. Senators and Representatives. Published every other year.

Sales Guide to High-Tech Companies
CorpTech, Woburn, MA
Covers over three thousand company profiles and twelve thousand executive contacts. Includes specific details on each company's products and services. Published quarterly; a yearly subscription is $185. Call 617-932-3939 for more information.

Transportation Officials and Engineers Directory
American Road and Transportation Builders Association, Washington, DC
Lists over four thousand state transportation officials and engineers at local, state, and federal levels. Published annually.

Associations

Air and Waste Management Association
1 Gateway Center, 3rd Floor
Pittsburgh, PA 15222; tel: 412-232-3444
http://www.awma.org/

American Chemical Society
1155 16th Street NW
Washington, DC 20036; tel: 202-872-4600 or 800-227-5558
http://www.acs.org/

American Institute of Biological Sciences
1444 Eye Street NW, Suite 200
Washington, DC 20005; tel: 202-628-1500
http://www.aibs.org/

American Institute of Chemists
501 Wythe Street
Alexandria, VA 22314-1917; tel: 703-836-2090

American Institute of Physics
1 Physics Ellipse
College Park, MD 20740-3843; tel: 301-209-3100
http://www.aip.org/

American Society for Biochemistry and Molecular Biology
9650 Rockville Pike
Bethesda, MD 20814-3996; tel: 301-530-7145

American Society of Microbiology
1325 Massachusetts Avenue NW
Washington, DC 20005; tel: 202-737-3600
http://www.asm.org/

American Society of Biological Chemists
9650 Rockville Pike
Bethesda, MD 20814-3996; tel: 301-530-7145

American Zoo and Aquarium Association (AZA)
Office of Membership Service
Oglebay Park, Route 88
Wheeling, WV 26003; tel: 304-242-2160
http://www.aza.org/

Association of American Geographers
1710 16th Street NW
Washington, DC 20009-3198; tel: 202-234-1450
http://www.aag.org/

Botanical Society of America
1735 Nell Avenue
Columbus, OH 43210; tel: 614-292-3519

Center for American Archeology
P.O. Box 366
Kampsville, IL 62053; tel: 618-653-4316

Department of Energy Headquarters Operations Division
1000 Independence Avenue SW, Room 4E-090
Washington, DC 20585; tel: 202-586-4333
(hotline for job vacancies, updated every Friday)

Environmental Protection Agency Recruitment Center
401 Main Street SW, Room 3634
Washington, DC 20460; tel: 202-260-2090/3308

Federation of American Societies for Experimental Biology
9650 Rockville Pike
Bethesda, MD 20814; tel: 301-530-7000
http://www.faseb.org/

Genetics Society of America
9650 Rockville Pike
Bethesda, MD 20814-3998; tel: 301-571-1825

Geological Society of America
3300 Penrose Place, P.O. Box 9140
Boulder, CO 80301; tel: 303-447-2020

National Accrediting Agency for Clinical Laboratory Sciences
8410 West Bryn Mawr Avenue, Suite 670
Chicago, IL 60631; tel: 312-714-8880

National Solid Wastes Management Association
4301 Connecticut Avenue NW, Suite 300
Washington, DC 20008; tel: 202-244-4700

Natural Resource Conservation Service, Personnel Division
P.O. Box 2980
Washington, DC 20013; tel: 202-720-4264

ENGINEERING

Associations

American Association of Engineering Societies
1111 19th Street NW, Suite 608
Washington, DC 20034; tel: 202-296-2237
http://www.aaes.org/

American Chemical Society
1155 16th Street NW
Washington, DC 20036; tel: 202-872-4600 or 800-227-5558
http://www.acs.org/

American Institute of Chemical Engineers
345 East 47th Street
New York, NY 10017; tel: 212-705-7338 or 800-242-4363

American Society for Engineering Education
1818 N Street NW, Suite 600
Washington, DC 20036; tel: 202-331-3500
http://www.asee.org/

American Society of Civil Engineers
1801 Alexander Bell Drive
Reston, VA 20191-4400; tel: 800-548-ASCE
http://www.asce.org/

American Society of Mechanical Engineers (ASME)
345 East 47th Street
New York, NY 10017; tel: 212-705-7722
http://www.asme.org/

Institute of Electrical and Electronics Engineers
345 East 47th Street
New York, NY 10017; tel: 212-705-7900
http://www.ieee.org/

Institute of Industrial Engineers
25 Technology Park
Atlanta, GA 30092-0460; tel: 770-449-0460

Society of Manufacturing Engineers (SME)
1 SME Drive, P.O. Box 930
Dearborn, MI 48121; tel: 313-271-1500

INFORMATION TECHNOLOGY

Publications

Access
1900 West 47th Place, Suite 215
Shawnee Mission, KS 66205; tel: 800-362-0681

(initial six-month nonmember listing, $15; each additional three
months, $15; initial six-month listing for members of the Data
Processing Management Association, $10)

AIIM Job Bank Bulletin
Association for Information and Image Management
1100 Wayne Avenue, Suite 1100
Silver Spring, MD 20910; tel: 301-587-8202
(four-month subscription: nonmember, $100; member, $25;
issued semimonthly)

Associations

ASIS Jobline
American Society for Information Science
8720 Georgia Avenue, Suite 501
Silver Spring, MD 20910-3602; tel: 301-495-0900
(free; monthly)
http://www.asis.org/

Association for Computing Machinery
1515 Broadway
New York, NY 10036; tel: 212-869-7440
http://www.acm.org/

Association for Systems Management
1433 West Bagley Road, P.O. Box 38370
Cleveland, OH 44138; tel: 216-243-6900

COMPUTERS

Publications

ComputerWorld
500 Old Connecticut Path
Framingham, MA 01701-9171; tel: 508-879-0700 or 800-343-6474
(annual subscription: U.S., $39.95; Canada, $110; issued weekly)

ComputerWorld, Campus Edition
500 Old Connecticut Path
Framingham, MA 01701-9171; tel: 508-879-0700
(annual subscription, $5; free to students; published each October)

High Technology Careers Magazine
4701 Patrick Henry Drive, Suite 1901
Santa Clara, CA 95054; tel: 408-970-8800
(six issues per year, $29)

Technical Employment News
P.O. Box 1285
Cedar Park, TX 78613; tel: 512-250-9023 or 800-678-9724
(weekly subscription, $55; annual subscription, $88, U.S. and
Canada)

Associations

IEEE Computer Society
1730 Massachusetts Avenue NW
Washington, DC 20036; tel: 202-371-0101
(available to members only)

CU Career Connection
University of Colorado, Campus Box 133
Boulder, CO 80309-0133; tel: 303-492-4727
(two-month fee for passcode to the job hotline, $30)

Data Processing Management Association
505 Busse Highway
Park Ridge, IL 60068; tel: 708-825-8124

Institute for Certification of Computing Professionals
2200 East Devon Avenue, Suite 247
Des Plaines, IL 60018; tel: 708-299-4227
http://www.iccp.org/

Quality Assurance Institute
7575 Philips Boulevard, Suite 350
Orlando, Fl 32819; tel: 407-363-1111

Semiconductor Equipment and Materials International
805 East Middlefield Road
Mountain View, CA 94043; tel: 415-964-5111
http://www.semi.org/

BUSINESS AND PROFESSIONAL

Publications

The Almanac of American Employers Corporate Jobs Outlook
Boeme, TX
Lists five hundred of the country's most successful, large
companies; profiles salary ranges, benefits, financial stability, and
advancement opportunities.

America's Fastest Growing Employers
Adams Media Corporation, Holbrook, MA
A national career guide for those seeking employment with the
most rapidly growing firms in the country. Includes names,
addresses, and vital statistics for more than 275 companies in
today's economy. Each profile gives key facts about the
company's growth and development.

Corporate Jobs Outlook
Corporate Jobs Outlook, Inc., Dallas, TX
Each issue reviews fifteen to twenty major (five thousand
employees or more) firms. The report rates the firms and
provides information on salaries and benefits, current and
projected development, where to apply for jobs, potential layoffs,
benefit plans, the company's record for promoting women or
minorities to executive positions, and college reimbursement
packages. Also includes personnel contact information for each
firm. Published bimonthly; a yearly subscription is $159.99. Call
210-755-8810. Note: This resource is also available online
through NewsNet (800-345-1301) or the Human Resources
Information Network (800-638-8094). Call for more details.

Directory of Corporate Affiliations
Reed Reference Publishing Company, New Providence, NJ
Lists key personnel in 4,700 parent companies and forty
thousand divisions, subsidiaries, and affiliates. Includes addresses
and phone numbers of key executives and decision makers.
Published once a year, with quarterly updates. For more
information, call 800-323-6772.

Directory of Leading Private Companies
National Register Publishing Company, Wilmette, IL
Profiles over seven thousand U.S. private companies in the
service, manufacturing, distribution, retail, and construction fields.
Includes companies in such areas as health care, high technology,
entertainment, fast-food franchises, leasing, publishing, and
communications. Published annually.

Encyclopedia of Associations
Gale Research, Inc., Detroit, MI
Published in three volumes. Volume 1 lists national organizations
in the U.S. and includes over twenty-two thousand associations,
including hundreds for government professions. Volume 2
provides geographic and executive indexes. Volume 3 features full
entries on associations that are not listed in Volume 1. Note: This
resource is also available online through Dialog Information
Services (800-334-2564). Call for more information.

International Directory of Corporate Affiliations
National Register Publishing Company, Wilmette, IL
Lists over fourteen hundred major foreign companies and their
thirty thousand U.S. and foreign holdings. Published annually.

The JobBank Series
Adams Media Corporation, Holbrook, MA
A top-notch series of paperback local employment guides. The
1997 editions profile virtually every local company with over fifty
employees in a given metro area. Company listings are arranged by
industry for easy use; also included is a section on the region's
economic outlook and contact information for local professional
associations, executive search firms, and job placement agencies.
The series covers twenty-nine major metropolitan areas, including
Atlanta, Boston, the Carolinas, Chicago, Dallas/Ft. Worth, Denver,
Detroit, Florida, Houston, Los Angeles, Minneapolis/St. Paul,
Missouri, New York, Ohio, Philadelphia, Phoenix, San Francisco,
Seattle, Tennessee, and Washington, DC. Many listings feature
contact names, common positions hired for, educational
backgrounds sought, benefits, fax numbers, internship information,
staff size, and more. Available at most bookstores. Updated yearly.

The National JobBank
Adams Media Corporation, Holbrook, MA
The 1999 edition includes over twenty-one thousand company
profiles. Many listings feature contact names, common positions
hired for, educational backgrounds sought, benefits, fax numbers,
internship information, staff size, and more. Updated annually.

National Trade and Professional Associations of the United States
Columbia Books, Washington, DC
Lists information on over sixty-five hundred trade and
professional associations. Published annually.

Resume Bank
American Corporate Counsel Association
1225 Connecticut Avenue NW, Suite 302
Washington, DC 20036; tel: 202-296-4522
(six-month registration: nonmembers, $65; members, $25;
complete job-matching application, and five copies of resume free)

FINANCIAL SERVICES

Associations

BANKING

American Bankers Association
1120 Connecticut Avenue NW
Washington, DC 20036; tel: 202-663-5000

American Institute of Banking
1213 Bakers Way
Manhattan, KS 66502; tel: 913-537-4750

Association of Master of Business Administration Executives
AMBA Center
South Summit Place
Branford, CT 06405; tel: 203-315-5221

Banking Federation of the European Economic Community (BFEC)
Federation Bancaire de la Communaute Europeenne (FBCE)
c/o Umberto Burani
10, rue Montoyer, B-1040
Brussels, Belgium; tel: 32-2-5083711; fax: 32-2-5112328

Banking Law Institute (BLI)
22 West 21st Street
New York, NY 10010; tel: 212-645-7880 or 800-332-1105; fax: 212-675-4883

BANKPAC
(formerly: Bankers Political Action Committee; Banking Profession Political Action Committee)
c/o Meg Bonitt
American Bankers Association
1120 Connecticut Avenue NW
Washington, DC 20036; tel: 202-663-5115/5076 or 202-663-7544 (fax)

Electronic Banking Economics Society (EBES)
P.O. Box 2331
New York, NY 10036; tel: 203-295-9788

Savings and Community Bankers of America Educational Services
Center for Financial Studies
900 19th Street NW, Suite 400
Washington, DC 20006; tel: 202-857-3100

U.S. Council on International Banking (USCIB)
1 World Trade Center, Suite 1963
New York, NY 10048; tel: 212-466-3352; fax: 212-432-0544

Women in Banking and Finance
55 Bourne Vale
Bromley, Kent BR2 7NW, England; tel: 44-181-4623276

Women's World Banking—USA
8 West 40th Street
New York, NY 10018; tel: 212-768-8513; fax: 212-768-8519

SECURITIES

Association of Securities and Exchange Commission Alumni
West Tower, Suite 812
1100 New York Avenue NW
Washington, DC 20005; tel: 202-408-7600; fax: 202-408-7614

International Securities Market Association—England
7 Limeharbour
London E14 9NQ, England; tel: 44-171-538-5655; fax: 44-171-538-4902

National Association of Securities Dealers (NASD)
1735 K Street NW
Washington, DC 20006-1506; tel: 202-728-8000; fax: 202-293-6260

National Association of Securities Professionals (NASP)
700 13th Street NW, Suite 950
Washington, DC 20005; tel: 202-434-4535; fax: 202-434-8916

North American Securities Administrators Association (NASAA)
1 Massachusetts Avenue NW, Suite 310
Washington, DC 20001; tel: 202-737-0900; fax: 202-783-3571
http://www.nasaa.org/

Securities and Futures Authority
Cottons Centre, Cottons Lane
London SE I 2QB, England; tel: 44-171-378-9000; tel: 44-171-403-7569

Securities Industry Association (SIA)
120 Broadway
New York, NY 10271; tel: 212-608-1500; fax: 212-608-1604

Securities Transfer Association (STA)
55 Exchange Place
New York, NY 10260-0001; tel: 212-748-8000

Western Pennsylvania Securities
Industry Agency
1 Oxford Centre, 40th Floor
Pittsburgh, PA 15219; tel: 412-731-7185

ACCOUNTING

Academy of Accounting Historians (AAH)
University of Arkansas, Department of Accounting
Fayetteville, AR 72701; tel: 501-575-6125; fax: 501-575-7687

Accounting Aid Society of Detroit (AASD)
719 Griswold, Suite 2026
Detroit, MI 48226; tel: 313-961-1840; fax: 313-961-6257
E-mail: itpass@igc.apc.org

Affiliation of Independent Accountants
9200 South Dadeland Boulevard, Suite 510
Miami, FL 33156; tel: 305-670-0580; fax: 305-670-3818

American Accounting Association
5717 Bessie Drive
Sarasota, FL 34223; tel: 941-921-7747

American Institute of Certified Public Accountants (AICPA)
1211 Avenue of the Americas
New York, NY 10036-8775; tel: 212-596-6200 or 800-862-4272 or 212-596-6213 (fax)
http://www.aicpa.org/

American Society of Tax Professionals
P.O. Box 1024
Sioux Falls, SD 57101; tel: 605-335-1185

American Society of Women Accountants
1255 Lynnfield Road, Suite 257
Memphis, TN 38119; tel: 901-680-0470
http://www.aswa.org/

American Women's Society of Certified Public Accountants
401 North Michigan Avenue, Suite 2200
Chicago, IL 60611; tel: 312-644-6610
http://www.awscpa.org/

Associated Accounting Firms International (AAFI)
(formerly: Association of Regional CPA Firms)
1000 Connecticut Avenue, Suite 1006
Washington, DC 20036; tel: 202-463-7900; fax: 202-296-0741

Associated Regional Accounting Firms (ARAF)
3700 Crestwood Parkway, Suite 350
Duluth, GA 30136; tel: 770-279-4560; fax: 770-279-4566 (fax)

Association for Accounting Administration (AAA)
136 South Keowee Street
Dayton, OH 45402; tel: 513-222-0030; fax: 513-2212-5794

Association of Accounting Technicians (AAT)
154 Clerkenwell Road
London EC I R 5AD, England; tel: 44-171-837-8600/814-6999;
fax: 44-171-837-6970
E-mail: aatuk@pipex.com

Association of Government Accountants
2200 Mount Vernon Avenue
Alexandria, VA 22301; tel: 703-684-6931

EDP Auditors Association
3701 Algonquin Road, Suite 1010
Rolling Meadows, IL 60008; tel: 708-253-1545

European Accounting Association (EAA)
European Institute for Advanced Studies in Management
13 Rue d'Egmont, B-1050
Brussels, Belgium; tel: 32-2-511-9116; fax: 32-2-512-1929
E-mail: vandyck@ciasm.be

Foundation for Accounting Education (FAE)
530 Fifth Avenue, 5th Floor
New York, NY 10036; tel: 212-719-8300 or 800-537-3635

Governmental Accounting Standards Board (GASB)
401 Merrit 7, P.O. Box 5116
Norwalk, CT 06856-5116; tel: 203-847-0700; fax: 203-849-9714
http://www.gasb.org/

Information Systems Audit and Control Association
3701 Algonquin Road, Suite 1010
Rolling Meadows, IL 60008; tel: 708-253-1545
http://www.isaca.org/

Institute of Certified Management Accountants (ICMA)
10 Paragon Drive
Montvale, NJ 07645; tel: 201-573-9000 or 800-638-4427; fax:
201-573-8438

Institute of Internal Auditors
249 Maitland Avenue
Altamonte Springs, FL 32701-4201; tel: 407-830-7600

Institute of Management Accountants
10 Paragon Drive
Montvale, NJ 07645; tel: 201-573-9000; fax: 201-573-9000

InterAmerican Accounting Association (IAA)
(formerly: InterAmerican Accounting Conference)
275 Fontainebleau Boulevard, Suite 245
Miami, Fl 33172; tel: 305-225-1991; fax: 305-225-2011

National Association of State Boards of Accountancy
545 Fifth Avenue
New York, NY 10168-0002; tel: 212-490-3868

National Society for Public Accountants
1010 North Fairfax Street
Alexandria, VA 22314; tel: 703-549-6400

INSURANCE

Publications

Insurance Field Directories
Insurance Field Company
P.O. Box 948
Northbrook, IL 60065; tel: 708-498-4010
($55; published each September)

Insurance Phone Book and Directory
US Directory Service
121 Chanlon Road
New Providence, NJ 07074; tel: 908-464-6800
($67.95, plus $4.75 shipping)

Associations

ACFE Job Bank
Association of Certified Fraud Examiners
716 West Avenue
Austin, TX 78701; tel: 512-478-9070 or 800-245-3321
(membership fee $75; send two copies of resume and cover letter
indicating salary requirements and where you are willing to relocate)
http://www.acfe.org/

Actual Training Program Directory Society of Actuaries
475 North Martingale Road, Suite 800
Schaumburg, IL 60173-2226; tel: 708-706-3500
(free; published each January)

American Academy of Actuaries
1100 17th Street NW, 7th Floor
Washington, DC 20036; tel: 202-223-8196

American Agents & Brokers
330 North 4th Street
St. Louis, MO 63012; tel: 314-421-5445

Best's Insurance Reports, Property/Casualty Edition
A.M. Best Company
Ambest Road
Oldwick, NJ 08858-9988; tel: 908-439-2200
(annual fee $70)

Independent Insurance Agents of America
127 South Peyton
Alexandria, VA 22314; tel: 703-683-4422 or 800-962-7950
http://www.iiaa.org/

Insurance Information Institute
110 William Street
New York, NY 10038; tel: 212-669-9200
http://www.iii.org/

Insurance Institute of America
720 Providence Road
Malvern, PA 19355; tel: 610-644-2100

Life Insurance Marketing and Research Association
P.O. Box 208
Hartford, CT 16141-0208; tel: 203-777-7000

National Association of Professional Insurance Agents
400 North Washington Street
Alexandria, VA 22314; tel: 703-836-9340

National Association of Life Underwriters
1922 F Street NW
Washington, DC 20006; tel: 202-332-6000

Professional Insurance Agents
400 North Washington Street
Alexandria, VA 22314; tel: 703-836-9340

Society of Actuaries
475 North Martingale Road, Suite 800
Schaumburg, IL 60173-2226; tel: 708-706-3500

FINANCIAL MANAGEMENT

Associations

American Education Finance Association (AEFA)
5249 Cape Leyte Drive
Sarasota, FL 34242; tel: 941-349-7580; fax: 941-349-7580
E-mail: gbabigianc@aol.com

American Finance Association (AFA)
Stern, 44 West 4th Street, Suite 9-190
New York, NY 10012; tel: 212-998-0370

Association of Commercial Finance Attorneys (ACFA)
1 Corporate Center, 18th Floor MSN 712
Hartford, CT 06103; tel: 203-520-7094; fax: 203-240-5077

Commercial Finance Association (CFA)
225 West 34th Street
New York, NY 10122; tel: 212-594-3490 or 212-564-6053

Financial Analysts Federation
P.O. Box 3726
Charlottesville, VA 22903; tel: 804-977-8977

Financial Management Association International
College of Business Administration
University of South Florida
Tampa, FL 33620-5500

Financial Management Service
Department of the Treasury
401 14th Street SW
Washington, DC 20227; tel: 202-874-6750

Financial Managers Society
8 South Michigan Avenue, Suite 500
Chicago, IL 60603; tel: 312-578-1300

Government Finance Officers Association of United States and Canada
ISO North Michigan Avenue, Suite 800
Chicago, IL 60601; tel: 312-977-9700; fax: 312-977-4806

Institute of Certified Financial Planners
3801 East Florida Avenue, Suite 708
Denver, CO 80210; tel: 303-751-7600; fax: 303-759-0749
http://www.icfp.org/

Institute of Chartered Financial Analysts
P.O. Box 3668
Charlottesville, VA 22903; tel: 804-977-6600

Institute of International Finance (IIF)
2000 Pennsylvania Avenue NW, Suite 8500
Washington, DC 20006-1812; tel: 202-857-3600; fax: 202-775-1430

International Association for Financial Planning
2 Concourse Parkway, Suite 800
Atlanta, GA 30328; tel: 404-395-1605
http://www.iafp.org/

National Association of County Treasurers and Finance Officers
c/o National Association of Counties
440 First Street NW, 8th Floor
Washington, DC 20001; tel: 202-393-6226

National Society for Real Estate Finance (NSREF)
2300 M Street NW, Suite 800
Washington, DC 20037; tel: 202-973-2801

New York State Consumer Finance Association (NYSCFA)
90 South Swan Street
Albany, NY 12210; tel: 518-449-7514; fax: 518-426-0566

New York State Government Finance Officers Association
119 Washington Avenue
Albany, NY 12210-2204; tel: 518-465-1512; fax: 518-434-4640
http://www.nysgofa.org/

North American Economics and Finance Association (NAEFA)
Department of Finance
Syracuse University
Syracuse, NY 13244-2130; tel: 315-443-2963; fax: 315-443-5389

Securities Industry Association
120 Broadway
New York, NY 10271; tel: 212-608-1500

HUMAN RESOURCES

Publications

HR Magazine
606 North Washington Street
Alexandria, VA 22314; tel: 703-548-3440

Associations

American Society for Training and Development
1640 King Street, Box 1443
Alexandria, VA 22313; tel: 703-683-8100
http://www.astd.org/

Employment Management Association
4101 Lake Boone Trail, Suite 201
Raleigh, NC 27607; tel: 919-787-6010

Institute of Management Consultants
521 Fifth Avenue, 35th Floor
New York, NY 10175; tel: 212-697-8262

International Personnel Management Association
1617 Duke Street
Alexandria, VA 22314; tel: 703-549-7100

National Training Laboratory
1240 North Pitt Street
Alexandria, VA 22314; tel: 703-548-1500
http://www.ntl.org/

Society for Human Resource Management
606 North Washington Street
Alexandria, VA 22314; tel: 703-548-3440
http://www.shrm.org/

LAW

Publications

ALA Management Connections
Association of Legal Administrators
175 E. Hawthorn Parkway, Suite 325
Vernon Hills, IL 60061-1428; tel: 708-816-1212
(free; updated weekly)

Federal Careers for Attorneys
Federal Reports, Inc., Washington, DC
A guide to legal careers with over three hundred U.S. government general counsel and other legal offices in the U.S. Explains where to apply, the types of legal work common to each field, and information on special recruitment programs.

Judicial Staff Directory
Staff Directories, Ltd., Mt. Vernon, VA
Lists over eleven thousand individuals employed in the 207 federal courts, as well as thirteen thousand cities and their courts. The book also has information on court administration, U.S. marshals, U.S. attorneys, and the U.S. Department of Justice. Includes eighteen hundred biographies.

NDAA Membership Directory
National District Attorneys Association, Alexandria, VA
Lists all district attorneys' offices across the U.S.
$15 for nonmembers, $10 for members. Call 703-549-9222 for more information.

Paralegal's Guide to Government Jobs
Federal Reports, Inc., Washington, DC
Explains federal hiring procedures for both entry-level and experienced paralegals. The volume describes seventy law-related careers for which paralegals qualify and lists over one thousand federal agency personnel offices that hire the most paralegal talent. Also profiles special hiring programs.

Associations

American Association for Paralegal Education
P.O. Box 40244
Overland Park, KS 66204; tel: 913-381-4458

American Bar Association Information Services
750 North Lake Shore Drive
Chicago, IL 60611; tel: 312-988-5000 or 800-621-6159

Internships for College Students Interested in Law, Medicine, and Politics
Graduate Group, 86 Norwood Road
West Hartford, CT 06117; tel: 203-236-5570 or 203-232-3100
($27.50, published annually)

National Association for Law Placement
1666 Connecticut Avenue, Suite 328
Washington, DC 20009; tel: 202-667-1666
http://www.nalp.org/

National Association of Legal Assistants
1516 South Boston Avenue, Suite 200
Tulsa, OK 74119; tel: 918-587-6828
http://www.nala.org/

National Federation of Paralegal Associations
P.O. Box 33108
Kansas City, MO 64114; tel: 816-941-4000

National Paralegal Association
Box 406
Solebury, PA 18963; tel: 215-297-8333

NCRA Employment Referral Service
National Court Reporters Association
8224 Old Courthouse Road
Vienna, VA 22182; tel: 703-556-6272
(six-month registration: nonmembers, $20; free to members)

Paralegal Placement Network Inc.
P.O. Box 406
Solebury, PA 18963; tel: 215-297-8333
(regular fee, $10; Nat. Paralegal Association members, $15)

MEDIA/COMMUNICATION/PUBLIC RELATIONS

Publications

P.R. Reporter
P.O. Box 6000
Exeter, NH 03833

Public Relations Consultants Directory
American Business Directories Inc.
5711 East 86th Circle
Omaha, NE 68127; tel: 402-331-7169

SMPS Employment Referral Society for Marketing Professional Services
99 Canal Plaza, Suite 250
Alexandria, VA 22314; tel: 703-549-6117 or 800-292-7677
(nonmembers, $100; members, $50; five copies resume and SMPS application on file for three months)

Associations

American Society for Health Care Marketing and Public Relations
American Hospital Association
1 North Franklin
Chicago, IL 60606; tel: 312-422-3737

American Society of Journalists and Authors
1501 Broadway, Suite 302
New York, NY 10036; tel: 212-997-0947
http://www.asja.org/

Council of Sales Promotion Agencies
750 Summer Street
Stamford, CT 06901; tel: 203-325-3911

Dow Jones Newspaper Fund
P.O. Box 300
Princeton, NJ 08543-0300; tel: 609-452-2820

Editorial Freelancers Association
71 West 23rd Street, Suite 1504
New York, NY 10010; tel: 212-929-5400

Institute for Public Relations Research and Education (IPRRE)
University of Florida
P.O. Box 118400
Gainesville, FL 32611-8400; tel: 904-392-0280

International Advertising Association
521 Fifth Avenue, Suite 1807
New York, NY 10175; tel: 212-557-1133

Investigative Reporters & Editors
University of Missouri
26A Walter Williams Hall
Columbia, MO 65211; tel: 314-882-2042
http://www.ire.org/

League of Advertising Agencies Directory
2 South End Avenue #4C
New York, NY 10280; tel: 212-945-4314

National School Public Relations Association (NSPRA)
1501 Lee Highway, Suite 201
Arlington, VA 22209; tel: 703-528-5840
http://www.nspra.org/

PR Newswire Job Bank
865 South Figueroa, Suite 2310
Los Angeles, CA 90017; tel: 213-626-5500 or 800-321-8169
(send resume and cover letter)

Promotion Marketing Association of America, Inc.
Executive Headquarters
257 Park Avenue South, 11th Floor
New York, NY 10001; tel: 212-420-1100

Public Relations Society of America
33 Irving Place, 3rd Floor
New York, NY 10003; tel: 212-995-2230
http://www.prsa.org/

Public Relations Student Society of America (PRSSA)
33 Irving Place, 3rd Floor
New York, NY 10003; tel: 212-460-1474
http://www.prssa.org/

Society for Technical Communication
901 North Stuart Street, Suite 904
Arlington, VA 22203; tel: 703-522-4114
http://www.stc.org/

Writers Guild of America
555 West 57th Street
New York, NY 10019; tel: 212-767-7800

SALES AND MARKETING

Associations

TRAVEL

Adventure Travel Society
6551 South Revere Parkway, Suite 160
Englewood, CO 80111; tel: 303-649-9016; fax: 303-649-9017

Airline Employees Association, Intl.
Job Opportunity Program
5600 South Central Avenue
Chicago, IL 60638-3797

Air Transport Association of America
1301 Pennsylvania Avenue NW, Suite 1100
Washington, DC 20004-7017; tel: 202-626-4000

American Travel Inns (ATI)
(formerly: American Travel Association)
36 South State Street, Suite 1200
Salt Lake City, UT 84111-1416; tel: 801-521-0732; fax: 801-521-0732

Association of Flight Attendants
1625 Massachusetts Avenue NW
Washington, DC 20036; tel: 202-328-5400

Association of Retail Travel Agents (ARTA)
845 Sir Thomas Court, Suite 3
Harrisburg, PA 17109; tel: 717-545-9548 or 800-969-6069; fax: 717-545-9613

American Society of Travel Agents (ASTA)
IIO1 King Street, Suite 200
Alexandria, VA 22314; tel: 703-739-2782; fax: 703-684-8319

Cruise Lines International Association
500 Fifth Avenue, Suite 1407
New York, NY 10110; tel: 212-921-0066

Freighter Travel Club of America
3524 Harts Lake Road
Roy, WA 98580; tel: 360-458-4178

Future Aviation Professionals of America
4959 Massachusetts Boulevard
Atlanta, GA 30337; tel: 404-997-8097 or 800-JET-JOBS

Greater Independent Association of National Travel Services (GIANTS)
2 Park Avenue, Suite 2205
New York, NY 10016; tel: 212-545-7460 or 800-442-6871; fax: 212-545-7428

Independent Travel Agencies of America Association (ITAA)
5353 North Federal Highway, Suite 300
Fort Lauderdale, Fl 33308; tel: 305-772-4660 or 800-950-5440; fax: 305-772-5797

Institute of Certified Travel Agents (ICTA)
148 Linden Street, P.O. Box 812059
Wellesley, MA 02181-0012; tel: 617-237-0280 or 800-542-4282;
fax: 617-237-3860

International Association for Air Travel Couriers
P.O. Box 1349
Lake Worth, FL 33460; tel: 407-582-8320; fax: 407-582-1581

International Association of Travel Exhibitors (IATE)
P.O. Box 2309
Gulf Shores, AL 36547; tel: 205-948-6690; fax: 205-948-6690

International Association of Travel Journalists (IATJ)
P.O. Box D
Hurleyville, NY 12747; tel: 914-434-1529

International Federation of Women's Travel Organizations
(IFWTO)
13901 North 73rd Street, #210B
Scottsdale, AZ 85260-3125; tel: 602-596-6640; fax: 602-596-6638

Travel Industry Association of America
1100 New York Avenue NW, Suite 450
Washington, DC 20005-3934; tel: 202-408-8422

U.S. Travel Data Center
(affiliate of the Travel Industry Association of America)
2 Lafayette Center
1100 New York Avenue NW, Suite 450
Washington, DC 20005; tel: 202-408-1832

Yours in Travel Personnel Agency
12 West 37th Street
New York, NY 10018; tel: 212-697-7855

MARKETING/ADVERTISING

American Advertising Federation
Education Services Department
1101 Vermont Avenue NW, Suite 500
Washington, DC 20005; tel: 202-898-0089
http://www.aaf.org/

American Marketing Association
250 South Wacker Drive, Suite 200
Chicago, IL 60606-5819; tel: 312-648-0536
http://www.ama.org/

The Convention Liaison Council
1575 Eye Street NW, Suite 1190
Washington, DC 20005; tel: 202-626-2764

Direct Marketing Association
1120 Avenue of the Americas
New York, NY 10036-6700; tel: 212-768-7277

Meeting Planners International
Informant Building, Suite 5018
1950 Stemmons Freeway
Dallas, TX 75207; tel: 214-712-7700

Retail Advertising and Marketing Association
500 North Michigan Avenue, Suite 600
Chicago, IL 60611; tel: 312-251-7262

Sales and Marketing Executives International
977 Statler Office Tower
Cleveland, OH 44115; tel: 216-771-6650
http://www.smei.org/

Sales and Marketing Management
355 Park Avenue South
New York, NY 10010; tel: 212-592-6300

FOOD SERVICES

Associations

Alaska Culinary Association
P.O. Box 140396
Anchorage, AK 99514; tel: 907-265-7116

American Culinary Federation
10 San Bartola Road, P.O. Box 3466
St. Augustine, FL 32085-3466; tel: 904-824-4468

Berks Lehigh Chef's Association
2012 Redwood Avenue
Wyomissing, PA 19610; tel: 610-678-1217

National Food Broker Association
2100 Reston Parkway, Suite 400
Reston, VA 22091; tel: 703-758-7790

National Restaurant Association
1200 17th Street NW
Washington, DC 20036; tel: 202-331-5900

SUPPORT SERVICES

Associations

American Society of Corporate Secretaries
521 Fifth Avenue
New York, NY 10175-0003; tel: 212-681-2000
http://ww.ascs.org/

California Federation of Legal Secretaries
2250 East 73rd Street, Suite 550
Tulsa, OK 74136; tel: 918-493-3540

National Association of Executive Secretaries
900 S. Washington Street, No. G-13
Falls Church, VA 22046; tel: 703-237-8616

PUBLIC SERVICES/SOCIAL SERVICES

Publications

Directory of Legal Aid and Defender Offices in the U.S. and Territories
National Legal Aid and Defender Association, Washington, DC
Lists legal aid and public defender offices across the U.S.
Published annually.

Associations

ACTION International
120 Beacon Street
Somerville, MA 02143; tel: 617-492-4930

American Counseling Association
5999 Stevenson Avenue
Alexandria, VA 22304; tel: 703-823-9800 or 800-347-6647

American Friends Service Committee
1501 Cherry Street
Philadelphia, PA 19102; tel: 215-241-7000
http://www.afsc.org/

American School Counselor Association
801 North Fairfax Street, Suite 301
Alexandria, VA 22314; tel: 703-683-2722

American Vocational Association
1410 King Street
Alexandria, VA 22314; tel: 703-683-3111 or 800-892-2274

Child Welfare League of America
440 First Street NW, Suite 310
Washington, DC 20001; tel: 201-638-2952
http://www.cwla.org/

Council for Standards in Human Service Education
Northern Essex Community College
Haverhill, MA 01830; tel: 508-374-5889

Council on Social Work Education
1600 Duke Street, Suite 300
Alexandria, VA 22314-3421; tel: 703-683-8080
(send $10 for Directory of Accredited BSW and MSW Programs)
http://www.cswe.org/

Educators for Social Responsibility
23 Garden Street
Cambridge, MA 02138; tel: 617-492-1764

Human Service Council
3191 Maguire Boulevard, Suite 1150
Orlando, FL 32803; tel: 407-897-6465

National Association of Social Workers
750 First Street NE, Suite 700
Washington, DC 20002-4241; tel: 202-408-8600

National Center for Charitable Statistics
1828 L Street NW, Suite 1200B
Washington, DC 20036; tel: 202-223-8100

National Civic League
1445 Market Street, Suite 300
Denver, CO 80202-1728; tel: 303-571-4343

National Exchange Club Foundation for the Prevention of Child Abuse
3050 Central Avenue
Toledo, OH 43606; tel: 419-535-3232 or 800-760-3413

National Network for Social Work Managers
1316 New Hampshire Avenue NW, Suite 602
Washington, DC 20036; tel: 202-785-2814

National Organization for Human Service Education
Fitchburg State College, Box 6257
160 Pearl Street
Fitchburg, MA 01420; tel: 508-345-2151

Save the Children Federation
54 Wilton Road
Westport, CT 06880; tel: 203-221-4000

Social Service Association
6 Station Plaza
Ridgewood, NJ 07450; tel: 201-444-2980

EDUCATION

Publications

Who's Who in Special Libraries and Information Centers
Gale Research Inc., Detroit, MI
Lists special libraries alphabetically and geographically. Published annually.

Associations

Academy for Educational Development (AED)
1875 Connecticut Avenue NW
Washington, DC 20009; tel: 202-884-8000; fax: 202-884-8400
E-mail: admind@aed-org
http://www.aed.org/

American Association of School Administrators
1801 N Moore Street
Arlington, VA 22209-9988; tel: 703-528-0700
http://www.aasa.org/

American Association of School Librarians
50 E. Huron Street
Chicago, IL 60611; tel: 312-944-6780

American Association of University Administrators
1012 14th Street NW, Suite 500
Washington, DC 20005; tel: 202-737-5900
http://www.aaua.org/

American Association of University Professors
1012 14th Street NW, Suite 500
Washington, DC 20005; tel: 202-737-5900
http://www.aaup.org/

American Educational Studies Association (AESA)
University of Cincinnati
Graduate Studies and Research
Cincinnati, OH 45221; tel: 513-556-2256

American Federation of Teachers
555 New Jersey Avenue NW
Washington, DC 20001; tel: 202-879-4400
http://www.aft.org/

American Library Association
50 East Huron Street
Chicago, IL 60611; tel: 312-944-6780
http://www.ala.org/

Association for Community Based Education (ACBE)
1805 Florida Avenue NW
Washington, DC 20009; tel: 202-462-6333 or 202-232-8044

Association for Educational Communications and Technology (AECT)
1025 Vermont Avenue NW, Suite 820
Washington, DC 20005; tel: 202-347-7834; fax: 202-347-7839
http://www.aect.org/

Center for Adult Learning and Educational Credentials (CALEC)
1 Dupont Circle NW
Washington, DC 20036; tel: 202-939-9475; fax: 202-775-8574

College and University Personnel Association
1233 20th Street NW, Suite 301
Washington, DC 20036-1250; tel: 202-429-0311
http://www.cupa.org/

Council on International Educational Exchange (CIEE)
205 East 42nd Street
New York, NY 10017; tel: 212-661-1414; fax: 212-972-3231
http://www.ciee.org/

Earthwatch
(formerly: Educational Expeditions International)
680 Mount Auburn Street, Box 403
Watertown, MA 02272; tel: 617-926-8200 or 800-776-0188; fax:
617-926-8532
E-mail: info@earthwatch.org
http://www.earthwatch.org/

Educational Research Service (ERS)
2000 Clarendon Blvd.
Arlington, VA 22201; tel: 703-243-2100; fax: 703-243-1985
http://www.ers.org/

Federal Librarians Round Table
American Library Association, Washington Office
1301 Pennsylvania Avenue NW, No. 403
Washington, DC 20004; tel: 202-608-8410

High/Scope Educational Research Foundation
600 North River Street
Ypsilanti, MI 48198-2898; tel: 313-485-2000 or 800-40-PRESS;
fax: 313-485-0704

Independent Educational Services (IES)
(formerly: Cooperative Bureau for Teachers)
353 Nassau Street
Princeton, NJ 08540; tel: 609-921-6195 or 800-257-5102; fax:
609-921-0155

Institute for Educational Leadership (IEL)
1001 Connecticut Avenue NW, Suite 310
Washington, DC 20036; tel: 202-822-8405; fax: 202-872-4050
http://www.iel.org/

Intercultural Development Research Association (IDRA)
5835 Callaghan Road, Suite 350
San Antonio, TX 78228; tel: 210-684-8180; fax: 210-684-5389
http://www.idra.org/

International Association for Educational Assessment (IAEA)
P.O. Box 6665
Princeton, NJ 08541; tel: 609-921-9000; fax: 609-520-1093

Madison Center for Educational Affairs (MCEA)
455 15th Street NW, Suite 712
Washington, DC 20005; tel: 202-833-1801; fax: 202-467-0006

National Association of Educational Office Professionals (NAEOP)
P.O. Box 12619
Wichita, KS 67277; tel: 316-942-4822; fax: 316-942-7100
http://www.naeop.org/

National Association of Secondary School Principals
1904 Association Drive
Reston, VA 22091; tel: 703-860-0200
http://www.nassp.org/

National Association of Student Personnel Administrators
1875 Connecticut Avenue NW, Suite 418
Washington, DC 20009; tel: 202-265-7500
http://www.naspa.org/

National Council for Accreditation of Teacher Education
2010 Massachusetts Avenue NW, Suite 500
Washington, DC 20036; tel: 202-466-7496
http://www.ncate.org/

National Council of Educational Opportunity Associations (NCEOA)
1025 Vermont Avenue NW, Suite 1201
Washington, DC 20005; tel: 202-347-7430

National Council on the Evaluation of Foreign Educational
Credentials
c/o AACRAO
1 Dupont Circle NW, Suite 330
Washington, DC 20036; tel: 202-293-9161 or 202-872-8857
aacrao@umdd (E-mail)

National Education Association
1201 16th Street NW
Washington, DC 20036; tel: 202-833-4000
http://www.nea.org/

National Rural Education Association (NREA)
Colorado State University
230 Education Building
Fort Collins, CO 80523-1588; tel: 970-491-7022; fax: 970-491-1317

Special Libraries Association
1700 18th Street NW
Washington, DC 20009-2508; tel: 202-234-4700; fax: 202-265-9317
http://www.sla.org/

University Council for Educational Administration (UCEA)
Pennsylvania State University
212 Rackley Bldg.
University Park, PA 16802-3200; tel: 814-863-7916/7917 or 814-
863-7918 (fax)
http://www.ucea.org/

GOVERNMENT

Publications

The Capitol Source
National Journal, Inc., Washington, DC
Includes names, addresses, and phone numbers for key figures in
the District of Columbia; also features information about
corporations, interest groups, think tanks, labor unions, real estate
organizations, financial institutions, trade and professional groups,
law firms, political consultants, advertising and public relations
firms, private clubs, and the media. Published twice a year.

Congressional Yellow Book
Monitor Publishing Co., New York, NY
Gives detailed information on congressional staff positions, committees and subcommittees, and top staff in congressional support agencies. Published annually.

COSLA Directory
The Council of State Governments, Lexington, KY
Provides information on state library agencies, consultant and administrative staff, plus ALANER numbers, electronic mail letters, and fax numbers. Published annually.

American Federation of State, County, and Municipal Employees
1625 L Street NW
Washington, DC 20036; tel: 202-429-1000

Directory of Federal Libraries
Includes library's administrator and selected staff for three thousand special and general, presidential and national libraries, as well as library facilities in technical centers, hospitals, and penal institutions.

Federal Executive Directory
Carroll Publishing Co., Washington, DC
Profiles a broad range of agencies, both executive and legislative, including cabinet departments, federal administrative agencies, and congressional committee members and staff. The directory also outlines areas of responsibility for legal and administrative assistants. Published six times a year; an annual subscription is $178. Call 202-333-8620 for more information.

Federal Organization Service: Military
Carroll Publishing Co., Washington, DC
Lists direct-dial phone numbers for 11,500 key individuals in fifteen hundred military departments and offices. Updated every six weeks; an annual subscription is $625. Call 202-333-8620 for more information.

Washington Information Directory
Congressional Quarterly Inc., Washington, DC
Provides important information on the federal government as a whole, and on each federal department and agency. The volume also provides details on regional federal information sources, nongovernmental organizations in the Washington area, and congressional committees and subcommittees. Published annually.

Washington '92
Columbia Books, New York, NY
Contains addresses, phone numbers, and profiles of key institutions in the city. Includes chapters on the federal government, the media, business, national associations, labor unions, law firms, medicine and health, foundations and philanthropic organizations, science and policy research groups, and educational, religious, and cultural institutions. Published annually.

Associations

American Planning Association
122 South Michigan Avenue, Suite 1600
Chicago, IL 60603; tel: 312-431-9100

Civil Service Employees Association
P.O. Box 7125, Capitol State
Albany, NY 12210; tel: 518-434-0191 or 800-342-4146

Council of State Governments
P.O. Box 11910, 3560 Iron Works Pike
Lexington, KY 40578; tel: 606-244-8000
http://www.csg.org/

International Association of Fire Fighters
1750 New York Avenue NW
Washington, DC 21006; tel: 202-737-8484
http://www.iaff.org/

International City/County Management Association
777 North Capitol Street NE, Suite 500
Washington, DC 20002; tel: 202-289-4262
http://www.icma.org/

National Association of Counties (NACO)
440 First Street NW, 8th Floor
Washington, DC 20001; tel: 202-393-6226
http://www.naco.org/

National Association of Government Communicators
669 South Washington Street
Alexandria, VA 22314; tel: 703-519-3902

National Planning Association
1424 16th Street NW, Suite 700
Washington, DC 20036; tel: 202-265-7685

New York State Professional Firefighters Association
111 Washington Avenue, Suite 207
Albany, NY 12210; tel: 518-436-8827

State Services Organization (SSO)
444 North Capitol Street NW
Washington, DC 20001; tel: 202-624-5470
http://www.sso.org/

DISABILITIES

ADA Regional Disabled and Business Assistance Centers

Connecticut, Maine, Massachusetts, Rhode Island, and Vermont:
New England Disability and Business Technical Assistance Center
145 Newbury Street
Portland, ME 04101; tel: 207-874-6535 (voice/TDD)

New Jersey, New York, Puerto Rico, and Virgin Islands:
Northeast Disability and Business Technical Assistance Center
354 South Broad Street
Trenton, NJ 08608; tel: 609-392-4004 (voice), 609-392-7044 (TDD)

Delaware, District of Columbia, Maryland, Pennsylvania, Virginia, and West Virginia:
Mid-Atlantic Disability and Business Technical Assistance Center
2111 Wilson Boulevard, Suite 400
Arlington, VA 22201; tel: 703-525-3268 (voice/TDD)

Alabama, Florida, Georgia, Kentucky, Mississippi, North Carolina, South Carolina, and Tennessee:
Southeast Disability and Business Technical Assistance Center
1776 Peachtree Street, Suite 310 North
Atlanta, GA 30309; tel: 404-888-0022 (voice/TDD)

Illinois, Indiana, Michigan, Minnesota, Ohio, and Wisconsin:
Great Lakes Disability and Business Technical Assistance Center
1640 West Roosevelt Road (M/C 627)
Chicago, IL 60608; tel: 312-413-1407 (voice/TDD)

Arkansas, Louisiana, New Mexico, Oklahoma, and Texas:
Southwest Disability and Business Technical Assistance Center
2323 South Shepherd Boulevard, Suite 1000
Houston, TX 77019; tel: 713-520-0232 (voice), 713-520-5136 (TDD)

Iowa, Kansas, Nebraska, and Missouri:
Great Plains Disability and Business Technical Assistance Center
4816 Santana Drive
Columbia, MO 65203; tel: 314-882-3600 (voice/TDD)

Colorado, Montana, North Dakota, South Dakota, Utah, and Wyoming:
Rocky Mountain Disability and Business Technical Assistance Center
3630 Sinton Road, Suite 103
Colorado Springs, CO 80907-5072; tel: 719-444-0252 (voice/TDD)

Arizona, California, Hawaii, and Nevada:
Pacific Coast Disability and Business Technical Assistance Center
440 Grand Avenue, Suite 500
Oakland, CA 94610; tel: 510-465-7884 (voice), 510-465-3167 (TDD)

Job Accommodation Network
P.O. Box 6123
809 Allen Hall
Morgantown, WV 26505-6123; tel: 800-526-7234 (voice/TDD)

The President's Committee on Employment of People with Disabilities
1331 F Street NW
Washington, DC 20004; tel: 202-376-6200 (voice), 202-376-6205 (TDD)

U.S. Department of Justice, Civil Rights Division
Office of the Americans with Disabilities Act
P.O. Box 66118
Washington, DC 20035-6118; tel: 800-514-0301 (voice), 800-514-0383 (TDD)

APPENDIX

C | **Index to the Questions**

What do you think of your current or last boss? See page 151.
What have you done that shows initiative and willingness to work? See page 206.
What have you done that shows initiative? See page 154.
What have you learned from jobs you have held? See page 138.
What have your other jobs taught you? See page 159.
What interests you least about this job? See page 182.
What interests you most about this job? See page 141.
What is an adequate reward for your efforts? See page 224.
What is the least relevant job you have held? See page 137.
What is the most difficult situation you have faced? See page 153.
What is the worst thing you have heard about our company? See page 178.
What is your current salary? See page 225.
What is your energy level like? Describe a typical day. See page 135.
What is your general impression of your last company? See page 183.
What is your greatest strength? See page 141.
What is your greatest weakness? See page 174.
What is your salary history? See page 225.
What kind of decisions are most difficult for you? See page 175.
What kind of experience do you have for this job? See page 135.
What kind of people do you find it difficult to work with? See page 185.
What kind of people do you like to work with? See page 184.
What kind of salary are you worth? See page 228.
What kind of things do you worry about? See page 153.
What levels are you most comfortable with? See page 164.
What makes this job different from your current or last one? See page 148.
What personal characteristics are necessary for success in your field? See page 156.
What qualifications do you have that will make you successful in this field? See page 207.
What religion do you practice? See page 189.
What type of decisions did you make on your last job? See page 144.
What type of position are you interested in? See page 207.
What was the last book you read? How did it affect you? See page 144.
What was the last movie you saw? How did it affect you? See page 144.
What was there about your last company that you didn't particularly like or agree with? See page 182.
What was your salary progress on your last job? See page 225.
What were some of the minuses on your last job? See page 184.
What were you making on your last job? See page 225.
What would you do when you have a decision to make and no procedure exists? See page 166.
What would you like to be doing five years from now? See page 139.
What would you say about a supervisor who was unfair or difficult to work with? See page 157.
What would you say if I told you your presentation was lousy? See page 187.
What would your references say? See page 143.
What's your idea of how industry works? See page 207.
When do you expect a promotion? See page 159.
When you joined your last company and met the group for the first time, how did you feel? See page 165.
Which of the jobs you have held have you liked least? See page 204.
Who else have you applied to? See page 148.
Why aren't you earning more at your age? See page 178.
Why did you leave your last job? See page 182.
Why do you feel you are a better _____ than some of your coworkers? See page 158.
Why do you think you would like this type of work? See page 207.
Why do you want to leave your current job? See page 182.
Why do you want to work here? See page 135.
Why have you changed jobs so frequently? See page 181.
Why should I hire an outsider when I could fill the job with someone inside the company? See page 179.
Why should I hire you? See page 142.
Why were you fired? See page 146.
Why were you out of work for so long? See page 180.
With hindsight, how could you have improved your progress? See page 175.
Would you be willing to take a drug test as a condition of employment? See page 243.
Would you like to have your boss's job? See page 151.
Wouldn't you feel better off with another firm? See page 187.
You have a doctor's appointment that conflicts with an emergency meeting. What do you do? See page 158.
You have been given a project that requires you to interact with different levels within the company. How do you do this? See page 164.

Index

Your Two Cents' Worth

Comments, questions, or suggestions? Please complete this questionnaire and mail it to me:

Martin Yate
c/o Adams Media Corporation
260 Center St., Holbrook, MA 02343

Hey Martin,

Here's how I used *Knock 'em Dead*:

By the way, I'm thinking of changing my will and naming you as my major beneficiary if you . . .

1. Give me some additional information about the following issue.

   _____

2. Tell me how to find the resource described below, since I drew a blank. (Circle one: This is something I came up with. / You mentioned it on page _____.)

   _____

3. Add a chapter on the following topic, since it would really be helpful to people like me.

   _____

   I guess that's it. No, wait—please stick my name in the hat when you're done reading this. I deserve a shot at a free dinner for two at the restaurant of my choice as much as anyone else who fills this out.

Name: _____

Address: _____

_____

Daytime phone: _____

Evening phone: _____

Occupation: _____

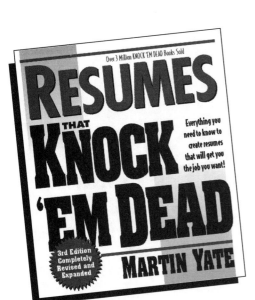

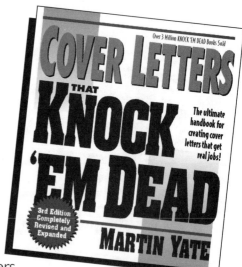

The JobBank Series

There are 34 local JobBank books, each providing extensive, up-to-date employment information on hundreds of the largest employers in each job market. The #1 best-selling series of employment directories, the JobBank series has been recommended as an excellent place to begin your job search by the *New York Times*, the *Los Angeles Times*, the *Boston Globe*, and the *Chicago Tribune*. JobBank books have been used by millions of people to find jobs. All JobBank books are $16.95 and over 300 pages. Titles available:

The Atlanta JobBank ▪ *The Austin/San Antonio JobBank* ▪ *The Boston JobBank* ▪ *The Carolina JobBank* ▪ *The Chicago JobBank* ▪ *The Connecticut JobBank* ▪ *The Dallas/Fort Worth JobBank* ▪ *The Denver JobBank* ▪ *The Detroit JobBank* ▪ *The Florida JobBank* ▪ *The Houston JobBank* ▪ *The Indiana JobBank* ▪ *The Las Vegas JobBank* ▪ *The Los Angeles JobBank* ▪ *The Minneapolis/St. Paul JobBank* ▪ *The Missouri JobBank* ▪ *The New Mexico JobBank* ▪ *The Metropolitan New York JobBank* ▪ *The Upstate New York JobBank* ▪ *The Northern New England JobBank* ▪ *The Ohio JobBank* ▪ *The Greater Philadelphia JobBank* ▪ *The Phoenix JobBank* ▪ *The Pittsburgh JobBank* ▪ *The Portland JobBank* ▪ *The Salt Lake City JobBank* ▪ *The San Francisco JobBank* ▪ *The Seattle JobBank* ▪ *The Tennessee JobBank* ▪ *The Virginia JobBank* ▪ *The Washington DC JobBank* ▪ *The Wisconsin JobBank* ▪ *The JobBank Guide to Computer & High-Tech Companies* ▪ *The JobBank Guide to Health Care Companies*

Hiring the Best, 4th edition *by Martin Yate*

Interviewing is a skill that must be developed, and Martin Yate shows just how to identify the person who provides the best "fit" for any given position. Includes sections on interviewing within the law and hiring clerical help, as well as prewritten interview outlines. 6" x 9", 240 pages, paperback, $10.95. ISBN: 1-55850-282-3

Available wherever books are sold

If you cannot find these titles at your favorite retail outlet, you may order them directly from the publisher. BY PHONE: Call 1-800-872-5627 (in Massachusetts 781-767-8100). We accept Visa, Mastercard, and American Express. $4.50 will be added to your total order for shipping and handling. BY MAIL: Write out the full titles of the books you'd like to order and send payment, including $4.50 for shipping and handling, to: Adams Media Corporation, 260 Center Street, Holbrook, MA 02343. 30-day money-back guarantee.